A History of
the Gardens of Versailles

PENN STUDIES
IN LANDSCAPE ARCHITECTURE

John Dixon Hunt, Series Editor

This series is dedicated to the study and promotion of
a wide variety of approaches to landscape architecture,
with special emphasis on connections between theory
and practice. It includes monographs on key topics in
history and theory, descriptions of projects by both
established and rising designers, translations of major
foreign-language texts, anthologies of theoretical and
historical writings on classic issues, and critical writing
by members of the profession of landscape architecture.
The series was the recipient of the Award of Honor in
Communications from the American Society of
Landscape Architects, 2006.

A History of
the Gardens
of Versailles

Michel Baridon

Translated by Adrienne Mason

PENN

UNIVERSITY OF PENNSYLVANIA PRESS

PHILADELPHIA

Publication of this volume was aided by a grant from
Centre National du Livre

Originally published as *Histoire des jardins de Versailles*
Copyright © Actes Sud / Établissement public du
musée et du domaine national de Versailles, 2003

Copyright © 2008 University of Pennsylvania Press

Published by
University of Pennsylvania Press
Philadelphia, Pennsylvania 19104-4112

Printed in the United States of America on acid-free
paper
10 9 8 7 6 5 4 3 2 1

Library of Congress Cataloging-in-Publication Data
Baridon, Michel.
    [Histoire des jardins de Versailles. English]
    A history of the gardens of Versailles / Michel
Baridon; translated by Adrienne Mason.
        p. cm.—(Penn studies in landscape architecture)
Includes bibliographical references and index.
ISBN 978-0-8122-4078-8 (alk. paper)
    1. Parc de Versailles (Versailles, France)—History.
2. Gardens—France—Versailles—History.   I. Title.
SB466.F83P37213   2008
712′.609443663—dc22   2008005507

CONTENTS

CHAPTER FIFTEEN
History, Gardens, and Landscape   238

Introduction

THE FIRST THING that strikes you as you approach the château of Versailles is the sheer size of the three wide avenues that converge and seem to draw the whole town toward the entry gates. Beyond the gates a massive array of buildings creates a skyline of brick, slate, and stone. Almost at once, the stone reaches out toward you, since as soon as you are inside the walls, the Pavé du Roi leads you across the Place d'Armes and imperceptibly upward to an outer courtyard where you are flanked by the Ailes des Ministres. You leave the open space behind as you move toward the equestrian statue of Louis XIV and the two pediments with their inscription TO ALL THE GLORIES OF FRANCE. This tells you exactly what is happening. You are entering the heart of the nation's heritage, a place where Louis XIV, the Sun King, is remembered alongside other great men and great moments in a history that is still unfolding and in which, if only by virtue of your presence here, you have a part to play.

The first courtyard leads into a second, the Cour Royale, and finally to a third, the Cour de Marbre. In each of these three stages of your approach to this vast complex of buildings, the space around you becomes progressively less open. Imperceptibly, the buildings that blocked the horizon when you arrived have surrounded and virtually closed in on you. You are right at the center, the hub from which everything radiates. But the logic of your approach dictates that you continue through the last screen ahead of you. As you move closer, you can see that in the middle of the screen, at its base, are three glazed doors, lit as it were from within. As you get nearer, you discover that this light is coming from three other corresponding glazed doors in the wall of a vestibule opposite. From that vestibule, at a slightly lower level, you can see an esplanade, which leads to a broad canal that stretches away to the horizon. Just when the palace seems to have tightened its grip around you, the light from the gardens reaches you through the palace itself and five marble steps are clearly visible in the vestibule, beckoning you to walk down toward them, losing the height you gained as you came up from the gates.

If you cross the few yards of the vestibule, you will be stopped in your tracks by a breathtaking spectacle. The space opens up completely, right up to the heavens as far as the eye can see. Then you can understand why Louis XIV began his famous guide on the gardens of Versailles, *Manière de visiter les jardins de Versailles,* by saying, "Leaving the château by the vestibule in the marble courtyard, one reaches the terrace. One should pause at the top of the steps to contemplate the layout of the parterres, the *pièces d'eau,* and the Fontaines des Cabinets."

In front of you lies the whole expanse of the terrace, where two long *miroirs d'eau* lead you to the top of the Parterre de Latone. From there, you can look down toward the bosquets and up along the Grand Canal stretching off to the west. Your eyes follow the line of the hills, whose gentle slopes close off the horizon to the north and the south. There is a total contrast between the world of stone and marble behind you and the sight of the trees, *bassins,* and *allées* that lie at your feet. Here, outside the walls, you can feel free to wander where you will. If you turn back to face the palace, you will see a very long façade with hundreds of windows, enhanced by columns whose recurrent motifs serve to emphasize its unbroken uniformity. A substantial *avant-corps* juts out toward you and, at the center of its base, three splashes of light remind you that the marble courtyard is on the other side of the walls. It is as if there were a huge theater curtain between you and the town, cutting the gardens off and drawing your gaze back toward them.

From here onward, you are in another world. The palace is behind you, the complex layout of its buildings reminding you how difficult it is to approach the inner sanctum: three avenues funnel into one single courtyard, and only a long trudge across the cobbles entitles you to walk on marble. After that, you enter an enchanted landscape where the shimmering water and the gleaming white statues scatter patches of light among the greenery. Just as you felt the weight of political authority growing as you approached the center of the palace, now you are discovering the splendor of the place in which it is exercised.

History remembers this kind of lesson, and the palace of the Sun King survived the fall of the ancien régime that it had been built to glorify. Versailles ceased to be the seat of government in 1789, but in 1837 the grandchildren of the Parisians who had lived through the Revolution saw a constitutional monarch, Louis-Philippe, accord it the high status it still has today as the place, above all others, where the nation can celebrate the splendor of its past. At the end of the 1870s, after the revolt by the Commune of Paris had been violently put down by the provisional government, the seat of which was Versailles, the Third Republic continued the traditions established by the July Monarchy. For more than a century, the two houses of government have met in the Salle des Congrès to elect the president of the republic or to modify the constitution, two defining moments for the institutions of government in France.

The historical importance of Versailles is so clearly acknowledged that for a long time it has been recognized far beyond France. The preliminary articles of peace granting independence to the United States were signed there in January 1783, and the Galerie des Glaces has been the scene of other ceremonies, which for better or worse have marked some key moments in world history. It was there that Bismarck proclaimed the creation of the German Empire in 1870 after the collapse of France, and there in 1918 that the Allies signed the treaty that marked the end of World War I. The Allies went even further, since they laid the foundation for the League of Nations and gave Versailles the coveted distinction of being the palace where the first international peacekeeping institution came into existence. The League of Nations did not survive World War II, but its heir, the United Nations, still carries the fragile but bright flame of the hopes that were kindled at Versailles.

For more than three centuries the political role that the Sun King assigned to Versailles has continued, albeit in a different form. Everyone is aware of that aspect, but what part do the gardens play in our perception of it? The château itself is emblematic: a magnificent theater set, an explicit and eloquent statement of political authority. But what about the gardens? They, too, are vast. They, too, are richly ornamented. But what is their proper function? Are they simply a luxuriously green setting for the château? An extension of the palace, carved out of the natural world? Or are they a creation in themselves, of a quite different order, with their own particular meaning?

To answer these questions, imagine for a moment that the gardens just disappear, that they are wiped off the map. Not by a storm like the one in December 1999 that flattened thousands of trees in the space of a few minutes but by some cataclysm that sweeps everything away: the bosquets, the Orangerie, the bassins, the statues—in other words, the whole structure that has been there for centuries. What would be left of Versailles? If it were stripped of everything but its buildings, the life force of the château would be irremediably lost. Inside its walls, only the shades of a long-dead past would remain, and the palace would be left stranded on its hill like the wreck of a beached ship. It is because of the trees, the bosquets, the reflections of the clouds drifting across the water, and the breezes rippling through the landscape that Versailles can change with the rhythm of the seasons and survive the passage of time.

Paradoxically, the enduring life of the architecture is made possible by the transience of the vegetation, and the gardens themselves, an achievement of extraordinary diversity, accommodate the changes that three centuries have wrought. It is thanks to the gardens that the grandeur of the baroque design, the rustic delicacy of the Hameau de la Reine, and the *corbeilles de fleurs* that Dufour placed in the Bosquet de l'Ile Royale in the Romantic era can coexist harmoniously. Through the gardens, these different styles and different moments in history can continue, in their own way, the destiny of the château. As long as the gardens continue to be restored and maintained, Louis XIV's grand political project, which brought them into being, can be perpetuated and show us what it has become. Even the least-informed visitor will become aware of the political nature of this project by seeing how an immense expanse of land has been conquered and given identity and form by human endeavor; it is through human endeavor that the gardens retain that form and are continually renewed. And what is political action, in the best sense, if it is not the impulse that it gives to the effort of a whole society?

It is not overstating the lessons of history to say that the palace and gardens of Versailles were the result of a new and triumphant vision of the power of the state. That vision is still ours today, even if the way the world has changed means that our horizons are wider and include an international perspective. The scale of political action, constraining us because it is beyond our complete control, is something we can live with and accept when, from high on the Terrasse de Versailles, we see how this vast expanse of nature has been ordered by human intelligence.

PART I

The State, the King, and the Gardens

Classical France, as the monarchy sought to define it: it is at Versailles, in the château itself you might say, that its essence can be captured.
   —Robert Mandrou

CHAPTER ONE

The Monarchy and the Gardens Before the Reign of Louis XIV

WHEN LOUIS XIV decided in 1677 to establish the seat of government outside Paris in the château he had created, it was the culmination of a plan he had clearly begun sixteen years earlier when he took over the reins of government after the death of Mazarin. As a clever tactician, Louis had felt then that it was time to cross a sort of political Rubicon and make the person of the king not just the symbol of monarchical authority but the agent through whom that authority was actively exercised. Lavish from the first with his gestures, he began to take an interest in Versailles, and it is clear that the creation of the gardens must have held a particular attraction for him; he always gave them priority over the buildings, pushing ahead with the work so that their final structure was in place long before the palace was as it is today.

Leaving the Louvre and establishing the court and the administration of a powerful and highly centralized monarchy in a new capital more than five leagues from Paris was a veritable revolution, which provided a definitive framework for the new political order. The king's liking for his gardens was an important factor and because, historically, no grand design has ever been realized without a number of different circumstances coming together to serve the purposes of an exceptional individual, we have to show, on the one hand, what the gardens of Versailles owe to a well-established tradition in the history of the French monarchy and, on the other, what they owe to the initiatives of a young king on whom fortune smiled for the first twenty years of his reign.

Taking the long view, two factors seem to predominate: first, the concept that the Valois dynasty, and after them the Bourbons, had of their role, and second, the advent of the Medici in the royal family.

The House of Valois, Catherine de Médicis, and the Gardens

As Machiavelli observed at the beginning of the sixteenth century, France had in its favor the power of a strongly centralized regime. In his *Treatise on Affairs in France* he wrote, "There is another very powerful reason for the greatness of the king: the kingdom was formerly divided between powerful barons who unhesitatingly took arms against their feudal overlord, as did the dukes of Guyenne and Bourbon; nowadays his authority over them is complete and all the greater for it."[1] He might have added that the kings of France knew how to create a powerful image of this centralization, and their relations with Italy helped construct it. And it was a conscious construction. To understand this, you only have to look at their vast expenditure on palaces and gardens. The role of François I was, in this respect, primordial. This king, whose household budget rose from 200,000 to more than a million livres in twenty-five years, was responsible for making Fontainebleau into a royal residence for hunting and for work. He also contrived to surround himself with a court that rapidly grew larger and more magnificent.[2] Its magnificence was in no small measure due to the gardens, which were considered the most beautiful in France. "Everything the king could collect of the very best," said Androuet du Cerceau, "went to Fontainebleau." It was at Fontainebleau that Cardinal Jean Du Bellay introduced the king to Hippolyte d'Este, to whom he was related through his wife. An immediate understanding grew up between these two men, young but already powerful and open to all the humanist ideas and projects in literature, architecture, and gardens. François I died before the Villa d'Este became one of the great gardens of the world, but the conversations he had with its creator certainly contributed to the making of Fontainebleau. Primatice, Vignole, and Serlio were invited there, as Leonardo had been to Amboise, and the king continued the work begun by Charles VIII. He remodeled the gardens in the Italian style that had become recognized as a work of art in its own right after the publication of *Hypnero-tomachia Poliphili* and the printed version of Alberti's *De re aedificatoria*.

Thus the world of Italian gardens made its appearance in Fontainebleau, where its galleries, grotto, art gallery, and frescoes brought a whole new style of living, just when the monarchy was establishing its power by setting up the apparatus of the modern state. François I capitalized on the splendor the Renaissance conferred upon the person of the monarch, not least through patronage of the arts, but whenever the occasion warranted it he also took care to maintain the image of a king who was a hunter-warrior and excelled in physical pursuits whenever he could. The first gentleman of the kingdom bore arms and used them, whether to contain the house of Austria, open up a road to Italy or, almost daily, hunt the animals that roamed in his parks. Physical exercise and the pleasures of the chase came with being a prince. In Fontainebleau, as later in Versailles, the park was a ready-made setting and it expanded like the gardens and like the royal household, which was already four times as large under Charles VIII as under his predecessor, Louis XI, and would double in size during the first half of the sixteenth century.

Henri II succeeded François I, and the influence of Henri's wife, Catherine de Médicis, was quickly felt at the French court. François I had arranged this marriage to unite the royal family with an illustrious line of manufacturers and bankers who had supplied Christendom with two popes and whose links to Florentine artists and humanists were as well-known as their economic power. Catherine was the granddaughter of Lorenzo the Magnificent, himself the grandson of the elder Cosimo, who had transformed his villa in Fiesole into a leading intellectual center. That example was followed by his descendants, who made their gardens a favorite place to mix with intellectuals and artists, allowing them to carry out a cultural policy that would do no harm either to their business interests abroad or to the role they played in the city.[3]

The Medici were powerful enough to set themselves up as governors of Florence, and this became evident later when they established a dynasty. Their gardens were conceived as a visible illustration of their role in history, a living image of a well-governed town and province. They followed a tradition exemplified by Pierre de Crescens and by Lorenzetti's frescoes for the Palazzo Pubblico of Siena, the rival town to Florence. By presenting the contrast between good and bad government simply through the appearance of the countryside, these frescoes established a direct link between nature and politics. The Medici learned from this and represented themselves as governors whose power was sufficiently great for Florence to reap the benefits. Their gardens mattered so much to them that they had them painted in the last decade of the sixteenth century by the Dutch artist Giusto Utens, whose "lunettes" are now well-known.

In this context, Valori wrote,

Lorenzo the Magnificent, realising that agriculture was an agreeable and
useful pursuit, well worthy of a prince, took an extraordinary interest in
all the revenues and profits to be had from it. In the countryside around
Pisa, he established a very pleasant estate, by draining the marshes and
wetlands. This was most useful to the neighbouring properties and
would be even more so today had the estate still survived. Similarly, he
had the barren, wooded land around Volterra so successfully cultivated
that both he and the local population found it very profitable.[4]

Following the family tradition, Catherine de Médicis appreciated the importance of gardens as the ideal image of the state. Since three French kings
were her direct descendants, one concludes that Louis XIV was continuing
the same tradition when he created such magnificence from the unpromising
soil of Versailles. In the sixteenth century, the house of Valois owned, in the
Ile-de-France alone, a number of gardens: the Tuileries, Tournelles, Vincennes,
Madrid (in the present Bois de Boulogne), Saint-Germain, and Fontainebleau.
Catherine de Médicis never missed the opportunity to make sure her name was
associated with them. In addition, she had her own gardens in the château of
Chenonceau where she was often in residence after Diane de Poitiers, Henri
II's mistress, had left. Catherine built waterfalls there and an aviary for her
tropical birds; she also bred silkworms so that the estate would yield a good
profit.[5] She organized fêtes in honor of François II and Mary Stuart in 1560,[6]
during which triumphal arches, obelisks, and small open-air amphitheaters appeared in the gardens. There was even an oratory in a clearing where the silence encouraged meditation.

In 1563 Chenonceau was the setting for other fêtes, this time to celebrate
the defeat of the Huguenots at La Charité-sur-Loire. There were perform-
ances of pastorales, such as Tasso's *Aminta* and Guarini's *Il pastor fido*, which
were also played at Fontainebleau in 1564. Anticipating Louis XIV in her love
of spectacle, Catherine de Médicis wrote to Henri III a few years later, "I have
heard it said by the king your grandfather that you need to do two things if
the French are to live at peace and love their king. Keep them entertained and
keep them occupied."[7]

When she was in Paris, Catherine de Médicis particularly enjoyed going
to the gardens that Charles V had created in what is now the Marais. She had
bought a piece of land adjoining the Louvre, which was known at that time as

"Thuileries" (tile works), probably because of its clay soil. Then, having secured the help of Antoine de Gondi, she began a program of building and laid out the Grand Jardin. Alfred Marie has described the key role this Florentine banker and his heirs played in the history of the royal gardens:[8] Saint-Cloud was bought from Jean-François de Gondi, his grandson, by the king's brother (who was known as "Monsieur"), and the same Jean-François de Gondi sold the seigneury of Versailles and the surrounding lands to Louis XIII. In the Tuileries, Catherine de Médicis employed men who had a profound influence on French garden history. It seems Bernard Palissy built a grotto for her: an estimate and a description have survived and its remains may have been rediscovered.[9] One Venetian ambassador greatly admired these gardens where, he said, "the arrangement of trees and plants is admirable. Not only do we find mazes, bosquets, streams, and fountains, but even the seasons of the year and the signs of the zodiac are represented. That is truly a marvel."[10]

It was in the Tuileries in 1564 that the monarchy established the link between their gardens and great political events: a celebration was organized to mark the reconciliation of Protestants and Catholics and to make the assassination of the duke of Guise a cause for public rejoicing. On that occasion, mermaids swam in the garden's canals and saluted the king, while Neptune kept them company on a chariot drawn by four horses. The Tuileries were used for the same purpose when envoys from Warsaw came to offer the duke of Anjou, the future Henri III, the crown of Poland. Sixteen of Catherine de Médicis's ladies-in-waiting came down from a rock where they had been seated to symbolize the sixteen provinces of France and recited poems, written by Ronsard, in honor of France and Poland.

This is how the royal gardens were directly associated with the political life of the kingdom, an example Louis XIV would follow with spectacular success a century later. As Kenneth Woodbridge observes, these celebrations anticipate those of Louis XIV's fêtes, the Plaisirs de l'Ile Enchantée.[11] One might add that they even more clearly anticipate the fêtes marking the end of the War of Devolution in 1668 and the acquisition of Franche-Comté in 1674. The fêtes arranged by Henri III in honor of the marriage of one of his favorites, the viscount of Joyeuse, were long renowned: "The garden was converted into a huge tiltyard and at eight o'clock at night, lit by torches and flambeaux, the king took part in a joust, fourteen white knights against fourteen yellow." During the ballet, put on in the great hall of the Bourbon mansion by the queen mother on the same occasion, the gardens made another appearance: "Scattered around the vast hall were little clumps of trees, lit by gold lamps in the shape of ships, grottoes, and an artificial garden planted with tropical shrubs; beyond could be seen a host of stars and a town with its spires silhouetted against the night sky."[12]

This was an evocation of the garden at night, where temporary structures were often built. Artificial mountains, Olympus or Parnassus, would be created, on whose seats not the nine classical muses but mythological figures personifying the provinces of France took their place. These structures, draped with cloth of gold and silver, were not fixed and could be wheeled round the wide paths of the gardens. Alongside these movable mountains would be a garden stage set, a sort of open-air theater, where the whole court would watch ballets performed. This taste for the magical in a natural setting was characteristic of the many Renaissance court fêtes.[13]

The Bourbons and the Gardens

Under Henri IV, the "gardener king" who also did a great deal for the gardens of Fontainebleau,[14] the appearance of the Tuileries changed. The gardens had suffered considerably in the war against the Ligue[15] and the king immediately set to work to repair the damage. He swiftly began a program of renovation under the direction of Pierre Le Nôtre, followed by the latter's son Jean, and André Tarquin, Claude Mollet, and Guillaume Moisy. He redesigned Catherine de Médicis's Grand Jardin and created the new garden between the Tuileries and the canal that separated them from the other buildings of the Louvre. After the harsh winter of 1609, when frost killed the cypresses in the borders, he agreed that they should be replaced by box, which had the advantage of being hardier but up until then had been considered to have too unpleasant a smell. But it was above all for the terrace known as the Feuillants on the north side of the Louvre, where the present Rue de Rivoli runs, that we associate Henri IV's name with the Tuileries. He had the terrace planted with a double row of white mulberries, supplied by the famous agronomist, Olivier de Serres, and set up a silk farm to the west of the gardens, thereby illustrating the arguments put forward by de Serres and Sully that the good government of France depended on the careful management of its agriculture. This was a modern version of an old iconographic theme of France as the garden of lilies, an emblem that evoked over the royal doorways the power of the king to bring fertility to the territories within his sway.[16]

This fact did not escape Claude Mollet, the author of *Théâtre des plans et jardinages*. In his first preface to the book, Mollet describes the king walking as he often did in the gardens, where he felt at home and free to behave in the same relaxed and easy way he had as a soldier.

> These words remind me of the pronouncements of that great king, the late Henri IV. Taking the air in the upper Allée of the great Tuileries gardens, at the time when the mulberries, which are still there to this day, were being planted, and seeing the care and diligence that I applied to my work, he said the following, while the Duc D'Espernon supported him on his right hand and I on his left: "Foresight makes a man rich; carelessness makes him poor. The gardener must heed that maxim, since the soil is only good if the man is good."[17]

This was the period when the idea that the prosperity of a great kingdom depended on economic factors was beginning to spread, and well beyond simply the upper echelons of the administration. Sully was very much aware of this. At Henrichemont in the Berry, he had a town built in Henri IV's honor as well as his own. It was designed as a square about five hundred meters along each side. He named the four streets that ran perpendicularly from the central square to each of the town gates after the queen and the king's three children and placed an inscription on the ramparts claiming credit for having "brought prosperity and plenty, banished want and established the rule of law."[18] The efforts he was making to ensure that the importance of the major sources of wealth was recognized were paralleled by rapid developments in economic thinking that led to a view of the state as a community whose members were all linked in some way or another by common national interests. Antoine de Montchrestien, at the same time he created the term "political economy" (the title he had given to his treatise), promoted the idea that national frontiers were porous boundaries through which political bodies could allow the circulation of wealth that they had created and for which they were accountable. Nothing could bring about political centralization more completely than the notion that national frontiers provided a kind of receptacle for the economic wealth of a nation. It was from this idea that the mercantilist doctrine emerged, according to which the wealth of a country was judged by its capacity to increase its own wealth at the expense of its neighbors and, as the means to that end, relied on improvements in road networks, waterways, and the banking system. In Montchrestien's view, "it is not a plentiful supply of gold

Fig. 1. Frontispiece of Olivier de Serres's *Théâtre d'agriculture et ménage des champs*, 1615 edition. Courtesy of Bibliothèque municipale de Dijon, 15 849. A garden placed on the top of a triumphal arch is used as an emblem of public prosperity as ensured by Sully's policy. Within its precise quadrature, the king, his scepter in hand, sits between the figures of Justice and Abundance while a gardener busies himself in the foreground. Like a garden, the kingdom is fertilized by the wise administration of the king and by the labor of all his subjects.

and silver or the quantity of pearls and diamonds that makes countries rich: it is the provision of clothing and the necessities of life."[19]

Colbert later put that principle into practice as did de Serres, who dedicated his book, *Théâtre d'agriculture et mesnage des champs* (Theatre of agriculture and land management), to Henri IV, a dedication that gave a new tone to the relationship between gardens and the monarchy. According to de Serres, agriculture restored to the kingdom the peace and plenty "which had been destroyed by the civil wars."[20] This proposition was illustrated in a frontispiece in which the figure of the king was enthroned in the middle of a garden, surrounded by figures representing justice, peace, and plenty (Fig. 1).

All these concepts show the influence of some of the ideas popular in Huguenot circles. The Huguenots, who had been responsible for Henri IV's education, made an important contribution to sixteenth-century garden history in France[21] because they stressed the need to embellish nature and make it bountiful, which is the very essence of garden design.

Henri IV was not content simply to make the Tuileries the image of good government in the center of his capital. He built other great gardens, which have not survived, at Saint-Germain-en-Laye (Fig. 2). These, designed by Dupérac, Claude Mollet's master, descended through a series of different levels from the present-day terrace to the level of the Seine. Inside the gardens were grottoes decorated with rocaille. These contained machines of which we can get some idea from the illustrations in Salomon de Caus's book, *Les raisons des forces mouvantes* (An explanation of mechanical movement). The

Fig. 2. Saint-Germain: the gardens in 1614. After Alexandre Francine, Kungliga Biblioteket, Stockholm. Saint-Germain was probably the finest Renaissance garden in France at the time of Henri IV and Louis XIII. Grottoes were dug out under its terraces, forming a succession of quadratures ascending from the level of the river to the summit of the hill on which the château stands.

steep drop gave sufficient water pressure to move automata so that Perseus could be seen coming to the aid of Andromeda and slaying a dragon with predictably copious amounts of blood splashing out. Louis XIII often went to Saint-Germain as a child, and Louis XIV was born there. These are all indications that the court found relaxed enjoyment there of a kind Paris did not offer, despite the building works that Marie de Médicis had instigated as soon as she took charge of the kingdom as regent after the death of Henri IV.

Marie de Médicis also came from the celebrated Florentine family and had married Henri IV after he repudiated Marguerite de Valois. She was the granddaughter of Cosimo I and her uncle was Ferdinand de Médici, who had helped the future king of France in his struggle against the Ligue and who intervened with the pope to negotiate Henri's readmission to the Catholic Church. That explains how France came to have a queen who had lived at Castello, the Pitti Palace, and the Boboli Gardens. Henri IV, who knew her tastes and was not without a sense of family, set her up at Montceaux, a château in Brie that he had bought back from Catherine de Médicis's creditors for his mistress, Gabrielle d'Estrées, who had conveniently died.

Once she became regent, Marie de Médicis, maintaining the traditions of her own family and of the French monarchy, set out to endow Paris with a palace and gardens stylistically and functionally that resembled the Pitti Palace. With Salomon de Brosse as the architect, Boyceau as the gardener, and the Francine brothers responsible for the fountains, she could not go wrong; from the start the Luxembourg gardens were indeed one of the jewels of Paris. Overlooked by the majestic buildings of the palace, which gave them their name, the gardens were magnificent, particularly for the abundance of water, the *parterre de broderie*, and the grotto. The water was brought in by a monumental aqueduct designed by the Francine brothers. It was a forerunner of the Aqueduc de Maintenon, which Louis XIV built to use the waters of the Eure for the fountains of Versailles. The parterre de broderie was the work of Boyceau, the most rigorous theoretician of the baroque garden, who also designed the Parterre de la Terrasse at Versailles for Louis XIII. The grotto, possibly the work of Alexandre Francine, closed off the transversal axis that ran as far as the Rue d'Enfer and formed a magnificent kind of screen with sculptures representing the Seine and the Rhône. Here, too, one is reminded of Versailles with its statues of rivers along the miroirs d'eau and, even more strikingly, of the Grotte de Téthys, which was demolished in 1684 to make room for the north wing of the château.

As far as gardens were concerned, Louis XIII was less ambitious than his parents were, but his minister, Richelieu, amply made up for that, and his name is associated with the château de Richelieu, the Palais-Royal, and Rueil. Style was the only thing they had in common. The gardens of the Palais-Royal (which are still one of the prides of Paris) rivaled the Tuileries and the Luxembourg gardens in size. Suffice it to say that Richelieu's intention was to signal the importance of his political role by taking up residence near the Louvre, at the political heart of the kingdom. Rueil functioned as his country residence when the court was at Saint-Germain, and visitors to it mention the extensive gardens. Its machines attracted a great deal of admiring curiosity, while some of the fountains created rather racy comic effects. The influence of Italian mannerism is detectable and is even more obvious in the entrance to the grotto, which represented a huge open mouth, rather similar to the one in Bomarzo. The scale of the gardens, which have now wholly disappeared, was impressive since the central allée was eight hundred meters long with an Italian cascade, an orangery, and fountains decorated with mythological statues, some of which had been bought in Florence.

A Forerunner of Versailles: Richelieu, the Château, and the Model Town

The cultural influence of Italy was again apparent in the château and gardens that Richelieu built in his native Poitou. Only a few outer buildings have survived but the grounds can be visited. The estate was built on a grand scale and Lemercier had some difficulty with the design of the château, since Richelieu (like, later on, Louis XIV at Versailles) was determined to preserve the main part of the building created by his father.[22] Five large walkways converge on a circle, with a diameter of 100 meters, which led into an initial courtyard of 140 meters in length. This then led into a second narrower courtyard (124 meters long by 112 wide) and finally into the front courtyard of the château itself (70 meters by 60), which one entered through a portico linking the two wings of the main building. From the château, you looked down on parterres that ran the length of the main axis to form a semi-circle at the end, its diameter the same as the one at the entrance. Other much larger parterres stretched away at right angles as far as the nearby town, whose main axis led straight to the front courtyard of the château. This impressive ensemble was lavishly decorated with statues of ancient Romans, almost all of them linked to the imperial period.

Richelieu had always admired classical Roman statuary. As early as 1623 he had sent his intendant to Italy to buy ancient marble statues,[23] and many of them found their way to his château in Poitou, the home of his ancestors. In his study of Richelieu's collection, which rivaled that of the earl of Arundel in England, Louis Batiffol tells us, "In the Richelieu château, there are one hundred and ninety four sculptures, busts, and statues. Of these, about a hundred are statues and all but a dozen are classical antiquities. They are everywhere: they decorate the interiors and the façades of the château, where statues and busts alternate, and also in the parterres, and here they are raised on pedestals."[24] Hercules and Mars watch over the entrance. The two slaves Michelangelo had intended for the tomb of Pope Julian II were used to decorate the main building, on the balcony of the *piano nobile*. But the strong political overtones of the entire place came primarily from the numerous busts and statues of Roman emperors. These were found on the "Roman" parterre, where Albinus and Pertinax stood alongside Venus and Bacchus. They were in niches along the Parterre de la Demi-Lune where Marcus Aurelius was placed next to Julian the Apostate and Vitellius was next to Brutus, Mars, and a hermaphrodite. At the entrance to the château the pillars of the gates were decorated with statues of Augustus, Claudius, Otho, Titus, and Drusus.

The buildings and their decoration were truly magnificent. "Of the great houses of Europe it is the most beautiful, with the sole exception of Fontainebleau," Bouthillier said in 1635.[25] What had been in Richelieu's mind when he had this truly royal château built? No one knows, since he died three years after completing the whole estate, but it looks as though he intended to make it an important seat of political power, an administrative capital away from Paris. This political intention took the shape of a model town (still in existence and an impressive sight) adjacent to the cardinal's estate. It was built to Lemercier's design and the layout was a perfect rectangle with perpendicular streets (Fig. 3).

The town Richelieu had built and that still bears his name was never home to the "officers" whom he had perhaps intended to live there. But even if Poitou is a long way from Paris and Richelieu never really governed France from his own château, there is a clear parallel with Versailles. The idea of building a town intended to be the dependency of a seat of power was realized for the first time at Richelieu. The town was supposed to serve, in fact, as a center of commerce supported by tax exemptions, but it was also intended to be the administrative hub of the duchy, with law courts, an academy, a printing press, and a mission house of the order of the Sisters of Saint Vincent de Paul, an order housed in only two other places, Paris and Saint-Germain, both royal residences. As Philippe Boudon has observed, the cardinal, clearly intending to centralize power, had brought together in the main town of the duchy "the economic, legal and cultural bodies that had previously been scattered in different places," and this was "a small-scale exemplar of his policy

Fig. 3. Richelieu. The town and the château, Bibliothèque nationale de France, Estampes, Paris. The château stands in the center of the illustration. One corner of the city rampart can be seen on the left. In this bold anticipation of Versailles, Richelieu associated vast gardens (now destroyed) with a brand-new administrative town that is still in existence.

for the nation."[26] Richelieu obviously meant to make the capital of his duchy the model for what the administrative capital of the kingdom might become.

After Richelieu's death, there was no other project on such a grand scale until the time of Louis XIV. Although Cardinal Mazarin was responsible for buildings in Paris as well-known as the Collège des Quatre-Nations (now the Institut de France) and the Salpêtrière, he preferred paintings, objets d'art, jewelry, and books to gardens and palaces. The clearest sign of his impact on Versailles can probably be best detected in the political ethic of Louis XIV. For Mazarin, a diplomat whose consummate skill was recognized by friend and foe alike, to divide and rule, and to exercise control by devious maneuvering were ruling principles from which he never deviated. He was a mentor, able to make a strong impression on a young man impatient for the throne. Louis XIV never forgot the way in which his minister outflanked the dangerous conspirators of the Fronde, nor the moment of triumph when the Treaty of the Pyrenees was signed: "His Holy Eminence is as powerful as God the Father at the moment of Creation," said Guy Patin.[27] The king would also remember the example Mazarin set in choosing people he could trust. Colbert is proof of that. Before being promoted to the post he held until his death as Louis XIV's *contrôleur général*, Colbert had managed Mazarin's finances throughout the two decades when the latter held high office in the French monarchy. The young Louis XIV learned much from the cardinal about the conduct of public affairs, so much so that he was convinced he could do equally well himself and, after Mazarin's death, become his own minister. He was heir to a long tradition he would carry forward in his own way, forging the state as he wished it to be.

CHAPTER TWO

The Nature and Splendor of the Monarch

A Change in the "Political Decor"

Politics is the art of the possible, and all politicians know that a situation can only be understood in terms of where it might lead. When Mazarin died, Louis XIV had already absorbed that lesson. He had seen how the political instinct and patience of his mentor had turned public opinion around, enabling the queen and her two sons to be brought back to Paris to a chorus of approval from the very people who had driven them away two years earlier. He had also appreciated that this change in public opinion would not have come about had the monarchy not been buttressed by a real desire, at the very heart of society, for peace and economic development.

After Mazarin's death the time was ripe to move forward. The power of the aristocracy, which had been weakened by Richelieu and undermined by Mazarin's exploitation of its inherent contradictions, could no longer prevent the centralization needed to stimulate the production and circulation of wealth. For thirty-seven years the two cardinals had, successively, governed the state, accepting the burden of their unpopular structural reforms with an apparent selflessness that did not prevent them from amassing huge personal fortunes. After them, a king, especially a young king, seemed like a savior.

Louis XIV knew how much he owed to his two former ministers. Now that the machinery of centralized government was in place, he set out to give it a renewed impetus. Instinct told him that the faceless masses had put their trust in his youth, his natural authority, and his sense of spectacle, enabling him to restore to the monarchy the prestige it had lost since the death of

Henri IV. On 10 March 1661, he announced to an expanded council of ministers, "The scene has changed. The principles that I will follow in governing the state, managing finances, and conducting foreign affairs will be different from those of the late cardinal. You know my wishes. It is up to you now, gentlemen, to carry them out."[1]

The king took two decisive steps: first, he transformed his Conseil d'En-Haut into a decision-making body and second, he had Fouquet arrested to ensure that the council would operate in a new way. The "political decor" was indeed changing.

Until then, when the king had been "in council," he had been surrounded by the highest-ranking men of the realm. For the sake of greater efficiency, the pomp and ceremony of this body had to be minimized. The only men remaining on the new council were Fouquet, who would keep his post as superintendent of finances for a few months, Le Tellier, secretary of state for war, and Lionne, who was responsible for foreign affairs. As a result of this first coup, the young king immediately had to accept a much higher level of personal responsibility. When, in the first decade of his reign, he wrote (or had his advisers write) his *Mémoires*[2] for the instruction of his heir, the Dauphin, he explained how he had learned the art of politics when still in the shadow of the cardinal. He was, he said, very pleased when "consummately skillful men" proposed solutions that he had worked out himself "privately and without the help of an adviser." In this way he had begun to look at the state "not as a neutral observer but as a ruler."[3]

But a ruler needs to have the resources to implement his policies. Thus, his next step was to remove the man in charge of the purse strings. Until then, all the kings of France had considered their superintendent of finances as a banker. But Louis XIV did not want a banker; he wanted an accountant. Colbert had carried out that role for Mazarin and he was happy to make his great skill available to the new master. The king, therefore, had to get rid of Fouquet, whose continuing presence had become particularly galling because the magnificence of his château at Vaux-le-Vicomte overshadowed the royal estate at nearby Fontainebleau. The deed was quickly done, and on the same day d'Artagnan arrested Fouquet, Louis XIV wrote to his mother from Nantes to "give her the details of this business." He proudly reported that he had hoodwinked Fouquet by telling him that he was looking for some papers while in fact he was watching for d'Artagnan to come through the courtyard so that he could arrest Fouquet. The king took no less pride in declaring publicly that from then on he would take personal charge of the Treasury. This was, he said, "his key to acquiring wealth and to relieving the suffering of his people."[4]

Immediately after this, he signed an edict by which he would personally endorse all public financial transactions. He also appointed the intendant de finances to the council and gave him the responsibility of looking after the accounts, with instructions to tell no one about them "without the express order of His Majesty."[5] Colbert thus became the king's right-hand man for public finance. He played the role of executor of the king's policy and kept his master informed about his wealth and liquid assets.[6] He reduced the tax on income (taille)—always a popular measure—and reduced the dues paid to the tax collectors from 25 percent to 4 percent. On the other hand, he doubled the income from the tax farms (indirect taxes, customs, gabelles, and customs dues), which increased the income from the royal domains almost sevenfold to 5,500,000 livres in 1671.[7] Even so, the network of *traitants* and *partisans*[8] was left in place, but the yield from the financial system increased substantially. This accounts in general for the large sums of money that the king was able to spend on Versailles and other projects.

One can understand how Louis XIV believed that he was imposing order throughout the realm and making the whole system clearer by taking measures he deemed salutary and fair because they were rational. He enjoyed being king, writing in his *Mémoires*, "I made it a rule to work regularly, twice a day, for two or three hours on each occasion, with different people. . . . I cannot tell you how immediately beneficial this proved to be. My spirits soared, my resolution doubled. I became a different person. I discovered myself anew. It seemed to me then that I was king and born to rule" (Fig. 4).[9]

These words herald the first twenty years of Louis XIV's reign, when the palace and gardens of Versailles grew and took shape. Those were the years that forged the reputation of the young king as a sort of genius, a reputation that persisted throughout his life and even into the following century. As Voltaire put it in his *Siècle de Louis XIV*,

> He showed how an absolute monarch who has the will to do good can readily achieve anything he wants. He had only to command and administrative triumphs followed as swiftly as his conquests in the field. It was truly wonderful to see new defenses, which were both beautiful and useful, spring up around the seaports that had lain abandoned and in ruins. They swarmed with ships and sailors, already containing sixty great vessels that he could equip for war. Everywhere, under his standard, settlers

Fig. 4. Louis XIV, king of France. This portrait attributed to Charles Le Brun shows the king at the beginning of his reign when the Versailles gardens were taking shape.

were leaving to found new colonies in America, in the East Indies, and on the shores of Africa. Meanwhile, in France, under the king's direction, the construction of huge buildings gave work to thousands of men, fostering all the arts that architecture brings with it. Within his court and in his capital, arts of a nobler and more brilliant kind bestowed on France pleasures and splendor undreamt of by former ages.[10]

Such a judgment, pronounced long after Louis XIV's death, and by a historian who was in fact critical of the institutions of absolutism, explains very well the excesses of some of the Sun King's contemporaries, particularly those who had the greatest interest in promoting a veritable cult of the royal person to avert any possible revival of the Fronde and in modernizing the state along the lines proposed by Colbert and his advisers.

The Monarch, Head of the Social Body

The images used in praise of the regime are often linked with nature and explain why gardens might have seemed appropriate for giving expression to these laudatory ideas. Even a mere chronicler, as far back as 1649, was able to put into words a view that became almost universal by the 1660s. The crown, he wrote, using the glittering panoply of metaphors linked to the solar myth, was "this brilliant star, this radiant sun, this endless day, this center to which all lines from the circumference point; in short, this prime mover who in turn moves all things in France."[11] The role of royal sovereignty is defined here in mechanistic terms, mirroring the scientific work of the period. But Bossuet, taking as his point of departure the scriptures, draws similarly lyrical comparisons: "Consider the Prince in his chamber. From him alone emanate the orders, which concert the efforts of magistrates and officers, citizens and soldiers, provinces and armies on land and on sea. It is the image of God, who from his throne on high, moves heaven and earth."[12]

How can we account for this strange mixture of ancient and modern, of sacred and profane, and the emphasis on the eternal laws of nature?

One explanation for this enthusiasm, displayed by a modest chronicler and a great churchman, lies in the deep and powerful groundswell of opinion in which the king felt himself caught up. The wars of religion were over, the king had triumphed over the Fronde, and divinely ordained absolutism was endorsed by a consensus resulting from several factors: popular belief, as exemplified by the royal touch to cure scrofula, a ceremony the king was careful never to neglect; the teachings of the Catholic Church, which was traditionally in favor of strong monarchical power; the support of the Protestants, who needed a strong power to enforce the Edict of Nantes, and, above all, the *noblesse de robe*, who owed their new social standing to the royal administration. This group knew how to wield the pen to honor the king as "the soul of the universe, second only to God, a buttress that supports the world."[13] They also knew that they had nothing to lose by implementing the king's centralizing policy, since centralization means rationalization, the struggle against provincial customs and particularities, and the imposition in public life of legal principles, which are by definition abstract and therefore universal. The king, who wanted to be seen as modern, could count on their support and they, in turn, served to promote his glory, that indissoluble symbiosis between the prestige of the state and the person of the sovereign.

However, Louis XIV, conscious as he was of the importance of support from the "*intelligents*," as the noblesse de robe was known, was equally aware of the tradition that had linked church and crown from time immemorial. There was nothing modern about this link, but it established a bond between the king and the very heart of his people. It comes as no surprise then that the voice of the old and the voice of the new were raised in unison, glorifying the royal person in images that were consciously universal and understood by all. And what could be simpler or more universal than the sight of the sun bathing the world in light?

This use of a pagan symbol raises the question of the king's faith. According to Voltaire, who claimed to have heard it from Cardinal Fleury, Louis XIV's belief was "naive and simple."[14] He probably saw no contradiction between the chapel at Versailles (a relatively late addition) and the daily flight of Apollo over his apartments. He was genuinely pious and observed all the rituals of worship. But his was the piety of the politician who would not be deterred by metaphysical questions; he concentrated on the pragmatic. His *Mémoires* show that he used religion to sanction the social hierarchy, whose structure is replicated in the order that the gardens of Versailles imposed on nature.

The *Mémoires* were written for the Dauphin at a time when Bossuet was his tutor and working on the first part of his *Politique tirée des propres paroles de l'Ecriture sainte* (Politics taken from the very words of scripture).[15] We can, therefore, be sure that during the years when the palace and the gardens of Versailles were under construction, the king and the bishop met on an almost daily basis and discussed "questions of mutual interest," as they say in diplomatic circles. As a result the relationship that developed between them was strong enough for Louis XIV to consult Bossuet thirty years later when he decided to clamp down on quietism and destroy Port-Royal-des-Champs. This likely explains why the bishop chose that time to complete his *Politique* and fulfill his self-appointed task as the theorist of absolutism and divine right.

According to Bossuet, the king is flesh and blood like every human being, but he is also the Lord's anointed and as such he has a mission, making him into the image of God and his minister in the affairs of this world.[16] This is the meaning of the famous sermon he preached in 1662 in Louis XIV's presence, just after the king had come to the throne: "You are gods . . . but gods made flesh and blood, earth and dust. You will die as mortal men. No matter.

You are gods, though you will die. Your royal authority lives on: its spirit passes to your heirs. . . . The man dies, it is true, but the king, we say, lives on: the image of God is everlasting."[17] Bossuet is stating a well-established principle that had been handed down through the centuries. It is as though ideas that had come down from the Middle Ages had been given a new lease on life by the development of absolutism in the baroque period. The decline of feudalism went hand in hand with centralization. As a result, the power of the crown, in which sovereignty was vested, seemed all the greater, since it seemed to come from a higher and more distant authority.

In his *Mémoires* Louis XIV, while not pretending to be a scholar, argues as though he had had the same intellectual training as Bossuet. In essence, they speak with one voice. In book 3 of Bossuet's *Politique*, titled "Où l'on commence à expliquer la nature et les propriétés de l'autorité royale" (In which we begin to explain the nature and character of royal authority), he starts with a single article containing only one premise: "There are four essential characteristics of royal authority: first, royal authority is sacred; second, it is paternal; third, it is absolute; fourth, it obeys the laws of reason."[18] For his part, Louis XIV says, "God who has set kings over men has decreed that they should be regarded as his lieutenants. Only God can hold kings to account. His wish is that whosoever is born a subject should obey without question."[19] The sacred character of the king's function confers upon him prerogatives that place him over all other men. As Bossuet puts it, "By virtue of his position, the king is father to his people and his greatness places him above petty concerns."[20] Similarly, Louis XIV says, "As I have told you elsewhere, since a sovereign is placed above other men, what his eye falls upon, he discerns more perfectly than they."[21]

This position is a consequence of his role as "God's lieutenant," which is the basis for his theory of sovereignty and his right to legislate for all. Again in his *Mémoires*, Louis XIV writes, "Our submission before God serves as the model and the rule for the obedience owed to us. Armies, councils—all the efforts of mankind—would not suffice to keep us on the throne if everyone believed that they had the same right to it as we do and did not revere a higher authority from which our own derives. The public homage we pay to this invisible power could in fact be justly held the chief and most important tenet of our policy, were it not that we have a higher and more disinterested reason for it."[22]

In the subtlest way, this shows that religion is useful to the supreme lawgiver in that it legitimates his authority. The "public homage" paid to God is mirrored by the homage due to princes and justifies all the ceremonial trappings surrounding their person. The king owes it to himself to live in the public eye, resplendent in all the pomp and ceremony of his role. As a living symbol of the state, he has to be omnipresent and to see into "the hearts of everyone," to borrow Primi Visconti's expression.[23] His palace and gardens are a theater in which he can display the splendor and majesty of the monarchy. Once again, Bossuet puts the king's thoughts into words: "The grandeur of God is manifest in the majesty of the prince."[24]

Ironically, Bossuet expresses these ancient ideas in a form that was consciously modern. His *Politique* is in fact constructed geometrically, namely, that the argument proceeds from a statement of principles that are then demonstrated as theorems. The method reminds us of Hobbes or the atheist Spinoza. However, this is hardly surprising. Bossuet had these authors' works in his library and the king had enough experience in politics to perceive their relevance personally when he thought about the sad destiny of Charles I of England or when he discussed the political theories of the English puritans and of the Dutch republicans.

The medieval image of the prince as God's representative on earth was thus modernized by references to astronomy and to seventeenth-century mechanics; the king became the pivotal point around which society, seen as a vast and unified whole, revolved. This corresponds to the definition of sovereignty given by Cardin Le Bret, one of Richelieu's advisors, in his book *De la souveraineté du roi*: "Sovereignty is no more divisible than a geometrical point."[25]

As a metaphor for the notion that the absolute nature of sovereignty made all subjects equal before the king, contemporary political discourse frequently evoked the circumference of a circle. Nivelon said that the king wins battles by sending orders "from the center of the state to its circumference," and Racine depicts him illuminating the whole world while "scarcely moving from the center of his kingdom."[26] This is reminiscent of the "bonds of authority" with which Pascal linked the king to other men, as well as of Hobbes's *Leviathan*, that great social body governed by economic solidarity (Fig. 5). Hobbes was also in favor of using a geometrical model to centralize the state along rational lines. He states unequivocally that for men to live in peace, they must "conferre all their power and strength upon one Man, or upon one Assembly of men."[27] To do that they have to construct a political body according to mathematical principles: "The skill of making, and maintaining Common-wealths, consisteth in certain Rules, as doth Arithmetique and Geometry; not (as Tennis-play) on Practise onely."[28]

Geometry and arithmetic are based on numbers and figures or, in other words, symbols with an eternal and universal value. The political thought of

Fig. 5. Frontispiece of Thomas Hobbes's *Leviathan*, 1651 edition. Bibliothèque nationale de France, Paris. Absolutism made visible: the "body politick" of the nation is composed of men, different but all standing together. The body has but one head, that of the monarch, in whose hands sovereignty resides.

the baroque period, trying to gauge the size of the gigantic Leviathan, attributed rational self-awareness to the monster, allowing him to understand how he was organized. Descartes understood this and he, too, developed a mathematized theory of absolute government. In a letter to the abbé Mersenne, he wrote, "The mathematical truths that you call eternal were established by God and depend entirely on him, as does all the rest of his creation. . . . I pray you; do not be afraid to declare firmly and publicly that it is God who has established these laws in nature, just as a king does in his realm."[29]

That premise led Louis to employ the term "reason" frequently and even the phrase *raison d'état*. It also explained his utter certainty that the king's actions should be inspired by a transcendent logic, the rational organization of all Creation itself. Doubtless Descartes was not one of the king's favorite writers, but if by any chance he could have read that letter to Mersenne, he would have thought it fit well with his conception of power. Indeed we find the same idea in his *Mémoires:* "Since we take the place of God, as it were, we seem to be privy to his knowledge, as well as his authority."[30]

If, by analogy with the laws of nature, the laws of the kingdom are sacred and rational, it is hardly surprising that on his deathbed the king said, "I am about to depart this life, but the state will never die."[31]

Phrases like this explain how the king could have seen gardens as extending the order he planned to impose on society into the landscape. For a man like him, always concerned about being a model of self-control and being able to hold the ring between different factions (Colbert's followers against those of Louvois, the supporters of the Gallican church against the pope, orthodox religion against first the Jansenists then the Quietists) or to persuade them to pull together to enlarge the state by wars, contemplating the order of nature must have seemed like "contemplating at length the calm of the gods."

But now that we have explained why the king saw himself as "God's lieutenant on earth," the "indivisible point" from which all the "bonds of authority" with other men radiated, we must turn to the man whose private decision it was to build Versailles. What do we really know about his artistic tastes, his love of nature, his sense of the landscape? He was so extravagantly praised in his lifetime and so vilified sometimes by posterity that we must revisit contemporary documents to see him as he really was.

Louis XIV, who had an instinctive sense of his hold on the public imagination, chose the sun, the largest visible body in the cosmos, as the image of regal majesty. He explained that decision in his *Mémoires.* The passage is rightly famous, but it is worth pausing to examine it.

We chose as the central image the sun, the noblest symbol of them all.
By its uniqueness, the effulgence that surrounds it, by the light it transmits to other stars that, like courtiers, attend on it, by the just, impartial

gift of that same light to all parts of the world, by the good it does everywhere, giving on all sides perpetual life and joy and the power of action, by its ceaseless motion beneath its surface calm, by its constant and unchanging course through the heavens, which never permits any deviation, it is undoubtedly the most vivid and most splendid image of a great monarch.

Clearly the king wanted a simple, powerful symbol that would strike the public imagination, and the idea conjured up by the image of the sun fit his political aim. Once again, he was linking old and new. In the time of Henri III, the sun had already been used as an emblem for the regal majesty. In the *Panégyrique pour le bienvenu et retour du très-chrétien Henry Roy de France de Pologne* (Panegyric for the welcome and return of Henry, most Christian king of France and Poland), we find, "For the poor who dwell in the country and those who dwell in the town, as well as other peace-loving people, you resemble the sun that shines impartially on all, bringing its life-giving warmth to every plant and animal on the earth."[32]

Louis XIV took this image and rejuvenated it. Its meaning was sufficiently impressive to make an impact on both the humblest and the most powerful. It was universal enough to evoke the "all-seeing eye" of the prince, and it could lend itself to a modern interpretation because of its link with astronomy, a science that since Copernicus had become increasingly popular. Through this image, the king became a modern political figure at the center of the social system. All human atoms gravitated around him at a greater or lesser distance, kept in motion by his irresistible and regular trajectory. He bathed them all in warmth and light, spreading the benefits of fruitfulness everywhere.

In his *Explication historique de ce qu'il y a de plus remarquable dans la maison royale de Versailles et en celle de Monsieur à Saint-Cloud*, the abbé Laurent Morellet said of Apollo, "He and his sister Diana divide the year between them and under their gentle sway, the earth brings forth all manner of plants."[33] According to Louis XIV himself, the power of the Sun King should "give life, joy, and the power of action to all." That was something Saint-Simon did not understand when he reproached Louis XIV for having chosen as the site for the gardens of Versailles "the most gloomy and unrewarding place of all. No view, no woodland, no water, and no soil. Because everything there is shifting sand or marshy ground, the place is airless: one will never be able to breathe there."[34]

In fact, an unappealing location was exactly what the king wanted to display his power over nature and create the image of a powerful, prosperous, and attractive monarchy. He wanted to take on the most difficult task possible so as compare favorably with his predecessors, crowning the long tradition that linked gardens and the monarchy with an achievement worthy of posterity. This is what Saint-Simon could not understand. He failed to perceive an essential trait of the king's character—not, for once, out of malice but out of simple myopia. This reaction raises the question of the king's relations with the people who saw how he operated. Among these were people like Dangeau and the marquis of Sourches, who simply report events without ever making a judgment or general statement about them. Others like Madame de Sévigné, the duchess of Orléans (the Princess Palatine), or the abbot of Choisy were just curious and with the odd word suggest a tiny flaw in the hieratic self-image the king had constructed. Finally, there were historians or memorialists, such as Saint-Simon, Voltaire, and Ezechiel Spanheim. Their testimony is vital, provided that it is used in the right way.

Voltaire does not claim to have firsthand knowledge. He begins his history, *Le siècle de Louis XIV*, in 1736, with the king already long dead. However, fascinated as he was by the brilliance of Louis XIV's reign, he goes out of his way to find eyewitness accounts to bring his narrative to life, sometimes getting a little carried away by his enthusiasm despite his real talent as a historian.

As for Saint-Simon, he was a true aristocrat, a *grand seigneur* from one of the ancient families of France. He detested "the bourgeois vulgarians" who surrounded the king and wrote to spite them and to defend the honor of the nobility. He used his pen as a weapon, and if he managed to score a point, he thought he was right. But he scored points because he saw things as they were, at least to his own way of thinking. And provided that one knows him well enough to spot the distortions, it is possible to see that his portrait of the dramatis personae in that splendid theater of Louis XIV's court rings true.

The erudite Spanheim, author of a famous treatise on numismatics, also claimed to be an eyewitness, but he was no duke or peer of the realm. He was a foreigner, sent as an envoy to the French court by the Elector of Brandenburg from 1680 to 1689. A scholar, he took to writing history, as did Pierre Bayle, with the genuine (if possibly self-deluding) intention of being objective. He was three-quarters French through his mother and paternal grandmother, and his *Relation de la cour de France*, written in French, bears the stamp of loyalty to the Protestant cause and a desire to tell the truth.

The testimony of these three historians is important for an understanding of the king's grand design for Versailles. Their accounts must be examined before moving on to witnesses who, though perhaps less ambitious, are nonetheless essential.

In Voltaire's eyes, Louis XIV was a second Augustus: "His words were always carefully chosen and loftily expressed, and he took care in public always to speak, as he acted, like a sovereign."[35] He admits that "Louis XIV had more judgment and dignity than wit" but admires him for having sought to "reform his kingdom, create beauty in his court, and encourage the arts." This program was carried out because, Voltaire goes on, "Louis XIV had a taste for architecture, gardens, and sculpture, and this taste was always for the grand and noble."[36] He has the highest regard for the king's character and gives him full credit for the cultural policy inaugurated in 1661: "Several writers have attributed solely to Colbert Louis XIV's munificence and the protection given to the arts, but in fact his only part in it was to lend support to the king's generosity and taste."[37] He adds, "If, one day, pieces like the baths of Apollo were found under the ruins and exposed to the elements in the bosquets of Versailles, . . . these modern-day artifacts would probably be compared with the finest of Greek antiquities."[38]

Saint-Simon did not share Voltaire's opinion. In his eyes, Louis XIV preferred quantity to quality: "Who could count the buildings he put up? Who could fail to be appalled by such arrogance, caprice, and bad taste?"[39] The château of Versailles was no exception: "All the buildings were built in quick succession with no overall plan; everything was jumbled together; lovely buildings sat cheek by jowl with undistinguished ones, vast spacious ones next to mean ones." However, some things did find favor: the Trianon, "a palace of marble, jasper and porphyry"; Clagny, "a magnificent château, with its fountains, gardens, and park"; and the ornaments in the gardens of Versailles: "Neither Asia nor Antiquity can rival these gardens in scale or variety. They have nothing so ornate, or so magnificent, nothing so perfect from recent centuries or so full of the rarest monuments from every other, in marble of every kind, bronzes, paintings, and sculptures."[40] Despite these praises, he was still scandalized by the amount of money spent on diverting "the whole of the river Eure" to supply the fountains, a piece of misinformation he gleaned from some unlikely source. In Saint-Simon's eyes, Versailles exemplified the overweening pride of a king who "in everything preferred splendor, magnificence, and abundance" and could not keep his obsession with appearances under control. He thought the gardens of Versailles had been created because of the king's "arrogant pleasure in imposing his will on nature," and if anyone had pointed out that it was Descartes who wanted to give mankind "mastery and owner-ship of nature," he would probably have riposted that the monarchy had come to a pretty pass if the king needed to turn to a philosopher for counsel.

Spanheim offers some useful correctives to the disparity of views between Voltaire and Saint-Simon. He presents himself as a diplomat with divided loy-alties: as a Protestant, he has every reason to dislike Louis XIV, but as a histo-rian he is bound to remain impartial. He praises the king for his "attention to affairs of state" and, like Voltaire and Saint-Simon, notes that his education was "neglected." However—and it is an important caveat—he emphasizes the transformation brought about by the exercise of power. He says that once the king had taken political control, "the power of his inspiration increased so much that he seemed able to carry the whole burden of state affairs and gov-ernment on his own."[41] He goes on: "Without being a scholar or a serious and enthusiastic reader, he writes well and judiciously. He appreciates the fine arts and protects them. He is particularly well versed in music, painting, and fine buildings. He has a fair and balanced judgment of things and of people insofar as they are known to him." This passage is significant in that it highlights what seem to have been Louis XIV's great merits: good judgment in the appoint-ments he made; his taste for the arts; and his choice of words.

As far as the arts are concerned, other testimonies are just as interesting, particularly an account by Daniel Cronström,[42] attaché to the Swedish em-bassy in Paris, of the presentation to Louis XIV of a Correggio Saint Jerome, which was a gift from the Swedish architect Nicodemus Tessin. Cronström describes the king gazing raptly at the painting and then after a while saying, "I can see it is very beautiful but I lack the expertise needed to appreciate all its beauties." However, he was still able to say, "The style of the drapery is dif-ferent from the other Correggio paintings, but since it is a sketch for the great painting in Parma, that is hardly surprising." All these observations came from a well-informed art lover who knew how to spot differences in the way the drapery was painted, differences that later raised questions about its attri-bution to Correggio. It is clear from this kind of evidence that Louis XIV was a man more sensitive to painting and architecture than to literature and suffi-ciently interested in things artistic to tell Le Brun that he would be "pleased to give up some moments of leisure to watch him paint."[43]

Of all the historians and memorialists who saw the king firsthand, it was Saint-Simon who best conveys the king's love of the gardens. Before quoting him again, however, let us turn to the marquis of Sourches who, in a simple sentence or two, describes the king walking alone in his gardens or, oblivious to bad weather, spending many hours in them: "In the evening, between five and six o'clock, after he had walked for two hours in his gardens as if to bid them farewell, the king took the carriage to spend the night at Meudon."[44] Similarly, six years later, when the king was seventy-four, "The king spent all morning in his gardens, despite the rain, and then went out again for the whole evening after dinner, despite the cold."[45] But here is what Saint-Simon says:

> The king loved to be out in the fresh air, and when he was deprived of it, his health would suffer, causing headaches and fits of the vapors. When he was younger, this had caused him to make excessive use of perfumes and, as a result, for many years afterward, he could not suffer any except the scent of orange blossom, and if you had cause to be near him, you had to take great care to have none about your person.

> Since he was tolerant of cold and heat, and even of rain, only extremes of weather deterred him from venturing outdoors every day. There were just three reasons for these excursions. At least once a week and often several times, he went stag hunting in Marly or Fontainebleau with his own pack of hounds and some others. Once or twice a week, particularly on Sundays or feast days when he had nobody working in the gardens and did not want to watch the big hunts, he went shooting on his estates and no man in France was such an accurate, accomplished, and elegant shot. At other times, he would walk in his gardens and buildings and inspect the work in progress. Sometimes on his walks he would be accompanied by ladies and in the forests of Marly and Fontainebleau where he would arrange for food to be served. And in Fontainebleau, the whole court would on occasion walk with him around the canal. It was a magnificent sight with some of the courtiers riding on horseback.[46]

Saint-Simon's testimony shows how the king, with all the physical delight of robust good health, reveled in the outdoor life. This established a link between the gardens and the château where the far corners of the ceiling in the Salon de Mercure were painted with allegorical images of "physical agility, knowledge of the fine arts; justice and royal authority." For Louis XIV, the splendor of the prince was linked to the aura emanating from his person, and the gardens allowed him to demonstrate that, to quote Bossuet, "the surroundings of greatness must themselves be great." As the king puts it in his *Mémoires*, "If a foreigner enters a state that is prosperous and well governed, expenditure on what may seem to be unnecessary extravagance creates a very favorable impression of magnificence, power, wealth, and grandeur. Moreover, physical skill and grace, which can only be achieved and maintained by such expenditure, always befits a prince and ensures that a favorable judgment of what can be seen will be extended to what cannot."[47]

And "what can be seen" or, more precisely, what he wanted to display, was the image of good government.

CHAPTER THREE

A New Image of Good Government

The Politics of Landscape: The Ineluctable Rise of Versailles

The king's temperament and outlook drew him to Versailles for personal reasons. His liaison with Mademoiselle de la Vallière, his love of hunting and open air have already been mentioned, and the memory of his father, Louis XIII, for whom Versailles had been a refuge in moments of depression, could be added to the list. But there was another reason, every bit as far-reaching and personal for someone who was creating a new form of government, namely, to have a very private place in which to work out his political strategy. He needed to be sure that he had somewhere to work in peace and, if necessary, in secret. This explains why he wanted to make Versailles comfortable enough to allow him to receive the Conseil d'En-Haut from time to time and to provide a place where he could hunt and work. He pursued this idea because it was attractive on two counts. If he could invite the court to join him there, it would enjoy a new setting that could be made sufficiently splendid so as to cut the nobility off from its power bases in the provinces. As for the bourgeoisie, who increased their own importance by increasing the power of the king, the most ambitious and promising of their number could also be cut off from Paris.

Louis XIV was enough of a politician and landscape artist to know this instinctively, but Colbert, his indispensable adviser and respected mentor, took a very different line. His true loyalties by birth and inclination lay with the bourgeoisie. In his view, the king of France ought to stay in Paris at the Louvre. All that was needed at Versailles was a hunting lodge. If the king wanted to improve the estate, he could replace the small Louis XIII château with a "fine house" that was suitably grand, but he should certainly not construct a completely new "envelope" around the existing buildings. As for the gardens, he would do better to leave those as they were. Colbert put all this in writing to Louis XIV in a memorandum quoted in the Colbert correspondence.

> It is impossible to construct a great house in that space. The terrain is hemmed in not just by the parterres but also by the village, the church, and the étang. The slope of the parterres and the avenues is so steep that it is impossible to extend the site or acquire more land without destroying everything at prodigious expense. It is true that the flower parterre is level with the château, but the other one slopes steeply. Added to that, from the château there must be a parterre that is flat or level with it or there must be a terrace, and that is impossible.[1]

However, the king did not want to abandon the idea of Le Vau's envelope, probably because it would be constructed on the three sides that overlooked the surrounding countryside, thereby revealing the potential for landscaping the site. He ordered work to begin and Colbert, availing himself of the frankness that the king had always encouraged, sent him a respectful but acerbic memorandum: "If your Majesty wishes to see where the five hundred thousand écus and more that have been spent on Versailles in the last two years have gone, he will be hard put to discover it. . . . How sad that Versailles should be the yardstick by which the greatest and most virtuous king, possessed of that true virtue that characterizes the greatest of princes, will be measured. And yet one has reason to fear this misfortune."[2] He added, in the hope of averting this "misfortune,"

> May it further please your Majesty to observe that he is in the hands of two persons who have hardly known him at all except at Versailles, that is to say, in the context of pleasure and entertainment. These persons are not acquainted with your Majesty's love of kingly glory, from whatever quarter it might derive. The range of their minds, their station in life, their various private interests, their concern to wait attentively upon your Majesty, together with the patronage they enjoy, mean that they will lead your Majesty from one design to the next in an effort to ensure the immortal reputation of these creations, unless your Majesty guards against this.[3]

Who were these two men who were known to Louis XIV only at Versailles (or "hardly known") and whose "interests," "station in life," and "range of mind" conspired to make the king's reputation dependent on that place? Surely Le Vau and Le Nôtre?[4] It cannot have been Le Brun, since he was in charge of the Académie de peinture and on excellent terms with Colbert, whose portrait he had painted. By contrast, in the eyes of the king's minister, Le Vau was out to make money and despite good judgment was as much a *maçon* or entrepreneur as an architect, and this may possibly explain why the Académie d'architecture was not founded until after his death. As for Le Nôtre, he was undoubtedly a garden designer whose parterres in the Tuileries were widely admired, but he was equally likely to have had ambitions for a whole landscape—as had been seen at Vaux-le-Vicomte—which meant that absurd sums of money were swallowed up by places whose sole function was to be visually pleasing. That was no way, in Colbert's view, for a king to forge a glorious reputation.

It seems, however, that a sort of complicity had already been established between the garden designer and the king, one grounded in the potential that the site of Versailles offered. Le Nôtre knew enough about human nature to understand that a great minister could be completely unaware of landscape, whereas a young king could fall in love with a place and project onto it the image of his tastes and aspirations. Like Louis XIV, he saw in the infertile plain of Versailles possibilities for a design far grander than that of Vaux-le-Vicomte. He had in mind a completely open perspective, free of all obstacles, where the path of the sun itself determined the median axis. The eye would then travel downward along it toward the pièce d'eau—which could be seen from the windows of Le Vau's envelope—and from there to a Grand Canal, even longer than the one at Fontainebleau, which would stretch toward the horizon like a stream of liquid light.

When it became quite clear that the king would not give up the idea of Le Vau's envelope nor the great gardens he could already see in his mind's eye, Colbert gave way. True, expenditure at Versailles was reduced in 1667, which may indicate that the king had perhaps heeded his minister—unless the War of Devolution against Spain had depleted the coffers—but the work began again in earnest in 1668 and expenditure doubled in 1669.[5]

Once he had resigned himself to the project, Colbert served the king with his usual competence and scrupulous attention to detail, keeping his master in touch with everything that went on. In a letter of 1672, when the king was in Flanders, Colbert wrote, "The stem of the cast-iron tree for the

Bosquet du Marais has been put in place and several branches have been sol-dered on. All the foliage has been beaten out and is ready to be attached to the branches. I have had a small supporting wall built in the Bassin du Marais to carry the beds of reeds, so there is no fear of their falling into the water as they have done previously."[6]

It is hard to believe that the same man could supervise the building of one of the bosquets in Versailles while issuing orders to the director of the Académie de France in Rome. But Colbert managed to do both at once. Was he hoping to flatter the king by writing to him about things that particularly interested him? Or was it rather that, having once accepted Versailles, he had been persuaded by Le Nôtre that gardens could be just as effective as buildings in forging the glorious reputation of the king? Documentary evidence does not provide a definitive answer, but it does appear that Colbert developed a genuine interest in garden design. He began to consider the impact gardens made, and in 1670 he even formulated an aesthetic judgment in a letter to the king, something Colbert rarely did: "We found that the increase in height of four inches in the designs for the figures in the Allée d'Eau will work well, as will moving the figures four feet further apart, in the Bassin du Dragon."[7]

This is evidence of real interest in gardens. It increased sufficiently for Colbert to ask Le Nôtre to design a garden for his château at Sceaux. He had probably discovered that the latter had a mind of sufficient "range" to en-hance the king's reputation and that of his minister. But how was the glorious reputation of the king to be expressed in landscape?

Hierarchies of Rank, Hierarchies of Space

The official political ideology, that of Bossuet and the king, offered a precise conception of society. This is how Louis XIV's *Mémoires* describe the social body, that vast, shifting, working mass governed by the "state."

> Every trade and every profession lends its support to the monarchy in its own way. The toil of the laborer provides food for all this great social body; the industrious artisan supplies all the needs and convenience of the public; and the merchant garners from a thousand different places all the goods that are both useful and pleasurable so that each individual may have them as they are needed. The financiers, by collecting public funds, ensure the survival of the State; the judges, by applying the laws,

ensure the safety and security of all; and the men of the Church, by instructing the population in religion, draw down the blessings of heaven by safeguarding peace on earth. This is why, far from holding any condition of men in contempt, we must be father to all to bring them all, if possible, to the pinnacle of perfection that befits their rank.[8]

Society is presented here as a harmonious entity, a living body in which every organ supports the life of every other under the supreme authority of the king, who is unique and set apart from all other groups: this puts him in a position to bring them to "the pinnacle of perfection that befits their rank." This last phrase makes clear that a harmonious society is a hierarchical society. If, as Louis XIV says elsewhere in his *Mémoires*, "we are the head of a body of which [the subjects] are the limbs,"[9] then some are made to fulfill one function, others a different one, but each must stay in his allotted place. The social order depends on rank, and rank depends on birth. The *Mémoires* represent the common people as an undifferentiated mass whose subsistence is earned through work; this makes them worthy of respect and they should not be unduly burdened by taxes. Individuals within that group have no right to consider the conduct of affairs of state, which should be left to princes and their advisers. It was in these terms that Louis XIV would describe Cromwell, a commoner, as "a man whom talent, opportunities, and the misfortunes of his country had inspired with ideas far above his station."[10]

Similarly, the clergy, who were always quick to point out to others where their duty lay, should remember their own obligations. What the king has to say about this allows him to consider all three orders of society: the aristocracy, the clergy, and the people.

> Would it be just if members of the aristocracy were to give their efforts and their blood for the defense of the kingdom, so often depleting their own resources to fulfill their role, and if the people, who possess so little and have so many mouths to feed, were forced to shoulder alone all the expenses of the state, while the clergy, exempt by their calling from the dangers of war, from the expenses of luxury, and the burden of family, enjoyed in their plenty all the advantages of the public weal, without ever contributing in the smallest measure to supply their own needs?[11]

The aristocracy is once again mentioned in the will Louis XIV drafted a year before his death, where he describes it as "the chief force" of the kingdom.[12]

And the king knew well how to harness that force. He never missed an opportunity to show that he shared their love of bearing arms and their sensitivity to slights on their honor. Knowing that Richelieu and Mazarin had considerably reduced the political importance of the nobility, he had contrived to retain their loyalty by removing the "usurpers" who had wormed their way into their ranks as proof that he wanted them seen as an elite linked to the ancient tradition of France and a repository of the values it represented.[13] And so the aristocracy, feeling that their special place had been recognized, had accepted to live at court around a king who acknowledged their special role and from whom they received favors in the form of *grâces*. Even so, they were not simply a foppish band whose talents were confined to the dance floor or the pageants of the court. There is ample evidence that demonstrates how the wars at the end of Louis XIV's reign decimated the ranks of the courtiers. The king considered the aristocracy as the traditional elite of French society, linked by birth to the country's history and summoned to Versailles to surround him as a guard surrounds the leader of an army (Fig. 6).

This royal guard had to have suitably distinctive accoutrements: status, living quarters, and dress that made them recognizable. Versailles supplied all of these. The aristocracy was to the realm what the marble courtyard and the bosquets were to the palace, gardens, and park as a whole. Since they were set apart by noble birth, they had to live in a world that was free from the limitations of the commonplace. They had the duty to bear arms but also to face the "expenses of luxury," both of which they shared with the king. Louis XIV makes that point unequivocally: "This sharing of pleasure (*société de plaisirs*) that allows members of the court 'une honnête familiarité' (a decent familiarity) with ourselves, moves and delights them more than words can express."[14]

Every word here is significant. By "société de plaisirs" Louis XIV means that the court shares the pleasures of the monarch. By "honnête familiarité" he is defining the code of politeness that enabled him to exclude from the court any trace of vulgarity, whether it arose from the country manners of the provinces, the coarseness of military behavior, or the lack of education among people of "low birth." Court society became a model for the rest of the realm. The court was part of the spectacle it offered and was itself an object of scrutiny for the rest of the king's subjects. It therefore played its part in the harmonious functioning of the whole social body and seconded the king in this task: "The people also on the other hand enjoy spectacles and it is always essentially our aim to please them; and all our subjects are, in general, delighted to see that we appreciate what they like and that what they do best

Fig. 6. Pierre-Denis Martin, *Vue du Bassin d'Apollon dans les jardins de Versailles,* 1713. Musée du Château de Versailles. The king on his promenade at the end of his reign. To avoid walking long distances, he used a "roulette," which was escorted by courtiers. The painter shows clearly the trees reflected in the Grand Canal to emphasize its function as a mirror.

also pleases us. In that way we sometimes govern their hearts and their minds, more completely perhaps than by means of rewards or benefits."[15]

But since the operation of this vast organization was based on the hierarchy of birth, the court had to follow the code of etiquette strictly. That alone, in fact, could remind all the members of this select group that their conduct somehow reflected in a purer, more clearly defined way what went on elsewhere in the country as a whole. And who could lay down the terms of this code and punish violations of it, if not the king himself?

This explains the elaborate ceremonies of which he was particularly fond, whether it was a review of the troops or the permanent spectacle offered by the court itself. As François Bluche puts it,

> Everyone accepted that you had to play by the rules of court etiquette since that determined who belonged to the elite and provided the outward evidence of the position of each individual. . . . The rules for attendance on the king were minutely detailed, fussy, and specific about the tiniest point. At first sight, they seem risible and derisory, but they obeyed political imperatives. . . . Everything was determined by niceties. When the Parlement of Paris met formally, the princes of the blood would cross the floor of the Grande Chambre diagonally to get to their benches. This was strictly forbidden to a duke, who had to walk around the walls.[16]

This geometrical organization of space, with some walking in a straight line and others obliged to turn at right angles depending on their rank, may seem slightly absurd, but it is a perfect illustration of what the whole court accepted; this ceremonial imposed a quasi-military display of a perfectly ordered world. This theatricalization of the political structure was perfectly suited to the two-dimensional surface of a floor, but it was even more effective in a three-dimensional setting. Take for example, the way in which Louis XIV staged the reception of the doge of Venice.

> When he arrived for an audience with the king, the Swiss guards (the Cent-Suisses) were lined up with their halberds on the great marble step; the royal bodyguards were lined up fully armed in the first two chambers of the apartment that served as the guard room. All the members of the court and all the other spectators stood in two lines from the second room right to the end of the gallery, where the king was seated on a silver chair, a sort of throne, raised on a platform covered with a Persian carpet. On the platform stood the Dauphin, Monsieur (the king's brother), Monsieur le Duc, the duke of Bourbon, the duke of Maine, and the count of Toulouse, in other words, all the princes of the royal

house, and behind the king, all the officers of the crown and the royal house who had the right to be there. At the foot of the platform were MM de Vendôme, Monsieur le Grand, and several other princes of the house of Lorraine, and Viscount St. Alban, the natural son of the late king of England, as well as the princes of the house of de Rohan. The rest of the nobility was crowded pell-mell into the gallery.[17]

By mentioning the great marble staircase, the two long lines of spectators, the length of the gallery, and the raised platform where everyone was at the right height for their rank, the marquis of Sourches shows how the political management of space was accomplished at court.

The same sense of hierarchy can be found in the gardens of Versailles. Near the château the statues of the Parterre d'Eau stretch out in a long line to create an effect such that the buildings look bigger. At the foot of the steps of the Parterre de Latone and the Orangerie, the bosquets are lined up along the allées. Below these again, trees are crowded pell-mell in the Grand Parc. Fortunately this symmetry, which might otherwise have seemed too cold, was broken up from the start by subtle variations, but even so, the backcloth against which the games, fêtes, and promenades of the court took place showed art at its most apparent and nature at its least "natural."

The Palace and the Iconographic Program of the Gardens

Historians sometimes use the term "myth" to mean a hybrid intellectual construct that fuses an image and an idea. We can thus say that the myth of Rome allows Louis XIV to be represented on medals as an emperor. The word "myth" thus links political concepts to literary or artistic forms, which is very useful as a means to analyze cultural history. However, there is a certain ambiguity in this term because of its link to the Greco-Roman pantheon. This is why the portmanteau word "idea-image" is preferable, since it encapsulates the thought processes by which the image of the sun becomes a symbol of absolutism as well a representation of nature, in terms of both natural order and fertility.

As Thierry Mariage, whose book is particularly useful in clarifying the process of administrative rationalization that began in 1661, puts it, "The Versailles project is indissolubly linked to Colbert's general policies. It fits with his efforts to bring about economic restructuring at that time, a process that was also based on a desire to change the underlying structures of French society."[18]

Colbert's own testimony is vital here. He was undoubtedly the agent of a centralizing form of absolutism that sought to rationalize everything, including weights and measures, and thus he prefigured the French Revolution. In one of his letters he advises the king to put in place "some grander design, such as bringing his whole realm under one system of laws, and of weights and measures," and he adds explicitly that it would be "a design worthy of Your Majesty's greatness, worthy of his mind and his age. Blessings and glory would be heaped upon Your Majesty, though the honor would be solely in the execution of the plan, since it was Louis XI, without doubt the cleverest of all our kings, who first conceived of it."[19]

But how could the gardens illustrate the implementation of this policy if not precisely by idea-images that could be interpreted from their statues or the way in which their structure was organized?

The first and simplest means of doing this was to establish direct relationships between the palace, where decisions were taken, and the gardens, where the king came to relax, even if politics was always present in his mind. As the eye travels along the broad sweep of the *grandes allées* toward the horizon, the gardens convey an implicit political message that is made explicit by the vases and statues whose symbolic value was then understood by all the residents of the palace.

As Yves Bottineau has put it, "The iconography of the north front, like that of the south, cannot easily be understood without taking account of the adjacent gardens."[20] And indeed the statues evoke the world of flowers, fruit, and even the table. On the Grand Perron, two marble vases correspond to the Salon de la Guerre and the Salon de la Paix, in different parts of the Galerie des Glaces. Tuby's Vase de la Paix depicts the treaties of Aix-la-Chapelle and Nijmegen, which marked the end of Louis XIV's first two wars and were his greatest triumphs. The sculptor has represented the king beneath a dais beside Hercules, while women bearing tributes pay him homage. The Vase de la Guerre de Coysevox shows a lion being tamed by Athena, an allusion to the diplomatic quarrel of 1662, which saw the Spanish ambassadors yield to those of France. It also shows the victory of the Austrians over the Turks, in which the French had played a part. Here again, Hercules is depicted alongside France, which is topped by the French cockerel. Hercules often figures in the Galerie des Glaces as well, particularly in Le Brun's sketch, *La conquête de la Franche-Comté*. Similarly the statue of *Renommée écrivant l'histoire du roi* (Renown writing the history of the king), which was set in place in 1686, evokes a theme that recurs frequently in the decoration of the Galerie des

Fig. 7. Bosquet de l'Encelade. Photograph by Jean-Baptiste Leroux. The triumph of political authority over sedition: the rebel giant has been thrown from the sky into the crater of Mount Etna. The effects of the fall are enhanced by hydrostatics: water fuses from his mouth and from his clenched fist, depicting the air expelled from his lungs by the pressure of the lava as well as his physical strength.

Glaces. The Enceladus (Fig. 7) also represents the theme of rebellion punished by supreme authority;[21] and in the Galerie des Glaces, this powerful statue by Gaspard Marsy is recalled by Le Brun's composition on the theme, *Le roi gouverne par lui-même* (The king in his own person rules), where one sees France, armed with a shield decorated with fleurs-de-lis, crushing the figure of Discord crowned with serpents. These are iconographic themes the king considered important since they linked the château and the gardens by the same series of images and representations.

An idea-image of much greater significance must be added to these iconographic themes, since it is linked to the structure of the gardens as well as their decoration. It is the myth of Apollo, which is found along both the east-west axis of the gardens, where the god emerges from the great bassin that bears his name, and the north-south axis, where the Python, defeated by Apollo, is pierced by arrows in the Bassin du Dragon. This theme recurs in one of the salons of the king's apartments where there is a mural, *Apollon sur son char, accompagnant les saisons avec la France en repos* (Apollo in his chariot, accompanying the seasons with France at rest). The contrast between the monster, who represents deformity, and the person of the king, the incarnation of order and harmony, shows the victory of supreme authority over all conspirators. As early as 1618, Louis XIII had been represented as Apollo to justify the murder of Concini.[22] After the Fronde, the theme was taken up again, notably in the *Ballet de noces de Pélée et de Thétis* (Ballet for the wedding of Peleus and Thetis), a court ballet by Isaac de Benserade in which Louis XIV, at the age of sixteen, played six different parts including Apollo, who with the Muses around him, spoke the following lines:

> J'ai vaincu ce python qui désolait ce monde,
> Ce terrible serpent que l'enfer et la Fronde,
> D'un venin dangereux avaient assaisonné;
> La Révolte en un mot ne saurait plus me nuire;
> Et j'ai mieux aimé la détruire
> Que de courir après Daphné.

> [I laid low the python, which held the world in bonds,
> That monstrous snake which Hell and the Fronde
> Had armed with deadly poison in its fangs.
> Sedition here shall ne'er cause me hurt
> Better by far that it be overthrown
> Than for Daphne I endure love's pangs.]

But in Versailles, Apollo is not simply an emblem. The idea-images he inspires can be found in the structure of the gardens as well as in the statuary, and since a garden is a representation of nature, it is nature itself that is supposed to illustrate it. The sun, the god of harmony and light, rises in his chariot and runs his course along the great axis around which the whole spectacle of the gardens and of the world is arranged. Each morning, Apollo appears in all his glory, endowing the universe with fertile warmth and marking for all creatures and all things the measure of day and night with its revolutions. If, as Louis XIV thought (and Bossuet as well), the functions of a monarch appointed by divine right are directly linked to the laws of nature, then the sun god is indeed his image. The king knows that he is mortal, but since "the state will remain forever," what he expects of the gardens is that the living world of water, trees, and flowers and the course of the stars in the sky should express both the ephemeral nature of all things and the imperishable majesty of political authority. That is what Colbert intended to convey when he ordered the great series of sculptures for the gardens: Les Quatre Continents, Les Quatre Saisons, Les Quatre Parties du Jour, Les Quatre Tempéraments de l'Homme, and Les Quatre Poèmes.

Louis XIV put this idea into words in his *Mémoires*, describing his role as king at the heart of the state, always taken up with a thousand different duties but pursuing his chosen path unhindered, like the sun.

> This is my tenth year on the throne and it seems to me that I have consistently followed the same path, never slackening in my devotion to duty. I am informed about everything, listen to the most humble of my subjects, and know at any and every moment the number and status of my troops and the state of the fortresses, straightway giving orders to supply their needs, negotiating directly with foreign ministers, receiving and reading dispatches, drafting part of the responses myself, and giving my secretaries the gist of the rest, managing the income and expenditure of my state, calling to account the people I have charged with important offices, keeping my affairs as confidential as my predecessors did, distributing favors and privileges according to my will, and keeping, to the best of my ability, those who serve me, however well they and theirs are rewarded, in a modest condition, far below the exalted position and power of the most important ministers.[23]

Saint-Simon was not exaggerating when he said that equipped with an almanac and a clock, one could know what the king was doing on any given day. This regularity of habit, together with the impassivity of his political persona, lent special force to the link Louis XIV sought to maintain with the

Olympian gods, the immortals who gave human form to the forces of nature but without experiencing decline and death. Here, too, the myth of Apollo was helpful in interpreting the way he saw his role, since it allowed the events in his personal life to have a kind of immortality that both glorified and universalized them. The infant Apollo had smitten the monster, and what was sedition if not a deformation of the body politic? The Bassin du Dragon was thus endowed with a symbolic meaning. The same was true for Latona, the mother of Apollo, who had been refused water by the peasants of Lycia as she fled with her two children. The parallel with Anne of Austria and the difficult moments she had lived through during the Fronde might indicate that the king was paying homage to his mother, since he identified with the sun god, god of harmony and destroyer of sedition.

As long as the Grotte de Téthys was still on the terrace of the château, the sun myth was only flawed because the figure of Apollo rising from the sea faced east, but even then it was reinforced by the fact that he finished his course in front of the building where the king slept, regaining his strength to face the new day. The subsequent demolition of the grotto and the construction of the chapel diluted the solar symbolism, but it was still clearly expressed through the great east-west axis that was organically linked to the structure of the palace and gardens as a whole. The myth of Apollo, the sun god, can thus be considered broadly coherent, or sufficiently so to accommodate the gardens within the daily cycle of natural life (Fig. 8). This idea-image is essentially a means to aestheticize the political. To go further than this and attempt to systematize links that are often fortuitous is a kind of intellectual exercise indulged in, even during the king's own lifetime, by some of his more sycophantic admirers. Everything that we know about the king's temperament (he was more naturally drawn to political action than metaphysical speculation) suggests that he was quite happy to let them say what they liked, provided it enhanced his reputation. Bossuet, who knew him well, gives us in his *Politique* a description that rings true: "Do not imagine the king with a book in his hand and a frown of concentration on his face, intent on the page before him. His book of choice is the world itself. The object of his study is to be attentive to all that happens so that he may profit by it."[24]

If he had not been that sort of man, Louis XIV would not have made the throwaway remark in his *Mémoires* that his motto might not be easily comprehensible, but since it appeared on all his buildings, he had no intention of changing it. Similarly, when he was building Marly, he would either have reused the solar symbolism in all the detail that is sometimes attributed to it

Fig. 8. View of the château from the Grand Canal at sunset. Photograph by Jean-Baptiste Leroux. The Grand Canal is already in the shade; the eye, as it rises instinctively toward the light, runs up the Tapis Vert, the powerful oblique lines of the Bassin de Latone, and finally reaches the façade ablaze with rays of the setting sun. Le Nôtre's mastery in the use of long oblique lines has never been equaled. Bold yet majestic, they enable him to establish his hold over a vast extent of ground.

or found a code to interpret nature that was considerably more complex than that of the planetary system he eventually chose.

The Power and the Influence of the State

Louis XIV used a very practical means to make the gardens the image of good government and of France's influence in the world: he introduced exotic plants and animals into the gardens to display the power of the state and to widen the political horizons of the kingdom. This reinforced his reputation as a monarch who was entirely devoted to the interests of the state and, through good administration, was able to ensure peace and plenty wherever his authority extended. Versailles was the symbol, the living image of this political ideal. Wherever the king was, wherever the signs of his political function and the reality of his person were apparent, opulence, order, and beauty had to be created as if by magic.

Visitors like La Fontaine, Madeleine de Scudéry, and the future Cardinal Fleury, then bishop of Fréjus, testify to this. In a letter to Colbert, the latter said about the waters that were being raised from the Etang de Clagny, "The water seemed to me to be brought up from the depths of an abyss and raised to a prodigious height without ever flowing back down. That is against its very nature, which art has subdued to carry it to the topmost point of the towers. . . . And so, one may venture to say that our king, having brought whole provinces under his yoke, has conquered the elements, having forced earth and air to nourish and protect the most sweet-scented plants, which in times past could not endure the cold of this land."[25] Madeleine de Scudéry describes the Grand Canal in the same way: "a canal 400 *toises*[26] long and 16 wide which, notwithstanding the setting and nature of the terrain, runs in a straight line toward the top of a knoll. On either side of it, woods seem to bow down as if they did not want to obscure the view that stretches into the distance beyond."[27] The "beautiful stranger" who figures in her *Promenade de Versailles* admires the gardens: "Everywhere, your prince delights in making art subdue or embellish nature."[28] Saint-Simon makes the same point but less graciously: "He took pleasure in tyrannizing and conquering nature with art and precious objects."[29] He is using an argument against Louis XIV that was often repeated later by the designers of the English landscape garden, for reasons that were both aesthetic and political.[30] For his part, the king realized that the modernity of these projects enhanced his reputation and strengthened his hold on the administrative organization of the realm. Among his most ambitious undertakings, and acknowledged as such since it is represented in the ceiling of the Galerie des Glaces, was the opening up of the Canal du Midi in 1681, linking the Atlantic and the Mediterranean. This was a huge project (it cost two million livres) of which Corneille said, "France—your great king speaks and the rock splits open."[31]

The overambitious nature of some of these developments—the diversion of the Loire and the Eure, for example—should not obscure the fact that Louis XIV, in his own way, wanted, like Henri IV, to make his gardens a political symbol. To do that, just as he used mastery of nature to demonstrate his power, he extended the political horizons of his realm by having ships from distant shores sail into Versailles. The Grand Canal, for those who knew how to read the signs, stood for the military and commercial presence of the royal fleets on the oceans of the world. Colbert had founded a series of trading companies—the Compagnie des Indes orientales (the French East India Company) in 1664; the Compagnie du Nord (for trade with the Baltic) in 1669; the Compagnie du Levant in 1670; and the Compagnie du Sénégal in 1673—and he encouraged the nobility to invest in the colonial trade.[32] At the same time he expanded the navy, taking his cue, as was so often the case, from the political principles of Richelieu, in whose opinion "whoever rules the waves rules the land."[33] The establishment of new enrollment procedures for the navy solved the problem of recruiting sailors, and by 1683 the navy, which had hardly existed in 1660, had 176 ships. This target had been achieved by adopting Dutch and British techniques and reducing shipbuilding time. The king, who did not share his minister's enthusiasm for naval matters, promised to visit the new rope-making factory at Rochefort in 1671, but not set foot aboard a ship until 1680.[34] However, he had a brigantine, a felucca from Naples, a Biscayan longboat, and two other longboats brought in on the Grand Canal. These were followed by a galliot, a miniature warship, complete "with carvings, gildings, small cannons, flags, pennants and pavesades,"[35] and, later, two gilded gondolas that had been a gift from the Republic of Venice. The small but symbolically important village where all the crews were housed was named after the Republic in its honor. This fleet was further increased in the 1680s. According to Pierre Verlet, this was when the attractions of the canal were enhanced by "a gilded galliot from Rouen in 1679, another from Dunkirk in 1682, and a vessel built on-site by the marquis of Langeron. The latter ship was made by ship's carpenters from Le Havre with wood from Amsterdam, and it was launched in the king's presence in August 1685. A galley, also built at Versailles, and a Dutch hoy were added in 1686 and two newly built ships, a gondola and a *peotta*, in 1687."[36]

The Menagerie and the Potager

Since early antiquity, royal gardens have frequently contained a menagerie. The kings of Assyria, the pharaohs of Egypt, and the caliphs of Baghdad all had menageries. Wild animals kept in captivity gave these rulers an opportunity to demonstrate their power and to display the extent of their empire to impress their subjects and foreign visitors. The kings of France also had their menageries, keeping wild animals in the Louvre and the Marais, as can be seen from the names of certain streets in the quartier of Saint-Paul.

In Versailles, the pattern was initially different (Fig. 9). Louis XIV ordered work to start at the beginning of the 1660s and probably put Le Vau in charge.[37] The octagonal building that was constructed at that time had a balcony around it at the first-floor level, overlooking a courtyard of a similar octagonal shape, beyond which were the animal enclosures. During the same period, on the south side of the menagerie a model farm—a perfect illustration of a well-governed France—was built with a drinking trough, barn, stable, and dairy that provided butter for the king's table. One had to pass by the farm, where domestic animals were housed, to get to the wrought iron balcony from which could be seen the enclosures housing ostriches, pelicans, and different kinds of wading birds, including storks, which had their own bassin. There was a whole population of animals that had originated from distant climes. At the end of the seventeenth century when the former menagerie at Vincennes was closed down, stags, lions, an elephant, and a rhinoceros were brought to Versailles. These animals were there to satisfy the curiosity of scientists as well as visitors; when one of the animals died, it was dissected in a specially designed building. Scientific concerns were therefore part of the setup of the menagerie, and it also served as an animal house for the members of the Académie des sciences. This was the case, too, for the potager.

The potager proved that even in the most unpromising terrain, good management of natural resources made it possible to grow the most exquisite fruits and vegetables. But this did not happen overnight. The earth dug out from the Pièce d'Eau des Suisses had to be used to fill in the proposed site. In 1679, a sum of 120,000 livres was allotted to "transport the earth and the walls of the enclosure for the new potager, which covered an area of twenty arpents."[38] Just

Fig. 9. Adam Perelle, The Menagerie. Musée du Château de Versailles. The menagerie, which no longer exists, stood at the southern extremity of the main arm of the Grand Canal and served as a matching piece to the Trianon. It sheltered exotic animals, particularly ostriches, which could be observed from an octagonal balcony that surrounded the building. It was meant to show that the king's power extended over distant lands, and it was used by the Académie des sciences. Claude Perrault used it as a laboratory for his dissections.

as much was spent the following year. A layer of topsoil had to be added to the earth that had been dug out and used to fill in the site. Once again, the king had triumphed over nature. In 1681, 18,000 livres was spent on what might be called the finishing touches: frames, tubs, an irrigation system, trellises, gates, and a central bassin. In 1682, during the completion of the terraces needed to ensure that the most fragile fruit trees could be planted against south-facing walls, La Quintinie moved into a house that had been built for him at the entrance to the potager.

By 31 July 1684, the works had been completed and Dangeau reported that the king walked in his gardens and his potager "where he allowed everyone who was with him to pick and eat the fruit."[39]

In La Quintinie's book, *Instruction pour les jardins fruitiers et potagers* (Practical advice for the cultivation of fruit and vegetable gardens),[40] which was published in 1690, two years after his death, one finds an address to the king. The tone and tenor of this are reminiscent of the *Commentaires* made by the art historian, Félibien on the portrait of Louis XIV by Le Brun: "Nature, who (it would seem) takes pleasure in granting all that Your Majesty wishes and indeed regards your person as her most perfect creation, has, without doubt, waited for this glorious reign to reveal the secrets that the earth has hidden from all earlier generations. . . . This earth, held by all to be so obdurate, finally consents with joy to every least command from a great prince whom all the elements rejoice in obeying."[41] La Quintinie is expressing the same idea we encountered earlier that the physical person of the king is a perfect production of nature and a guarantee that the world is as it should be.

One of the visible signs of a prince who has at last triumphed over nature was the cultivation of orange trees, native to hot climates and not previously able to survive in France. International trade, encouraged by Colbert and his successors—and, metaphorically, this is similar to the flotilla on the nearby Grand Canal with its exotic ships—overcame this difficulty through the relations it built up between France and the rest of world: "The Genovese merchants . . . each year in February, March, April, and May bring us large quantities of quite big and strong orange trees and let us have them at a very reasonable price whether or not they have a root ball" (Fig. 10).[42]

La Quintinie was particularly fond of these oranges and a whole "book," as he called it, of his magnum opus was devoted to them: "All oranges are either sweet, or bitter, or bittersweet, a mixture of sweet and bitter; bitter oranges should be used in sauces, the others may be eaten raw, like other fruit. In the first category, there are sweetish ones, and these are rather bland and disagreeable as a result, so one should avoid taking as many of these as are available. The best of the sweet ones are from Portugal and another kind of large, thin-skinned oranges from the Indies; the small oranges from China are also very good."[43]

No one knows whether La Quintinie is making an explicit reference to trade with China and the ships in the Indian Ocean, but he is keen to show that the orangerie and the Trianon were becoming a latter-day Garden of the Hesperides thanks to the knowledge of their gardeners and the methods of cultivation they used. From then on, the orange trees were perfectly at home: "What one sees and admires each year in the gardens of the Trianon can be used to guide and instruct those who are in a position to follow their example."[44] La Quintinie is undoubtedly flattering the taste of the king here, since we know from Saint-Simon that the only scent he could tolerate was orange blossom. He does the same with figs, devoting a chapter to them and mentioning

Fig. 10. Jean-Baptiste Martin le Vieux, *Perspective View of the Orangerie and of the Château de Versailles from the Hills of Satory.* Musée du Château de Versailles. The picture dates from the late 1680s. The chapel had not yet been built but the rest of the buildings had reached their present size. The new orangerie built by Jules Hardouin-Mansart is shown in its pristine glory with its parterre *à pans coupés* (with its corners cut off) reconstituted. On the left, below the Cent Marches, the labyrinth is visible.

"the pleasure that our great king takes in that fruit."[45] In his book, as is the case everywhere in Versailles, the king is omnipresent and the rest of the world follows in his wake. We know that the potager was directly linked with the food prepared for the royal table by the Service de la Bouche du Roi, and we also know about the impressively large amounts of food that were pre-pared and eaten in Versailles,[46] but we can see from La Quintinie's book that he was as well informed about the trade in fruit as Le Bouteux at the Trianon was about the trade in flowers.

This is not all. He does not simply tell us what has to be done; he gives us a reason for doing it and he is clearly taking a consciously modern attitude in an attempt to give garden design the status of a science. He takes a position in the debate about the circulation of sap and refutes the "old-fashioned dicta of unskilled gardeners," according to whom grafts and plantings must be carried out when the moon is waning. His pragmatic approach frequently places him in the camp of the Moderns as opposed to the Ancients. As Stéphanie de Courtois says, he made the potager "a real scientific laboratory, where he tested different methods of grafting, treatment, and plant breeding."[47] In that sense, his book, with its preface by Charles Perrault, reveals a great deal about the re-lationship between the gardens of Versailles and the sciences.

It is to this aspect of the gardens' history which we must now turn to ana-lyze the relationship between them and geometry. To this relationship they owe their form.

PART II

The Empire of Geometry

There are no subjects that suit me better than mechanics and geometry which can be seen in the works of nature.
　　　—Christiaan Huygens

CHAPTER FOUR

Versailles and the Academies

The Implementation of a Cultural Policy: Colbert and the Perrault Brothers

The creation of the gardens of Versailles was the product of a cultural policy directly linked to the system of government established in 1661. Since the king was its architect but Colbert and his advisers were responsible for its implementation, it was not monolithic and its complexity created a hitherto unknown intellectual climate in the corridors of power in France.

Once he had consulted his Conseil d'En-Haut and given his ruling, the king was free to assign different responsibilities to whichever scientists, artists, and writers he considered representative of the cultural life of the realm. His judgment was good, and he appointed men already highly regarded by their peers or likely to be so in the future. He offered them a pension to secure their services, and in return he expected them to add to the luster of his reputation and to make France the cynosure of the civilized world. By virtue of honors, in the form of *grâces* and titles that he bestowed, he was able to attract every talent both at court and in the academies of Paris. These individuals came from very different spheres, since their intellectual antecedents mattered little if they had proved their outstanding ability. This explains how people with wide-ranging backgrounds and views came to rub shoulders with one another, occasionally even in the king's immediate entourage. There were skeptics, like La Mothe Le Vayer, who had been the king's tutor for eight years; Huguenots—some who had recanted, some who had not—like Dusquesne and Turenne, Dangeau and Madame de Maintenon; some cradle Jansenists or those with strong Jansenist beliefs, like the Perrault brothers, Racine, and the great theologian Antoine Arnauld; and Catholics, some of whom (Father La Chaise, for example) had ultra-Montanist leanings, and others like Bossuet who supported Gallicanism.

Such was the climate of brilliant intellectual diversity in the first third of Louis XIV's reign. Men of letters knew whether they were on the side of the Ancients or the Moderns, but the open quarrels between them had not broken out at this point. Free speech was still allowed at court. Molière made fun of everyone and the king was on his side; he enjoyed Jean-Baptiste Lully's occasionally dubious sallies and even allowed Colbert to quote the songs satirizing the showy military reviews that he and Louvois had arranged at Moret, near Fontainebleau. Openness between the king and those who were close to him was the order of the day.

At first the diversity of this world, united in pursuit of a common goal and strengthened by new ideas, was paramount. But later tensions became more apparent and relations between those in power and some of the intellectuals became strained. The priorities of political authority prevailed. But it must be stressed again that the gardens of Versailles had already been created when religious orthodoxy became a matter for the state and the cultural life of the court lost its brilliance. The momentum was sufficient to carry the gardens forward despite this and they continued to grow in size and in variety because their pattern fostered creativity, as when a musical theme proves so rich that it allows different musicians to bring their own variations to it.

What was the source of this extraordinary richness that underpins the central theme of the gardens? Unquestionably it was the site itself. The magnificence of Versailles is certainly a function of its size, but it is also, and above all, the landscape, which is revealed as the eye travels along the two axes of the gardens: the north-south axis, which stretches along the Pièce d'Eau des Suisses, and particularly the east-west axis with the Grand Canal and the Course du Soleil. This perspective toward the west makes the Grande Terrasse a place where the eye can travel over an immense cradle of water and foliage before being drawn up toward the sky. When Louis XIV decided on this site, nothing of that yet existed and the Val de Gally was not at all attractive, as Saint-Simon remarked. But the art of garden design is no different from any other: one person's Eden is another person's cesspool.

There has been much speculation about the respective contributions of Le Nôtre, Le Brun, Le Vau, François d'Orbay, and later Hardouin-Mansart in the creation of these gardens where so much was achieved from so little.

However, the names of Colbert and the king himself should crown the list. The way in which they brought together many different talents to steer the project to completion remains exemplary. The collaboration between these two great political figures and the nation's best-known garden designer was particularly felicitous for the gardens of Versailles. Le Brun must be added as well: as we have seen, he had gained Colbert's trust and he knew enough about the relations between the king and his minister to give the latter a kind of privileged position in the discussion of his plans. About the Galerie des Glaces, where the decoration had been modified in 1679, he wrote to Colbert, "Monseigneur, here are the designs for Trianon and the one that the king ordered for the Galerie in Versailles. I await your order before beginning any work. . . . I should not wish to speak to His Majesty about them before I have your opinion, which I deem the most trustworthy of all those I may wish to seek."[1] The way in which Le Brun addresses his superior shows clearly that he considers that the team in charge of the work at Versailles was still tightly knit even after fifteen years of working together. Insofar as Colbert was the linchpin of the team, we must examine how he contrived to create and then coordinate the work of the artists and builders who designed the gardens.

Colbert had a finger in every pie. In 1664 he was appointed Surintendant des Bâtiments in charge of the building works. In 1665, he took control of the exchequer as contrôleur général des Finances, and the following year he was appointed secrétaire d'Etat à la Marine, secretary of state in charge of the navy. Then, in 1669, he took over the royal household as secrétaire d'Etat à la Maison du roi. The king could ask him to "hurry the works along" on one site or another just as easily as he could ask him to provide a personal report on the delivery of Mademoiselle de La Vallière's babies or the comings and goings of Madame—and Monsieur—de Montespan. The meticulous, hardworking Colbert demurred only when he considered the king's expenditure extravagant, particularly when he had to foot the bill for the sumptuous military parades that Louvois arranged near Fontainebleau. He was a workaholic and proud of his powerful position. He enjoyed being able to find posts for his own people and he knew that he could increase his personal wealth with an easy conscience, since the wealth of the realm was growing at the same time. He kept an eye on everything that went on. He knew that developments in science and technology and the aggrandizement of the state in the person of the king were an essential plank of his economic policy. Since the backdrop of power had changed, there was a new basis for the division of authority: all the credit for devising the new policies went to the king and the credit for carrying them out went to the minister. In this apparently subordinate role, Colbert had made himself indispensable. In the eyes of some he was a modest man, concerned with his political mission and nothing else; to others he was a clan chief, profiting astutely from his rise to power. But however one sees him, he was a great politician and as with any great politician, one has to accept the whole package. He is judged by his vision, the means he chooses to accomplish his purpose, and the sum of achievements that are his legacy. Colbert's vision was very broadly the same as the king's and it included an ambitious policy for development that harnessed the life forces of the realm, one might even say the nation. He obeyed the monarch while influencing his decisions, which was not always an easy task, given the king's strong personality and tendency toward what Saint-Simon called "a mania for the excessive." As for the sum of his achievements, these can still be seen all over France in the administrative system, in the ports, in the libraries, and, of course, in Versailles.

It was as Surintendant des Bâtiments that Colbert most successfully contrived to make his collaboration with the young Louis XIV indispensable. By founding the academies he was able to ensure that these distinguished institutions would further the new cultural policy. He knew that he needed the intellectuals, the "intelligents," as they were called, to achieve his objectives. Richelieu had already paved the way when he founded the Académie française. However, unlike the "Great Cardinal," as Richelieu was called—probably to distinguish him from Mazarin—Colbert was initially satisfied with discreet support before he launched his big projects. Charles Perrault, whom we find in this context also, writes in his memoirs that Colbert, who "either foresaw or already knew that the king would make him Surintendant des Bâtiments," began to prepare for the role as early as the end of 1662: "He realized that he would have the task not only to complete the Louvre, a project that had been started so many times and always been left unfinished, but also to put up numerous monuments in the king's honor, such as triumphal arches, obelisks, pyramids, and mausoleums, since the latter would deny himself no grand or magnificent project."[2]

Among these grand and glorious projects were also "entertainments fit for a king"—in other words, fêtes, masquerades, and carousels—and "all these things should be written down and recorded in a lively and trustworthy fashion for the benefit of other countries." To organize this, Colbert created a small council of people well-known in the cultural world who could give him advice and suggestions. This committee was known as the *petite académie* and it set to work at once.

The "small academy" was to the Académie proper what the new Conseil d'En-Haut was to its predecessor. One of its key members was Chapelain, who was by then a veteran of sixty-eight, a founding member of the Académie française and author of *Sentiments de l'Académie sur le Cid* (Opinions of the Académie on Corneille's *Le Cid*), a work that had in no small measure helped give tragedy the status it would have throughout the reign of Louis XIV, namely a literary genre that most nobly expressed the political thought of the baroque age. He was supported by Amable Bourzeis, an abbot from the diocese of Autun who was nearly as old as Chapelain and also a founding member of the Académie française. Bourzeis had a passion for foreign languages and was known for his sermons and his gifts as a Christian apologist. In addition to these stalwarts, Colbert had appointed two young men: the abbé Jacques Cassagnes, who at twenty-seven was the youngest of the group and whom Chapelain considered the leading orator of the time; and Charles Perrault, seven years his senior and, as secretary, in direct contact with Colbert. The four men were promptly presented to the king who told them, "I am entrusting you with what I value the most—'ma gloire' (my reputation as a glorious king)."[3]

The members of the petite académie interpreted their mission in the broadest sense, since they took responsibility for the medals struck to commemorate a victory or the completion of a large project, as well as the emblems and devices on buildings, collections of prints bearing the royal seal of approval, and in general anything that pertained to Louis XIV's reputation in the cultural sphere.

It fell to Perrault to coordinate and administer this massive program. He had made his reputation by composing two odes, one on the Peace of the Pyrenees and the other on the king's marriage. Mazarin had liked them and spoken highly of them to Colbert. The latter immediately saw in this young author a cultured and energetic man who could be of great service to him. The two men seemed natural allies. Both had links to the worlds of commerce and law; in both families there were administrators and men of learning; both shared a commitment to modernizing the state; and both were pragmatists, much attracted to new technical and scientific developments and the advancement of knowledge in all spheres. Moreover, there was a hint of Jansenism in the Perrault family, which made for a kind of austerity that was not displeasing to the man Madame de Sévigné had dubbed "The Chilly North."

The "Perrault Clan," as Antoine Picon called it, included impressive intellectuals. They had an impact on the creation of the Versailles gardens in that they established links between different academies. Charles Perrault, Colbert's right-hand man in the petite académie, was elected to the Académie française in 1667, the same year as Colbert himself. He had three brothers: Pierre, with whom he had written comic poetry and whose career as receveur des finances (a tax collector) was sabotaged by Colbert; Nicolas, a Jansenist theologian who had problems with authority; and Claude, an expert in human anatomy, a physicist, and an architect whose name is still associated with the grotto in Versailles, the Paris Observatory, and the Colonnade du Louvre and who was a founding member of the Académie des sciences in 1666. Within just the Perrault family, one can see a network linking almost all branches of the arts and new scientific and technical knowledge.

Charles Perrault had not succeeded in persuading Colbert, nor perhaps the king, that an "Académie générale"[4] bringing together all the intellectuals of note in the realm would be of any use. But the idea had some success in another form. The Académie royale de la danse was founded in 1662; the Académie de peinture et de sculpture, which had been founded in 1647, was restructured by Le Brun in 1663; the Académie des sciences began to meet in 1666; and the Académie royale d'architecture was granted its charter in 1671. The Académie française, founded in 1634, was the oldest and its members in-cluded all the most distinguished writers of the time (except Molière). In one way or another, their names are still associated with Versailles. La Fontaine, whose relations with the king were somewhat strained because of his loyalty to Fouquet and his links with libertine circles, did not become a member until 1684, but his poem *Les amours de Psyché et de Cupidon* is perhaps the most beautiful one that the gardens inspired. Quinault, the dramatist and li-brettist for Lully's operas, was elected in 1670, Racine in 1673, and Bossuet and Charles Perrault in 1671. Benserade, whose version of Aesop's Fables in rhyme, *Fables d'Esope en quatrains*, provided the subjects depicted in the Fontaines du Labyrinthe, became a member in 1674, and Boileau, who like Racine was a royal historiographer, was elected in 1684.

The prestige of the other academies was also enhanced by the intellectual distinction of their members. The Académie de peinture was given a great boost when Le Brun took over as its director. The role of this artist, who was completely loyal to Colbert, was not confined to painting the Galerie des Glaces but also extended to the gardens, where he redesigned the Parterre d'Eau. He worked on that occasion, as on others that we know less about, with Le Nôtre, who had also frequented Simon Vouet's atelier and been in-volved with the large team working at Vaux-le-Vicomte. Colbert appointed him director of the Gobelins in 1662 and he was ennobled that same year, after which he had a brilliant career as the leading royal painter, earning him the right to work in Versailles for eighteen years. He obtained the right for all painters officially recognized by a royal brevet to join the academy, and as a result all who were employed by the Bâtiments du Roi became part of the new organization.

The Académie d'architecture was founded in 1671 after the death of Le Vau (1670) who, since 1667 with Le Brun and Charles Perrault, had been a member of a "petite commission"—another small advisory group created by Colbert. After Le Vau's death, Colbert relied on a group of architects to control the profession through a state organization. This team included d'Orbay (1634–1697), who began working at Versailles as Le Vau's deputy; he had made the traditional artistic tour of Italy and for a while enjoyed Madame de Montespan's protection until Hardouin-Mansart supplanted him in the king's favor. Something similar happened to Libéral Bruant (1635?–1697), who was an engineer with the Ponts et Chaussées (public highways) for the districts of Paris, Soissons, and Amiens from 1669 to 1695 and had launched the major building project for the Invalides before being ousted in 1676. Another founding member, Daniel Gittard (1625–1686), had worked for Fouquet at Vaux and Belle-Ile, and he had collaborated with Le Nôtre and Hardouin-Mansart at Chantilly. Other founding members of the academy were Antoine Le Pautre (1621–1679), who came from a family of engravers and draftsmen and built the very baroque cascade that can still be seen in the lower part of the Saint-Cloud gardens, and Pierre Mignard (1612–1695), who became a member of the Académie de peinture only after the death of Le Brun, his great rival. The last two members of the team—and the most high-profile because of their posts in the administration—were André Félibien and François Blondel, who were secretary and president, respectively. Félibien, a historian who was also a theoretician, had published his *Entretiens sur les vies et les ouvrages des plus excellents peintres anciens et modernes* (Conversations on the lives and works of the most excellent ancient and modern painters) in 1666–68 and his *Conférences à l'Académie de peinture* (Lectures to the Academy of Painting) in 1669. His reputation was made when he produced his *Description sommaire du château de Versailles* in 1674. He knew Versailles well from his frequent visits there as keeper of the Cabinet des Antiques from 1673. Blondel (1618–1686) had had a much more checkered career since he had commanded a naval galley before making his name as a mathematician and, as such, drawing up plans for fortifications, notably those at Rochefort where his rope factory is today one of the highlights of the Jardin des Retours. His lectures at the academy established an official theory of the principles of architecture. They were published between 1675 and 1683 and remained authoritative until Charles Perrault challenged them in the 1680s after the structure of Versailles had already been erected.

With this group of people, one might think that these three academies sufficiently explain how the gardens of Versailles took shape. Not so. It would be a mistake to claim that the arts were the only formative influence. Since we are considering how the gardens were constructed, we need to remember that the aim of garden design is to represent nature, and as a result it is dependent on the means by which we observe and seek to understand the natural world. That is why the sciences play an integral part, not only through our knowledge of botany but by the techniques and experiments carried out by physicists to observe the actions and reactions of matter and to make sense of the world around us. If you visit Paris today and see the glittering sphere of the Geode that dominates the skyline above the Parc de la Villette, you know that the world is no longer as it was when Haussmann created the Parc des Buttes-Chaumont. If you reflect on why this should be so, you will conclude that science is a part of our life and an agent of constant change. And should you wonder when the state first became aware of that, it would be no illusion if you saw the bewigged shadows of some great seventeenth-century figures silhouetted against the Geode. First and foremost among them would be the Sun King himself, reveling in the rebirth of the solar symbol, even under the aegis of the republic.

Science and Its Technical Applications

Louis XIV was keen to demonstrate that the new cultural policy attached great importance to the scientific community (Fig. 11). The visit he made to the Académie des sciences and the words of encouragement he had for the assembled members are often evoked. Simple commonplaces, one might say. But what is less well-known is that Louis XIV personally knew certain academicians, particularly Jean-Dominique Cassini, whose memoirs were published by his grandson at the end of the eighteenth century. For example, Cassini says, "I had the honor of seeing the king on many occasions. He was greatly pleased to hear from me what had been observed by the astronomers. His Gracious Majesty appointed an hour for me to go to his chamber where I spoke at length of my plans to have astronomy serve to improve the study of geography

Fig. 11. Colbert presenting the members of the Académie royale des sciences (founded 1667) to Louis XIV. Sébastien Leclerc, frontispiece of *Mémoires for the Composition of a Natural History of Animals.* Bibliothèque nationale de France, Estampes, Paris. The instruments shown—an armillary sphere, a parabolic mirror, a telescope, a spyglass—are used by astronomers to observe and to represent the world. They were also used by geographers (see the map unrolled on the floor), by military engineers (see the plan of a fortified town to which Colbert points), and by garden designers as shown by the vast geometrical figures of the parterres visible from the Observatoire (under construction at the time).

and navigation." He adds, "Finding myself at the observatory in company with the king, His Majesty was gracious enough to compliment me on the progress I had made in the French language."[5]

Louis XIV wanted to be a modernist, and Colbert worked strenuously to foster his growing interest in the scientific world. In a memoir of 1667, titled *Pourquoy et comment l'observatoire a esté baty* (Why and how the observatory was built), Claude Perrault wrote,

> Monsieur Colbert, who was convinced that the arts and sciences make no less a contribution to the luster of a reign than all the military virtues and arms, had no sooner established the small Académie des inscriptions et des médailles (Academy of public inscriptions and medal design) than he persuaded His Majesty to create another larger academy with more members where . . . astronomy, geography, geometry, and all the other branches of mathematics, physics, botany, and chemistry would be studied and brought, if possible, to the highest point of perfection.[6]

When Louis XIV came to power, Galileo had been dead for nineteen years and Descartes for eleven, but these two men had acquired considerable intellectual sway by introducing scientific research into philosophical speculation and technical advances. Never before had the importance of science been so clearly apparent. Those who cared about the results had a common view of the world that was spread not just by a new vocabulary but also by new processes of manufacture, construction, and, above all, by new and constantly more sophisticated instruments.

Among the many interesting aspects of the period is the structure of the emergent Académie des sciences. In June 1666, just after it was founded, its initial members, known as "geometers," were Auzout, Buot, Carcavy, Frénicle, Huygens, Picard, and Roberval. A few months later the "physicists," another group, emerged: Cureau de la Chambre, Duclos, Gayant, Claude Perrault, Burdelin, Marchand, and Pecquet. They specialized in the study of the living world. Some of the most eminent figures in the academy—particularly Claude Perrault and Christiaan Huygens—who found the division between the two groups difficult to accept, persuaded their colleagues that they should meet together rather than separately. The gardens profited from this collaboration since questions as seemingly diverse as the circulation of sap, the design of the telescope, or methods of triangulation were discussed by everyone. And at Versailles, as we shall see, surveyors, engineers, and botanists were all needed.

Colbert and the king increased the influence of the Académie des sciences by inviting foreign scientists to join it and providing them with a pension. That was how France attracted Huygens, a Dutch astronomer and specialist in mechanics, Cassini, an Italian astronomer and cartographer, and Rømer, whom Picard, also an astronomer, had brought from Denmark because he was heir to part of Tycho Brahe's scientific legacy. The pensions paid to Huygens and Cassini amounted to 6,000 and 9,000 livres, respectively, considerably larger than the amounts paid to the most distinguished men of letters.[7] The *Comptes des Bâtiments du Roi* (Accounts of the royal household) show that for the year 1665, for example, pensions were also paid to scientists working abroad, such as Carlo Dati of the Accademia della Crusca, Viviani, the "leading mathematician of the duke of Tuscany," and Hevelius, an astronomer in Dantzig. Until the crisis that led up to the revocation of the Edict of Nantes and the departure of Huygens, the atmosphere of the Académie des sciences was liberal. This changed when Louvois took over. He reminded the academicians that the most important function of their work was to enhance the king's reputation, and it was not until Pontchartrain arrived that basic research itself took pride of place again.

But why should there have been so many astronomers among the ranks of the academicians? And why did one of the most famous of them, the abbé Picard, make such frequent visits to the gardens of Versailles?

CHAPTER FIVE

The Astronomers in the Garden

Measuring Nature

Why Astronomers?

This question can be easily answered. Gardens are representations of nature, and since every representation is a mental construct, the form they take is grounded in the knowledge of those who create them. Insofar as the garden architecture of Versailles is made up of steps, terraces, circular pools, straight allées, bosquets, and *salles de verdure* that make up an open-air palace, the calculations and measurements needed to create it are an integral part of the great scientific movement that began in Europe with the Renaissance.

That said, the differences between the gardens of the Renaissance (the age of Androuet du Cerceau) and the baroque gardens (the age of François Mansart and later Le Nôtre) are immediately apparent. The effects of perspective lengthen considerably, large canals make their appearance, and the palisades along the allées are higher. With these circumstances, different problems of measurement arise and the relationship with the landscape is no longer the same. The role played by light is also different. That is why the baroque style, in gardens as in other areas, was developed by artists who were consciously creating new forms, a fresh kind of beauty that represented the world in a way that was conceptually very unlike what had been done before. The passionate desire to construct an expression of truth through the imagination is familiar to creative artists. Other passions pale in comparison. To understand this creative drive, you have to study the process by which it regenerates the past by linking it to new discoveries. And the innovative power of the baroque can be understood only by putting it into a historical context that goes back to the Renaissance.

Historians of science agree that the seventeenth century was a turning point in the development of modern science. Robert Lenoble and Yvon Belaval credit the baroque period with "the unparalleled merit of looking at the world with new eyes"[1] and with having increased the number of works popularizing scientific discoveries. Never before had questions of geometry and astronomy created anything like the controversies surrounding the Inquisition's condemnation of Galileo in 1633 or the publication of Pascal's *Pensées* in 1670. With every refinement of the telescope, those "new eyes" could see a sky ever more crowded with stars. Because the king himself used cosmic symbolism and astronomers also worked in the gardens of the Sun King, the form of the parterres, the bosquets, and the bassins necessarily reflected their new vision of the world.

This vision was not that of the Renaissance, which in itself was different from the vision of the Middle Ages, for reasons being debated in the academies of Europe in the century that saw the creation of the gardens of Versailles. In 1603, Prince Federico Cesi had founded the Accademia dei Lincei in Rome with Galileo as one of its members. In 1657 Ferdinand II, the grand duke of Tuscany, had followed suit and created the Accademia del Cimento (Academy of experimental science) in Florence. Its members included scientists such as Viviani, a disciple of Galileo, to whom Louis XIV awarded a pension. This academy, which attracted a great deal of admiration in Europe, served as a model for Charles II in 1662 when he founded the Royal Society in London. Colbert saw how this institution brought together men of learning and those involved in industry and commerce, and the idea of the Académie des sciences was born. He appreciated the industrial, financial, and commercial strengths of the countries bordering on the North Sea and saw what was happening in Holland, where groups of prestigious scientists were working in towns such as Leiden and Amsterdam. Among them was Christiaan Huygens, the son of a philosopher and a friend of Descartes. The foundation of the Académie des sciences was, therefore, intended to give France a leading role in cutting-edge research of the day.

It was here that the astronomers had a part to play. They improved the instruments that could be used to observe and measure the world, creating an image of it that was quite separate from that of the Renaissance, albeit rooted in it. Their research fit within an existing long-established tradition from which "mechanical" physics was developing. At the end of the Middle Ages, physicists like Oresme, Buridan, and Albert of Saxony had disputed the physics taught in universities. This physics, called the Physics of Rest, derived from Aristotle and posited the earth as a motionless sphere in the center of the universe, with other spheres carrying the stars orbiting around it. Since the earth was at rest, no object could be set in motion on its surface or toward it unless it had itself been set in motion by another object. The physicists who disputed this pointed out that the stars moved without receiving impetus from another object and that the same was true for the surface of our planet: the cannonball is propelled through space without being followed by the cannon; the bow does not follow the arrow, nor does the sling follow the stone. This was the origin of Buridan's theory that the stars had been shot into space by God and would continue in their course until the end of time.

This type of observation led to the idea that the natural state of things was not rest but motion and that knowledge of the world would come from the study of that movement or, in other words, mechanical science. At that time, the universe seemed to be a space inhabited by bodies that moved because of a force inherent within them. The stars followed their course in the distant heavens as a result of the impetus they had received in the creation of the world. Cannonballs, arrows, and stones fell back to earth because their inherent impetus was weakened and destroyed by an opposing force—gravity. Yet, if the laws of motion were to be discovered, observation was essential, and that was the origin of the experiments on moving bodies—balls on sloping surfaces, pendulums—as well as systematic observation of the stars designed to lead to a great mechanical system of the universe. This branch of science, which was groundbreaking in its time, largely depended on progress in astronomy (Fig. 12). Its practitioners soon claimed that it had its origins in Greek science, particularly geometry, and they enthusiastically began to study the great classical texts on it. It did seem that only mathematics could provide an explanation for the movement of bodies in space. Geometry became all the more essential since the only way to observe the stars was to construct telescopes and use different lenses; through these lenses, beams of light appeared as geometrical figures where everything was just angles, lines, planes, and volumes. Euclid, who founded geometry and optics, was seen as the father of modern science.

The gardens of the Renaissance are living proof of contemporary scientific curiosities. Their creators initiated the style of fountains and machines, embodiments of mechanical physics. Making water rise as a "water jet" gave it

Fig. 12. Coquart's *View of the Observatoire de Paris and of the Tour de Marly*, 1705. Bibliothèque de l'Observatoire de Paris. The telescope of the astronomers is pointed toward the night sky. They provide an image of science with military (the protection of frontiers by fortifications), religious (Galileo's famous condemnation), philosophical (Pascal's discussion of the infinite world), and technical (Picard's glasses used at Versailles) implications. Louis XIV took an interest in eclipses, similar to Molière's *femmes savantes* and certain segments of the public.

the impetus that threw it into space, where gravity brought it back down in parabolas or columns; you could see it slowing down as it rose, then go faster as it fell, demonstrating mathematical forms in space. Then after it had shown the laws that govern the movement of liquids, it flowed away into grottoes, then dropped back into the bowels of the earth before rising again through the springs to reach the sea, then evaporating into clouds where gravity caused it to fall to back to earth as rain. Thus the endless cycle of water was completed, and the gardens were a spectacular example.

However, if you compare two gardens, one from the sixteenth century, Ancy-le-France, and one from the beginning of Le Nôtre's career, Vaux-le-Vicomte, the differences are immediately apparent.

Geometric forms are common to both, as is the general layout, but you can see that in less than a century these forms had become elongated as perspectives had lengthened. Parterres are extended and the median axis vanishes into the horizon. The vegetation seems higher and the shadows loom larger, giving the masses of greenery a whole new presence and power that change the relationship between the parterres and the surrounding landscape. Because of this extra length, the allées become broader and have palisades along them, which "compart" space, to use the contemporary term. As is always the case when styles change, there is an affective shift and the arrangement of forms follows another logic, since space is constructed differently.

The artists of the Renaissance constructed space using linear perspective, a discovery made by Brunelleschi in the Quattrocento. This meant that three dimensions could be represented in a single plane. Of course, medieval painters also used a single plane, but in their pictures different spaces with different perspectives sat alongside each other without the figures in them appearing particularly concerned. This corresponded to an image of the world inspired by Aristotelian physics, according to which the universe was composed of a series of different worlds, each with its own separate nature taking its place within a hierarchy. Mechanical physics could no longer accept this conception of the world, since the way the course of the stars was represented implied that they moved through a neutral environment. Space, therefore, had to be shown as homogeneous. Linear perspective succeeded in doing this by treating a picture as the intersection of a visual pyramid and the flat surface of the canvas. The straight lines of light leaving the artist's eye matched the lines that converged as they reached the vanishing point. Geometry triumphed once again, since it allowed any point in space to be situated relative to any other and any of these points to an observer. Gardens immediately changed to accommodate this new dynamic and took the form of paintings laid out on the ground. Bernard Palissy, like Alberti, suggested that they were best seen from above so that the proportions could be fully appreciated, and that is why they were often surrounded by walkways.

In the baroque period, this method of constructing space was not discarded. Quite the reverse: perspective continued to dominate painting, architecture, and garden design. What changed was the way in which the depth of space was represented by the play of light and shade. In his treatise of 1612, *La perspective avec la raison des ombres et des miroirs* (Perspective explaining shadows and mirrors), a title as movingly beautiful as a Georges de la Tour painting, Salomon de Caus, who also created the Hortus Palatinus at Heidelberg, explains that the painter must be careful to get the correct shape for the shadows because the depth of the painting depends on them: "Having adequately discussed and demonstrated how to represent all kinds of figures on a plane surface and effect the foreshortening, I shall now show how shadows should be added to the foreshortened figure." He then explains that the sun is a star of "immense size," whom some take to be one hundred and sixty-six times greater than the earth, and contrary to certain beliefs, it shines with a constant brilliance, even during an eclipse. The sun is "the only source of light that illumines the entire world," and any picture must take that into account if it wants to be true to life. He adds, "If you wish to depict a landscape or a scene with figures in it and only the sky above, you need to add a source of light that will illuminate the whole, and what cannot be seen because an object is in front of it will be in shadow."[2]

Thus all objects have a shadow, and that is what gives them depth. Other theorists of perspective, such as Allain Manesson-Mallet and Father Jean Du Breuil, would discuss the relationship between perspective and shade a few years later, sometimes using the gardens of Versailles as an illustration. It is to the latter that we owe developments in "the power of shadows," which are extremely helpful as a means of understanding the form of expression in the baroque period. In all of these areas, the curiosity of the age about astronomy and the use of telescopes to see the light from the stars are evident. "How many bodies whose existence was unknown to our earlier philosophers have spyglasses allowed us to discover?" asked Pascal.[3] The painters drew all the relevant conclusions from these discoveries. In the Renaissance, shadows drifted, but in a neutral, completely translucent space, a purely geometric presence. In the baroque period, particularly among the Caravaggists, shade animates and constructs space, both through the geometric pattern that leads to a vanishing point and by the contrast between light and shadow that fits into it. Gardens offer many examples of this (Figs. 13, 14).

There is another parallel with astronomy. At the beginning of the sixteenth century, Copernicus had left his native Poland to teach mathematics in Italy, where he developed a world system with the sun as a star whose light was cast on the planets that moved around it. The Sun King took up this image of the world a century and a half later, renewing an earlier idea-image and giving it a scientific connotation that suited his new cultural policy.

The discoveries of Copernicus were well-known. They had been spectacularly confirmed by the observations of Tycho Brahe, a Danish astronomer whose tables charting the movement of the stars were so highly regarded that the French academician Picard was financed by Colbert to go to Denmark and bring back any documents, giving the exact location of his laboratory. The French academicians knew that Tycho Brahe had given Kepler and Galileo reliable measurements on which to base their world systems. When Kepler had shown that the human eye was a sort of optical instrument at the back of which rays of light, refracted by the lens and reflected by the retina, re-created an image of the world, it seemed that the telescope was a sort of super eye capable of allowing astronomers a much greater degree of vision. (His *Dioptrics* dates from 1611.)[4] By continuing the work of his two predecessors in calculating the trajectories of the planets, Kepler was able to show that planets' orbits described ellipses that all followed the same laws, and these laws explained how the solar system functioned in the same way as one might explain the functioning of a machine. He concluded from this that the only way of thinking about the world was as a clock in which all the parts meshed together, each one contributing in its own way to the overall movement. And by putting his eye to the telescope, he could also see a world full of stars, and their path, which obeyed the laws of mathematics, expanded the field of human knowledge to the limits of the imagination.

That, however, was the whole problem. In Kepler's mind, the idea that the universe extended beyond the reach of the telescope undermined the validity of his conclusions. Seized by what he called "a kind of terror," he refused to admit to himself that the world could be infinite. But Galileo went beyond that and brought the concept of infinity into the world of scientific speculation. Carrying out more experiments on moving bodies and astronomical observations, he rapidly seemed to become a kind of prince of mechanics. His works, particularly *Siderius Nuncius* (The starry messenger), brought science into the public arena. Since he made stars into messengers revealing the

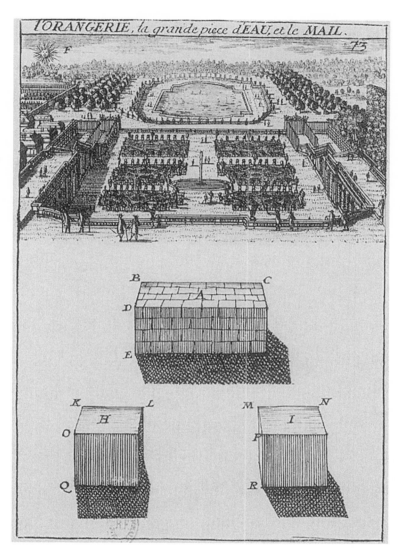

Fig. 13. Manesson-Mallet shows how to draw shadows projected by geometrical volumes lighted from one side. He thus follows in the steps of Salomon de Caus, who had inquired into the proper way to draw shadows and the reflection of objects in a mirror (*La perspective avec la raison des ombres et des miroirs*, 1612). De Caus and Manesson-Mallet take their place in a long succession of perspectivists whose construction of space relied on geometry and light distribution, thus playing a central part in the relationship between Caravaggism and the baroque. Versailles, with its solar symbolism, is an excellent illustration of this relationship. Bibliothèque nationale de France, Paris.

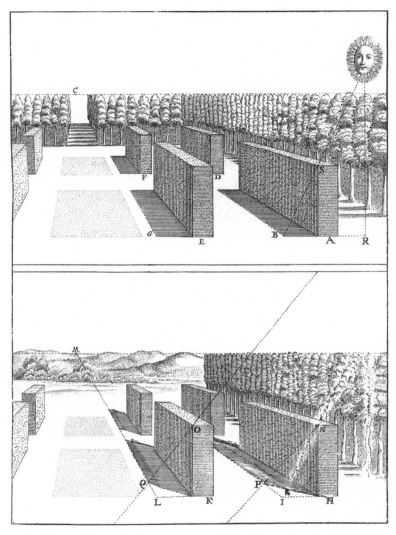

Fig. 14. The theory of light and shadows as demonstrated by the palisades, in Jean Du Breuil, *La perspective pratique* (1642–49). Bibliothèque de l'Institut de France, Institut de France, Paris. Réunion des Musées Nationaux/Art Resource, NY. Du Breuil, a perspectivist of great reputation, illustrates here the role played by shadows in baroque gardens. Palisades stand like walls of greenery whose shadow varies and slides sideways according to the sun's position in the sky. The sun, the emblem of the king, follows the central axis of the gardens, whose geometric forms are immobile. But shadows are not: they remain geometric but compose a network whose circular motion animates the gardens. Motion and geometry were central to seventeenth-century science.

true nature of the world to humanity, he thought it even more important to study its appearance. That is how he came to create the first relief map of the moon, calculating the height of the mountains by the length of the shadows they threw.[5] It was as if light made the image of the world more dramatic. The stars clustered in the heavens looked like shining spheres with huge cone-shaped shadows in their wake, stretching into the depths of space. From then on, all matter was given form by the contrast of light and shade, and this discovery, which resulted from the use of the telescope, appeared again by some mysterious process of osmosis in the work of Caravaggio, who had considerable influence on the work of other painters, whether Dutch, Spanish, Italian, or French. Perspective was no longer created in the translucent space of the Renaissance geometers but within the space of the baroque age, bathed in light and given depth by shadows. The academies Louis XIV had created were carried along with this vast movement. Le Brun had been the pupil of Vouet, who knew something of the work of Caravaggio. Similarly, Le Nôtre, who had also studied with Vouet, knew something about the part shadows played in the landscape.

Before turning to these aesthetic matters, let us look in greater detail at what gardens owed to astronomy in other ways, particularly through the improvement in measuring instruments and by the way in which the image of the world had been transformed by geometry and mechanics. If it was correct to assume that everything was in motion and that motion could be calculated and represented, mechanics made the world intelligible provided one was able to measure things accurately. In his *Principes de la philosophie,* Descartes wrote, "We shall know that the nature of matter or of any body in general is not determined by its having solidity, weight, or color or being present to our senses in some other way, but only that it is a substance extended in length, breadth, and depth."[6]

If matter is defined as a substance that has extension, it can be knowable only if it can be measured. The seventeenth century was passionate about measurements; Colbert, as we have seen, anticipated the French Revolution when he dreamed of a unified system of weights and measurements. Among the members of the Académie des sciences was Huygens, who used the pendulum to measure time as accurately as possible, while his fellow member Rømer was the first person to measure the speed of light. Scientists all over Europe were abandoning the old "qualitative" physics, to which Descartes is referring here, in favor of "quantitative." They did not all agree with the details of Descartes's system, but they were all geometricians, and that implied a rigor in reasoning apparent in all areas of intellectual life, whether literary criticism, grammar, or the arts. One could even speculate whether the sense of proportion, which according to the contemporary definition was one of the main characteristics of the "honnête homme," owes something to the discoveries of quantitative physics.

Descartes had been put on the index in 1663 and the Sorbonne, as always more anxious to preserve old ways than to promote new ones, had banned the teaching of his theories in 1663. But Boileau had responded to that with his *Arrêt burlesque* (Ridiculous decree), and that had not prevented him from becoming the royal historiographer six years later. Better still, Huygens, who was a convinced Cartesian and made no secret of it, dedicated his work on the pendulum, *Horologium oscillatorium*, to the king in 1673 at the time Holland was being invaded by the armies of France. In that work, he said specifically, "It is principally to France that we owe the renaissance and rehabilitation of geometry in our century." In other words, the Sorbonne decreed one thing and the academicians another, without the king's intervention. Whose side would he have taken? All the "intelligents" were aware that the work of the Académie des sciences was inspired by two main concerns inherited from the Renaissance: improving optical instruments and refining the mechanistic vision of the world. They all knew, too, as the king proved in his conversations with Jean-Dominique Cassini, that this work enabled maps to be drawn that were useful to commerce and essential to the military. These factors explain why everything to do with accuracy of measurement was encouraged and sometimes even funded by the state. Two examples will suffice. It was known that a ship could establish its longitude only if it had an accurate timepiece that allowed its position to be determined as a function of the difference between local time and the zero meridian. Huygens solved the problem by improving clock movements using the work of the geometricians on cycloids and by inventing a system of suspension to keep clocks horizontal onboard ship. Thus the measurement of time also enabled the measurement of space. It was also known that longitude could be determined by observing the satellites of Jupiter, since a given configuration of these satellites was visible from two different points on the planet. The Stathouder of Holland had offered a bounty of 25,000 florins to anyone who could produce tables of the movements of these satellites that were accurate enough for that purpose. Cassini succeeded in doing so in 1668.

It is easy to understand why Colbert and Louis XIV were able to procure the services of such a prestigious scientist the next year and proposed that

Cassini work in the new observatory which Perrault, dividing his time between Paris and Versailles, was building. Once he had moved to France, Cassini, with Picard, began work on a *Carte de France corrigée par ordre du roi sur les observations de MM. de l'Académie française* (Map of France revised by order of the king according to the observations of the members of the Académie française). Louis XIV pronounced himself satisfied with the map, albeit complaining to its authors, "You have lost me a third of my kingdom." This came from the redrawing of the Atlantic coastline, which had been thought to be further west than it actually was. This correction had been calculated using the triangulation method, which measured the length of a given line, say a fraction of the meridian, by charting a series of points along that line, for example a bell tower or a piece of high ground, and drawing triangles between these points (Fig. 15).

By measuring the angles with a protractor, it was possible, if you knew the length of one side of the triangle, to work out the length of the other two sides. You then proceeded from one triangle to the next and so on. This method, invented by the Dutchman Snellius, went back to the beginning of the century, but it had been improved by the screw micrometer, which had been described by Auzout in 1666, before he brought out his treatise *Manière exacte pour prendre le diamètre des planètes, la distance entre de petites étoiles et la distance des lieux, etc.* (The exact method for measuring the diameter of the planets and the distance between small stars, places, etc.). Auzout had shown how to improve the accuracy of the measurements by adding telescopes with fixed and mobile wires to the protractors so as to provide a more precise measurement of the distance between two angles of sight. This allowed scientists to measure the terrestrial meridian, a problem that seemed particularly important since the calculations done by the Ancients had been lost and there was no consensus among modern scientists. Louis XIV tasked the Académie des sciences with the solution of this problem, and Picard explained in his *Abrégé de la mesure de la Terre* (Short account of the measurement of the earth) how he had come to choose thirteen locations ("the center of Ville-juive mill; the corner of the Pavillon de Juvisy; the top of the bell tower in Brie-Comte-Robert; the center of Montlhéry tower," and so forth)[7] to trace his triangles in the countryside from high points that commanded a view of the whole area. One can see how the progress made in optics encouraged scientists to take an all-encompassing view of the landscape and readily understand how the paths of knowledge could follow large rectilinear diagonals, whether in the French countryside or in the Grand Parc of Versailles.

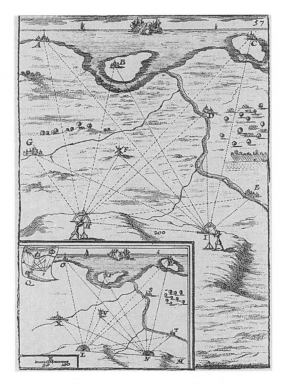

Fig. 15. Allain Manesson-Mallet, cartographers at work in *La géométrie pratique,* 1702. Bibliothèque nationale de France, Paris. The cartographers are measuring distances by the system known as triangulation. The long oblique lines drawn across the land-scape are virtual, but they assert man's intellectual power over space. In the parks of the period they become material on a smaller scale, corresponding to the surveying and to the rational maintenance of forests.

Versailles, the image of good government in France and, therefore, the image in landscape of France itself, could not be independent of a movement encouraged by the king. To get the measure of this landscape, you had to see things on a grand scale and the broad allées that traverse the park mirror the straight lines the cartographers were plotting across the countryside to make their measurements. Colbert had the same task of obtaining accurate meas-urements in the royal estates that he had made more profitable. He had very specific views about how this should be done. He wrote to Chamillart, whom he had appointed commissioner for the reforestation of the Ile-de-France, "It is essential that you make every conceivable effort to obtain both the old and the new figures, if possible, for all the forests in the Ile-de-France, with all the statements relating to the surveys that have been made of these, including even their boundaries, so as to be able to put them back into place after your redevelopment."[8] In Versailles itself, Colbert commissioned a survey of the Grand Parc. In the accounts of the *Comptes des Bâtiments du Roi* we find items of expenditure such as "6 September 1680—8 January 1681: To Claude Caron, surveyor, both for his trouble and for the payment of the workers who have charted the woods and lands of Versailles—1,715 livres 19 *sols*."[9]

Le Nôtre, for his part, planned his project on such a scale that he annotated his drawings with exact measurements. The layout he proposed for the Avenue de Picardie in Versailles includes the following directions: "From the Grand Chemin de Paris to the Rond de la Butte is 300 toises. From the said Rond de la Butte via the Clos de M. S. Sauveur to the Grande Avenue du Chasteau de Versailles, 1,100 toises. From the start of the Grande Allée of the château to the transversal allée, 350 toises. From the said transversal allée to the entrance to the Place du Château, 500 toises: that is to say, from the Grand Chemin de Paris, taking it from the little bridge to the château of Versailles, 2,300 toises."[10]

Then, as now, taking measurements was the first step toward building. Spyglasses designed the shape of towns and canals just as present-day computers streamline vehicles by visualizing air turbulences. The way things are made to appear depends on the instruments used to create them.

"Our Wonderful Telescopes"

A case that clearly exemplifies the concerns, both theoretical and practical, of the Académie des sciences is that of the abbé Picard, who is still associated with the gardens of Versailles because of his work on measurements. Picard (1620–1682) was educated by the Jesuits and was a friend of Auzout and Gassendi. He is a perfect representative of the contemporary sciences with his interest in astronomy, mechanics, and problems of measurement. In his *Mémoires*, Charles Perrault tells us that Colbert had appealed to Picard to find out whether it was possible to divert some of the water of the Loire at Orléans to Versailles to solve the problem of the water supply for the fountains. Le Nôtre and the king relished the project: "Two days ago Le Nôtre said to the king as they walked together along the Canal de Versailles that it would be wonderful to watch the ships, their sails billowing, sailing downstream from the Loire like sleighs on a slope, until they come floating into the canal."[11]

Pierre Paul de Riquet, basking in his newfound fame after building the Canal des Deux-Mers, had been consulted. He had observed that the Loire flowed faster than the Seine and deduced that the bed of the Loire must therefore be higher at Orléans than that of the Seine in Paris. In his view, therefore, it was possible to carry out the project so dear to the hearts of the king and his gardener. In his *Traité du nivellement* (Treatise on leveling), published by La Hire in 1684, Picard recounts how the story began and what ensued: "He [Riquet] had seen that the slope of the Loire was much steeper than the Seine and so he had formed the idea that the bed of the Seine was much lower than that of the Loire and on that basis he was convinced that a canal could be brought from the banks of the Loire to the château of Versailles. He even had no problem in suggesting that he could bring this water over the top of the Sataury Mountain, which is twenty toises higher than the ground floor of the château and this would have provided a reservoir to make the gardens more beautiful."[12]

Picard had the means to prove that Riquet was wrong. He had drawn up a table of "apparent rises in level" that he used to correct measurements of the earth's roundness. He had shown that if you place a pole vertically in the ground and look at a distant point, a church steeple for example, along a straight line at right angles to the pole, the distant point will seem lower than it really is because of the curve of the earth's surface. At a distance of 4,000 toises (about 16 kilometers), the difference is a little over 14 feet. It is true, Picard observed, that the observer's line of vision is sometimes distorted by the refraction caused by the layer of air, but this phenomenon is apparent only at distances of more than 600 toises.

Once these corrections had been made, he could establish the slope of a river with a calibrated telescope. By looking at the towers of Notre Dame from a point downriver in the Seine valley (in this case the Clos des Capucins near Meudon), he could work out the difference in altitude between the two chosen points. All he had to do then was to measure the distance that separated the level of the Seine from the two landmarks in order to establish how much lower the Seine was in Meudon than in Paris. Picard was thus able to prove that the Seine was sixty and a half toises lower than the ground floor of the château of Versailles. In the same way he was able to show, by taking a series of landmarks on a map that "Le Sieur Vivier had drawn up" of the Paris area, that the surface of the waters of the Loire at Orléans was in fact eleven toises below the ground floor of the château of Versailles (Fig. 16).

Given these conditions, it was not from Orléans that the waters of the Loire could be brought but from La Charité, further upstream, which meant

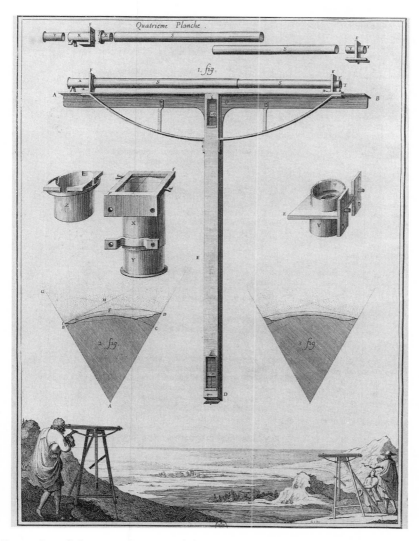

Fig. 16. Picard's lunette in his *Traité de la mesure de la terre,* 1684. Bibliothèque nationale de France, Paris. At the end of his *Traité,* Picard describes a level to which he had added a field glass to make long-distance observations. In a short presentation of the astronomer's works, the *Mémoires de l'Académie des sciences* indicates, "Shortly after [creating this instrument] he was given an important opportunity to demonstrate its capacities when the levels of the water circulation were examined at Versailles together with the height and slope of the beds of the Seine and the Loire."

that a canal more than two hundred kilometers long would have to be built. Riquet, apprised of Picard's work, seemed, according to Perrault, to be unsure of his ground and his project was abandoned. It was Picard who was approached about digging the tunnel that would bring the waters of the Bièvre to the canal. The calculations were so accurate that there was virtually no error when the earthwork contractors, starting at either end of the tunnel, met in the middle. The same was true for the Grand Canal. Its immense length had caused some concern about bringing in the water, but it turned out that once again the calculations had been accurate and the two ends were at the same level.

Telescopes—"these wonderful telescopes," as Descartes put it in his *Dioptrics*—seemed to be instruments that served every purpose. They could be used to calculate the diameter of the moon and to draw up a map of it; they could also establish the distance between the earth and the sun, the true location of the coast of Brittany, and the amount of earth that needed to be moved so that—despite what Colbert had said—the Bassin d'Apollon could be seen from the windows of the château of Versailles. The image of the world created by this optical instrument was an exhilarating one, since knowledge of the world was constantly expanding as a result of its power; by shortening the distances, it allowed the observer a level of control over the new landscape. This is how a whole network of large distances, which could be measured—and therefore controlled—by telescopes, allowed the artist to draw "optical views"—the name itself is revealing—where a château or garden could be seen from above, as if from a balloon. Similarly, the practice of changing the focus to bring parts of the landscape closer or make them more distant enabled effects of accelerated or decelerated perspective to be created in a garden so as to give a visitor the heady feeling that he was in control of space. These effects' dependence on optical devices applied to long perspective explains how the telescope produced and developed that sense of space and spectacle, which is one of the most original characteristics of the baroque aesthetic.

The work of two of Le Nôtre's great predecessors, François Mansart and Jacques Boyceau de la Barauderie, is illuminating in this respect. In the Château de Maisons the former cut long allées through woods, and in order to divide off the garden without destroying the long perspective, he dug out *sauts-de-loup* (sunken walls), the forerunners of the English ha-ha. The latter wrote in his *Traité du jardinage selon les raisons de la nature et de l'art* (Treatise on gardening following the rational order of nature and art), "Perspective can reveal the correct length of allées to anyone who looks at it to gauge perfection. But often people wish to make them longer, either as a means to contain the whole space that they want to ornament, or as a path to reach further into the distance."[13]

Simply glancing at the long straight paths which Le Nôtre cut through the woods of the Grand Parc shows how much he wanted to "reach further into the distance" and landscape the whole area for which he was responsible. And you can see how in this same Grand Parc, with the help of "wonderful telescopes," he calculated as accurately as possible the length of the Grand Canal and the gradual lengthening of its three bassins so as to establish his control over the landscape as far as possible. Similarly, in the Petit Parc, the calculation of the proper ratio between the length and breadth of the allées and especially the angle of their slope required exact measurements that only the cross-wires of spyglasses could provide. Such were the means he also employed to "gauge perfection." He had worked with Boyceau and Mansart, the first architects in France to define and demonstrate the freedom and the power afforded by the capacity to control space over a great distance. He also expressed this pleasure in the way that long perspective underpinned the new style, because he instinctively identified with the discoveries that guided those of his contemporaries who saw with "new eyes." It is easy to understand why Le Nôtre's debt to Mansart should have been clearly established by an orator— whose name, sadly, is unknown—who said of Jules Hardouin-Mansart, "One may say that the late Monsieur Mansart, whose nephew is the subject of my oration today, contributed in no small measure through his teaching and lessons, as the great architect he was, to opening the way to Monsieur Le Nôtre of whom I was speaking."[14]

Le Nôtre thus took his place in a tradition that derived from the science of measurement. The way he controlled the landscape can be explained by his skill in using geometry to remodel a site and make it blend with living nature through the effects of water within a harmonious mantle of vegetation. To an astute observer like La Quintinie, he seemed to be an innovator who knew how to transform garden design by taking it beyond the design of beautiful parterres. In the preface to his treatise *Instruction pour les jardins fruitiers et potagers*, he wrote, "Our century, which has excelled in everything human industry can imagine, has, through the efforts of M. Le Nôtre, brought ultimate perfection to this aspect of gardening. This is apparent in so many canals, water features, cascades, gushing fountains, mazes, lawns, terraces, etc., ornaments that are indeed new but in truth marvelously enhance the natural beauty of gardens."[15]

In other words, Le Nôtre transformed the design of gardens by using a complex series of large geometrical volumes to structure the grounds; by having terraced large esplanades and long inclines (he had a genius for oblique lines), he made plantations that showed vegetation to its advantage and, by creating a range of water features (canals and fountains), enhanced their natural beauty. We can, therefore, safely accept La Quintinie's testimony and see how the sciences were applied by examining first the design, then the water features, and finally the vegetation found there. That will allow us to proceed rather like the painters of the time, who initially drew their figures in the nude so as to get the form right before giving them life and expression by adding clothes and by painting in their faces.

CHAPTER SIX

Engineers and Gardeners

The Remodeling of the Gardens

The Earthworks

Colbert had been right when he predicted that the form of the gardens as they were in 1661 meant that they could not "be extended without overturning everything and incurring enormous expenditure."[1] Once the initial measures had been taken so that the installation could proceed, the terrain was next. The outlay involved in this was for the "earthworks" (excavating; shifting the earth; and leveling the ground) and waterproofing the bassins with a lining of clay known as *corroi* or *conroi*. In *Mémoire récapitulatif des dépenses faites à Versailles, Trianon et Clagny* (Summary account of expenditure at Versailles, Trianon and Clagny), which appears as an appendix to the *Comptes des Bâtiments du Roi*, the cost of the "excavations and *conroy* [*sic*]" is listed as 6,038,035 livres, or approximately 7 percent of the total, which amounted to 81,151,414 livres. This is the third largest sum after the stonework (21,186,012 livres) and the construction of the Eure Aqueduct (8,612,995 livres). This gives us some indication of how much it cost to redesign the site at Versailles.

In the *Comptes des Bâtiments du Roi*, year after year one finds items such as "To Edme Bourgeau for excavation and moving of earth, 3,604 livres. To Roch Ameau as total payment for having transported one hundred and fifty cartloads of topsoil into the small park." Sometimes more details are given. An entry for 1669 reads: "To reimburse him [Henri Dupuis] for his payment of the laborers who are leveling the ground around the canal." In 1671 a payment of 266,500 livres is recorded to Sieur La Massonière "against the deal he has struck, to shift the earth from the Grand Canal, as its length and breadth are increased."[2]

The excavation of bassins and the leveling of slopes meant that the excavated earth had to be moved and then reused to make embankments, taluses, and esplanades in which the earth was then leveled off. The gardens then took shape through the planes, lines, and angles that were created as a result of the remodeling. Once the distances had been fixed by the geometrical relationships that gave the gardens their overall structure (ends of a terrace, the difference in height between the top and bottom of a feature, or the positioning of a canal), the bosquets were put in place and decisions made about the width of steps and the siting of ornaments, such as vases, statues, and so forth.

At all of these stages of construction, instruments such as the protractor and the graphometer were essential. In his book *La théorie et la pratique du jardinage* (Theory and practice of gardening) (1709), Dézallier d'Argenville explains that with the help of these tools it was possible to "raise the height of a terrain, however large, and make it level." That had to be done by using poles set out along straight lines converging on a point. These poles were all the same height, and by looking along the line from the central pole their tops could all be fixed at the same level. The lines were then drawn on the ground and rigoles were used to get the right level.[3]

> Note that when you use the terms "rigole," "rayon," or "repaire,"[4] it is not like opening up the earth as if you were putting in a palisade, which should strictly speaking be called a "tranche" (trench); it is in fact bringing in earth along a cord stretched between poles so as to form a "rigole," which is used to level off the ground. These "rigoles" must be one or two feet wide; you tread the earth down and then rake it finely until the cord touches the surface of the earth, just brushing it lightly and evenly.[5]

When vast esplanades, vertugadins,[6] or slopes like those around the Bassin de Latone or in the Allée d'Eau were being built, out came the cords and with them calibrated scopes fitted with pinnules or, for greater accuracy, calibrated lenses. This allowed space to be organized and structured on a grand scale, mirroring the world as it appeared through the "wonderful telescopes" that observed it.

Garden Design and Military Engineering

A considerable volume of earth also had to be moved in order to build the system of canals that supplied the bassins and fountains and to apply the corroi and make it even more watertight by the addition of large tiles. These two kinds of earthworks involved such a major upheaval over such a wide area that in looking at paintings such as *Louis XIV visitant le réservoir d'eau de Montbauron* (Louis XIV visiting the Montbauron reservoir) or *Louis XIV donnant ses ordres à l'officier des chasses* (Louis XIV giving orders to the officer in charge of hunting), one is inevitably reminded of others, such as *Louis XIV dirigeant le siège de Maastricht* (Louis XIV commanding the siege of Maastricht) or *Louis XIV devant la tranchée au siège de Tournai* (Louis XIV at the siege of Tournai). The last three works mentioned are by Adam Frans Van der Meulen, who followed the king's campaigns in Flanders and Franche-Comté; the first is by Jean-Baptiste Martin, also known as Martin des Batailles.

It is easy to see why the earthworks that were needed to carry out a siege during that period, as well as the shape of the fortresses themselves, meant that the painters who put them on canvas had to be capable of representing a whole landscape and the geometrical mass of the structures that had been built within it. Garden design on the scale of Versailles required the same kind of "moving" and leveling of earth; it was probably because of this that the king invited Le Brun and Le Nôtre to be present at the siege of Valenciennes in 1677. He wrote about it to Colbert in April 1677: "Le Brun and Le Nôtre arrived this morning with Van der Meulen. I am content that Le Brun should see how this siege is organized, for it is very fine."[7]

This aesthetic parallel between the wholly peaceful art of garden design and the military scenes in question can be understood if one reflects on the kind of skills required by contemporary military architecture. Engineers had always served to further the ends of the monarch, particularly when the strongholds of the Huguenots or the aristocrats involved in the Fronde had to be demolished. Since the time of Sully, whom Henri IV had put in charge of fortifications, the state had relied on engineers to fortify frontiers and constrain free cities and feudal lords to obey the king. Among the engineers who supported Sully were Salomon de Brosse and Androuet du Cerceau, whose connections with garden design have already been discussed. By the time of Louis XIV, the same terms were being used by gardeners and military engineers. In the *Comptes des Bâtiments du Roi* for 1668, one can read, "To Léonard Saint Laurent and Jean Guinot in total payment for earth shifted in the construction of the Grand Canal, the two demi-lunes that are at each end and sundry other works—9,535 livres."

Other terms were common to the design of both gardens and fortifications. In Furetière's dictionary of the time, for instance, the definition of the term "glacis" gives the following as an example: the allées of this garden are *en glacis* (slope down). It also reminds us that "in respect of fortifications, a glacis is an earthwork that gradually slopes down to the ground and disappears into the surrounding land." Dézallier d'Argenville, too, points out that the space between two terraces is called "plain-pied," or "what is called the 'terre plein' in the case of fortifications."[8] It is easy to see why he drew this parallel, since he always emphasized the importance of surveying and knew that Father Jean Du Breuil had specifically said that towns should be fortified according to plans drawn up using the same optical instruments as those of the surveyor.[9] It is clear why engineers might have come to Versailles to do their training or finish it, as it was considered one of the state's great construction sites. It is equally obvious why the military should have found the Maintenon Aqueduct interesting: the leading member of the royal military engineering corps had been in charge of its earthworks. These engineers were either ingénieurs de tranchée, trench engineers essentially responsible for the earthworks, or ingénieurs de place, site engineers with high-level technical expertise who combined knowledge of architecture and urban planning.[10] For the former, a fast-track program of training was enough. However, for the latter, technical expertise in ballistics and work with well-known architects, such as those at Versailles, were needed. As Anne Blanchard puts it,

> They were recruited from the ranks of master masons and some were related to the architect d'Orbay. . . . These future ingénieurs de place, who were the sons of architects and artists and also sometimes from middle-class families eager for employment in the king's service, rather like civil servants *avant la lettre*, received their real training on the royal construction sites in Paris or elsewhere (Versailles, Clagny, Maintenon). There, they came into contact with the greatest architects of the period, Mansart, Le Vau, d'Orbay and very many others. They were trained to work on a grand scale and according to the principles of classical art. They were among the most efficient agents of royal centralization.[11]

Blanchard also observes that some of the ingénieurs de place had made the Grand Tour to Rome, which confirms the complex link, already highlighted by Thierry Mariage, between the design of gardens and of fortifications. You cannot look at the massive base of the grotto in Vaux, the Grande Terrasse in Versailles, or the esplanade in Chantilly without being reminded of the scarps and counterscarps of a Vauban fortress.

These building engineers knew that level ground was rare, and they also knew that the military designs required large-scale earthworks so that they could withstand enemy cannonballs and bullets. So in some places they had to level off the ground, in others infill it, and alter the surface of the ground to reproduce the forms that geometry had proved to be the most efficient: "At the siege of Mons in 1691, 20,000 pioneers, who had been requisitioned in the north of France, circumvallated the town with a ditch 27 kilometers long, 7.15 meters wide, and 2.6 meters high. The excavated earth was piled up at the back to form a parapet."[12] The landscape was thus redesigned to take into account the trajectory of projectiles and the siting of cannons and mortars. To work these out accurately, the cartographers and geographical engineers—a corps created at Vauban's behest—constructed three-dimensional relief maps, which were real landscapes in miniature.

These maps allowed the contours of the terrain to be visualized, and they provided a model of what were known as *profils,* not in the strict sense of the term illustrated by the figures produced by Vauban and Dézallier d'Argenville but in the sense of an overview in relief, as in the series of *Plans, profils, et vues de places* by Ponault de Beaulieu (1643–1697). In this work, each town is shown both in relation to the surrounding landscape and in the form of a plan. The clear and immediate view of the relief afforded by that allowed contemporary strategists to model their plans for attack and defense in the light of ballistic requirements and their supply of cannons and mortars. After Namur had been lost, Vauban wrote to Louvois in 1692, "There is a relief plan of Namur in the Tuileries; I will let you see and touch all the many defects of this site, and at the same time, I shall show you how the one for which I have been blamed could be corrected."[13]

By looking at a relief map, like looking at a landscape, a geographical engineer could forecast the trajectory of the projectiles and ensure that the constructions had the best defensive angle, in other words the best model to make bullets and shells ricochet off the surface rather than penetrate it. The shapes obtained in this way had a functional beauty, rather like the utopian cities of the Renaissance, in that they were governed by the physical laws of movement. Contemporary scientists were so convinced of it that in Testelin's painting *Visite du roi à l'Académie des sciences* (The king visiting the Académie des sciences), a treatise on fortifications can be seen among the glasses and telescopes.

Can we then say that, as in the time of Leonardo da Vinci, the soldier, the engineer, and the artist were sometimes one and the same? The truth is more complex than that. Le Nôtre was not a military man and Vauban's field of expertise was not his. But with hindsight we can see what they had in common: earthworks, and above all the same belief in the efficacy of geometry. The ingénieur de place traces on the ground the line of the defensive angles. Then he either digs out or fills in, using masses of earth as a means of defense and as a means of protecting the firepower of his own side. Once these works are finished, they form a geometrical figure in relief in the landscape that seems both to be gathered in on itself and to thrust outward as if to attack. It is the parabolic path of the projectiles that determines the form of walls and ditches. And it is thanks to that that the geometricians hold sway over the landscape.

The same is true for gardens. To make the most of a slope, a gardener can use three kinds of earthwork: he can construct terraces and subterraces at different heights, but the earth has to be held in position by stonework; he can create terraces "that will be self-supporting," as Dézallier d'Argenville said, "by using taluses or glacis [both terms used by military engineers] that can be cut at each end of the terrace";[14] or, finally, he can simply create *paliers* (levels) or *repos* (shelves) and then deploy all the resources at his disposal, such as platforms, steps, vertugadins, "turf taluses, and glacis," including a few fountains that put the "finishing touches" on these features.

If the jets of water in the fountains are to rise and spread out in a parabola, reservoirs have to be situated on the highest terraces such that as the water jets out at the lower level there will a powerful impetus to provide the necessary pressure. There has to be a slope to allow sufficiently high pressure and the reservoir has to be raised to a point where both it and the substantial base that supports it are concealed. To achieve this, earth has to be banked, shored up, and integrated into the structure of the gardens by means of the taluses, which are described by Dézallier d'Argenville. Similarly, to create effects of moving water, such as the Allée d'Eau, for example, the downward slope that is required must be regular and designed to produce a series of cascades. It is, therefore, no longer the path of a projectile that dictates the rules but another moving body, water; it is every bit as exacting, since it also obeys the laws of mechanics that govern the universe. Just over thirty years after the death of Le Nôtre, the engineer Belidor, a provincial *commissaire d'artillerie* (artillery steward) and Regius Professor of Mathematics, offered a striking example of the relationship between garden design and fortifications. In 1737 he published his *Architecture hydraulique* (chapter 5 deals with "the means of distributing and directing the jets of water for the ornamentation of gardens") and his *Bombardier français ou nouvelle méthode pour jeter les bombes avec précision, avec un traité des feux d'artifice* (The French Bombardier, or a new method of throwing bombs accurately, with a treatise on fireworks).

Le Nôtre's vertugadins, demi-lunes, and esplanades are not, of course, copied from bastions and counterscarps. But they are their counterparts, just as the Vase de la Paix is the counterpart of the Vase de la Guerre on the terrace at Versailles.

CHAPTER SEVEN

Hydraulics and Physics

Water and Air

LE NÔTRE WOULD certainly have assented to the views that Dézallier d'Argenville expressed in *La théorie et la pratique du jardinage*, nine years after the
former's death: "It would be quite difficult to find a material more suited to
gardens than water and fountains. They are the chief ornament of gardens.
They are the living force that animates them. Their sparkling brilliance and
the way they cascade banish solitude; it is often solely their cool murmuring
that brings us the pleasing restfulness gardens afford."[1]

If further proof were needed of garden design as an independent art, water
would provide it; of all the arts it is undoubtedly garden design that best ex-
ploits all its magic. The Renaissance garden had paved the way, offering, as we
saw earlier, brilliant examples of the physics of movement with its water jets,
fountains, and grottoes. The French baroque garden used these same features
and added a fourth: long canals that illuminated its design with large flat surfaces of light. This harnessed the natural resources of the damp climate in this
respect to make the most of the lengthening of perspectives and exploit for its
own purposes the new scientific advances in optics and all the contemporary
work on reflection and refraction. These also enabled its immense vistas to be
made more dramatic, as the calm of still water contrasted sharply with the controlled tumult of the fountains and the effervescent exuberance of the water jets.

But in Versailles, water was precisely the problem. When Le Nôtre visited
Rome and saw the pope, he showed him the plans of the gardens. The Holy
Father was most surprised to see that none of the cascades and fountains

appearing in them was directly supplied by any river.[2] Le Nôtre explained that the water came from étangs and was brought to reservoirs through iron or wooden ducts. But he did not dwell on the fact that the fountains only worked from time to time. There was already insufficient water for what was needed. We know from one of his rare extant letters how frustrating Le Nôtre found this. In a letter to Bentinck, William of Orange's adviser, who had come to visit the great French gardens, he apologizes for not having been able to go with him to Chantilly and cannot resist a plaintive comment: "If sheer youthfulness of spirit could have allowed me to go, I know the pleasure that I could have given His Highness, and I would have had the honor of showing you the beauties of the place. You would have had to admit that the sight of a river falling from an astonishing height and joining an infinitely long canal is a great natural beauty. It is better not to ask where the water for this canal comes from."

"The sight of a river falling from an astonishing height": if only Versailles could have had water from even one modest river, like the Anqueuil or the Nonette! Every possibility was explored; the history of the gardens of Versailles in Louis XIV's time is characterized by a constant, but abortive, search for water. Thirty years after the death of the Sun King, Blondel made a very sad observation: "When the water is playing in all the fountains, bassins, and bosquets of Versailles on days when it is open to the people or when the king orders it in honor of an ambassador or another great dignitary, a volume of 35,292 *muids* (9,458 cubic meters) of water is used in the two and a half hours that the spectacle lasts."[3]

Seventeenth-century scientific and technical advances had met their match here, though not for want of trying, and the best that contemporary science and technology could offer was pressed into service. In this instance, however, art could not defeat nature.

The story begins in 1664. The new shape of the gardens was becoming apparent, and the bosquets, bassins, and fountains designed by Le Nôtre needed a water supply. Le Nôtre himself grappled with the problem and signed a contract with Denis Jolly (the official engineer to the king who was responsible for the maintenance of the Pont-Neuf pump in Paris). Jolly was to construct a pump to direct the water from the Etang de Clagny, very close to the château, to a water tower, from which it would then be brought to a reservoir above the Grotte de Thétys.

It was stated in this contract, signed in the presence of "*noble homme* André Le Nôtre," adviser to the king, contrôleur général des Bâtiments, that this "great machine of a new design"[4] would have a two-horsepower capacity

Fig. 17. Adjutages (photograph by J. M. Manai). Musée du Château de Versailles. The water, under pressure when it reaches the end of the pipes, forces its way through the adjutages or ajoutoirs, which give the jet a distinctive form. It can be made into a *lance*, a *bouillon*, a *colonne*, or an *aigrette*, among other things. The sculpting of water jets enhanced the expressive capacities of the statues' posture and was in keeping with baroque aesthetics.

providing at least thirty inches of water. The pump mechanism is described precisely; in particular, it is specified that the pistons will have "strong leathers attached to eight large iron bars to draw in and compress the water."[5] The contract was signed in March 1664 and water began to flow into the reservoir and water tower in December 1665. Sieur Francine—whether this was Pierre or François is not known—had previously lined the reservoir with mastic-coated canvas, using his own secret process. The king came to see the machine on 21 December 1665, and the water could thus flow into the gardens where about half the bosquets we know today had been constructed.

In April 1666 the king, who was impatient to see the fountains working, was finally able to see the display they made. Reporting back to Colbert, one of his collaborators declared, "The king, who had come to see the work, went through the Bosquet Vert to see the effect created by the water jet, which was turned off immediately after His Majesty's departure. In the fruit garden His Majesty noticed that the water jet in the bassin at the foot of it only rose to a height of twenty-five feet. I think that it was buffeted too much by the wind and that the adjutage was too large" (Fig. 17).[6]

That day the king spent an hour and a half in the Petit Parc. To say that it was difficult to supply enough water for the bosquets and bassins is an understatement. Therefore, the volume of water had to be increased by constructing a lead reservoir with a capacity of 580 cubic meters above the grotto. This allowed a reserve supply to build up during the night so that the water jets could play during the day. The Jolly pump was powerful enough to raise the water level in the Etang de Clagny by slightly more than 32 meters. In 1667, the following year, three "clay" reservoirs, as they were called, were built at the site of what is now the north wing. Their capacity was almost ten times greater than that of the grotto reservoir. Thereafter, the water tower, built by Le Vau, functioned on two levels: the upper level supplied the grotto reservoir, and the lower one the clay reservoirs. This dual system was replicated in the gardens where only the parterres of the Grande Terrasse were supplied by the grotto reservoir.[7] Shortly afterward Le Vau built three waterwheels to support the Jolly pump. They used a bucket system called the "chapelet," and they were terraced to create a chain that raised the water though a series of levels from the étang to the clay reservoirs. Another waterwheel ensured that the water was recycled, bringing it back up from the Bassin d'Apollon to the Etang de Clagny.

A simple comparison of the 1665 plans and those of 1674 shows that the construction of almost all the bosquets in the present structure created the need for a considerable water supply. In 1670, the Latona and Apollo groups were put in place and the Marmousets were installed in the Allée d'Eau; the following year, three bosquets were created: the Marais, the Etoile (or Montagne d'Eau), and the Théâtre d'Eau. As their names suggest, they relied for their effect on the fountains, and in the case of the last mentioned these became a sort of aquatic display that could be varied by the use of taps. On the terrace of the château, the Girardon group was placed in the Grotte de Thétys in 1672 and, for this, the final refinements were added to the elaborate water effects planned by Perrault. Finally and most ambitiously, on this same terrace the elegant forms of the new Parterre d'Eau, a huge square as wide as the avant-corps of the château designed by the Le Brun atelier, were added to the ensemble.

All the bosquets and bassins built in 1670 needed more and more water, not least because the king insisted that the five jets of the new parterre, together with those of the Sirène and the Cour Royale (no longer there but shown on the 1674 plan), as well as those of the Parterre du Midi, should play constantly. Here again innovative solutions had to be found, and quickly, since the upper gardens depended for their water supply on the Grotte de Thétys where the capacity of the reservoir was not great. For all the jets supplied by the Thétys reservoir a recycling pump, similar to the one already installed in the Bassin d'Apollon, was used. Francine, who had already acted as adviser to Le Nôtre in 1664 in the negotiations with Jolly, recommended the installation of three high-capacity reservoirs on the terrace; water could then be raised from these to the top of the grotto by bucket chains powered by horse-drawn carousels. The 400 cubic-meter reservoirs were built in 1672 and were the subject of an exchange of letters between Colbert and Louis XIV, who continued to think of his gardens, despite being at war with Flanders. Colbert wrote to the king, "All the pumps are working well, the sieur Francine is doubling the chapelet of the pump that takes the water back from the parterre to the upper reservoir, so that I hope it will transport 120 inches of water." The king replied, "The pumps at Versailles must be kept in good order, especially those serving the upper reservoir; when I arrive, I must find that they are in good repair so that they do not cause me grief by constantly breaking down." In the same letter he asked Colbert to try out the new ten-fountain arrangement by having them play all at the same time so that on his arrival he could "decide how long they should play and how large the jets should be."[8] There has never been any doubt that Louis XIV was deeply attached to his gardens, but water features, it seems, were his passion.

This explains why, despite all the ingenuity that went into the water-wheels and the system of pumps, using first two, then three, horses, a way had to be found at this point to bring more water to Clagny, since water was lost at every stage of the process. There were three possibilities: the first, tried and tested, was to drain the huge expanses of land in the area around Trappes; the second, a big project but one that would provide much water, was to divert the course of a river other than the Loire; and finally, a modern, but risky, solution was to construct a large pump that would bring the water from the Seine, six kilometers away. These three projects were all carried out at the same time but with varying degrees of success.

The étangs around Trappes and Bois-d'Arcy were drained over several years under the supervision first of Picard and Colbert, then Louvois and Gobert. The idea had been suggested to Colbert by "sieur Francine" on the recommendation, according to Picard, of "sieur Vivier, who at that time was drawing up a map of the region round Orléans." The astronomer Picard was once more pressed into service. Calling on the support of his assistant and of Vivier, proving how closely cartography and leveling were linked, he showed once again that the operation was impossible. But while he had been carrying out his work on leveling, he had noticed that water flowed into the Bièvre from the Trappes and Bois-d'Arcy plateaus through gorges across which dikes could be constructed. The étangs created in that way were above the ground level of the château. To bring the water to the château, a tunnel had to be constructed under the Satory plateau. The *Mémoires de l'Académie royale des sciences* describes the initiative and shows how carefully Louis XIV followed the whole operation: "But what is even more important is that after the conduit pipes had been installed between the entry point in the Satory mountain and the top of the grotto in Versailles, His Majesty, having ordered the first trial of the water supply, had the pleasure of seeing the water gush out with such force that it undoubtedly could not have been much higher, given the leveling that had been done. When he came down from above the grotto, His Majesty told Monsieur Picard that he was very pleased indeed."[9]

It is noteworthy that Picard mentions the presence during this operation of Rømer, whom Picard had presented as a candidate for membership of the academy on his return from Denmark. Evidently the Danish scientist justified his membership in this august body with alacrity since he abandoned his work on the speed of light to measure the flow of water in the conduits of the Montbauron reservoir instead. But the king still dreamed of having enough water for all the fountains to play continuously, all at the same time. That is how the famous Marly machine came to be constructed (Fig. 18).

Work on it began in 1681. An enormous mechanism, the noise of which could be heard for miles around—the hum of reactors was not a familiar sound in the countryside of the Ile-de-France—it was constructed at the level of Bougival. Built by a team from France and Liège, with the hydraulics engineer Arnold de Deville and with Rennequin Sualem, it had fourteen bucket wheels, twelve meters in diameter, turned by the Seine. These bucket wheels poured water into conduits, and 221 pumps drove the water up the long slope of the riverbank to an aqueduct, which took it to Louvenciennes and thence to Versailles and Marly. Dézallier d'Argenville has described this elephantine machine which, incidentally, proved robust enough to be considered worth repairing as late as the nineteenth century under Napoleon III: "In the case of the Marly machine, the water is forced 500 feet upward, following the slope of the mountain; or, more precisely, 148 feet up to the first two catch basins halfway up, from where other pumps take over and carry it 175 feet up to the next catch basin, where it is taken another 175 feet up by other pumps to a further catch basin, where more pumps take over again and force it 177 feet

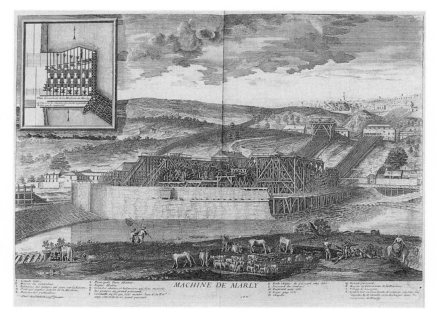

Fig. 18. The Marly machine. Musée du Château de Versailles. The water was retained upstream to provide the energy needed for the machinery; it was then collected by large wheels equipped with buckets, pumped up the hill into an aqueduct, and conveyed to either Marly or Versailles.

up to the platform of the tower of the aqueduct, which has 36 arches and is 330 toises long."[10]

Yet the loss of water and energy caused by weaknesses in the valves and the friction of the rudimentary transmission system meant that 221 pumps were not adequate. They provided water to supply Marly, but another solution had to be found for Versailles. That explains the proposed diversion of the waters of the Eure: this project did not come to fruition either for other reasons, but it demonstrated the potential of contemporary technology. Louis XIV announced the new project at his *lever*, in August 1684 at Fontainebleau.[11] Colbert was dead, as was Picard, but the cooperation that they had established between the upper echelons of the administration and the Académie des sciences had continued thanks to Louvois and Philippe de la Hire. The latter began his measurements in October 1684, estimating the height of the bed of the Eure at Maintenon, where the river was closest to Versailles. At that point, the river bed was thirty meters below the ground level of the château. But upstream there was a large bend in the river around Chartres, and by cutting off this bend one could join the river again at Pontgouin and the difference in height could be increased by seventy meters. This allowed some of the waters of the river to be diverted and brought to Versailles along a by-channel slightly more than seventy kilometers long.[12] The distance was not great but there were two problems along the route it had to follow: spanning the Larris valley at Berchères and the valley of the Eure at Maintenon.

Work began without delay and progress continued when Vauban was able to arrange for thirty thousand men, under the command of Maréchal d'Uxelles, to join the existing workforce. At the beginning of 1688, almost the entire canal had been completed, but the two major obstacles, Berchères and Maintenon, had not been overcome. The second, in particular, seemed formidable. Vauban had proposed building an aqueduct, which would be 5 kilometers long and 70 meters high in places. This work of art was to be three stories high and able to carry the waters of a canal 1.89 meters deep and 2.48 meters wide. By 1688, only the first story had been completed. Realizing that the war of the League of Augsburg was imminent, the king told Vauban and Louvois to speed the work up and abandon the idea of the aqueducts in favor of cast-iron siphons. At Maintenon, the siphon would be located on the story of the aqueduct that had already been constructed; at Berchères it would be at the bottom of the valley, which was admittedly not deep. In both cases, foundry masters from Champagne and Normandy had to be persuaded to supply hundreds of meters of large cast-iron pipes, and their leaders were promised letters of nobility if they honored the contract "from start to finish, in the specified time."[13]

But the war was getting inexorably closer, and soon the troops left Maintenon for billets closer to the frontiers. All that remains today are the majestic ruins of the Maintenon aqueduct and the memory of a great project on which the talents and resources of engineers like Vauban and scientists like La Hire had been employed. The works were abandoned and Louis XIV had to give up his ambition to bring all the water he needed to Versailles. We should remember, too, that it was Versailles in its entirety—not just the gardens—that was involved. Saint-Simon so successfully managed to have the Eure Canal dubbed a "cruel folly" that it is easy to forget that some of the water would have supplied the inhabitants of the town, like the waters of Roquencourt, which supplied fountains and water points on the public highway.

Despite this failure, as far as the construction of canals, fountains, and pumps is concerned, the technical achievements of the time were brilliant. The use of iron pipes—or, more accurately, cast-iron pipes—in the construction of canals was established in the early years. As Dézallier d'Argenville observed, "Iron pipes are smelted and cast into shape and are frequently used nowadays; there are two kinds: one with handles, one with straps. But only the latter are used, as they are better. Iron pipes have all the merits of lead pipes, last longer in gardens, and are infinitely cheaper. They can withstand an elevation of 177 feet in the conduit of water at Marly. These same pipes break in the streets of Paris because of the weight of carriages. Lead is easier to handle and much better for use in streets."[14]

But however successful lead was in Paris streets, iron worked well in Versailles and was used extensively, precisely because it was "infinitely cheaper." In this context, it is worth noting that the *Mémoires de l'Académie des sciences* for 1677 contains some interesting exchanges between Mariotte and Rømer about hydrostatic problems encountered in Versailles. Having established that the beauty of the water jets was a "wonderful sight, never before seen" and, moreover, one that "served the pleasures and grandeur of a great king," and having also established that "the water jets need the support of geometry," Rømer provided "a universal rule to evaluate the abundance of all the horse-driven machines serving to raise water." (These would have been the norias, or bucket waterwheels, which were used at that point to supply Le Vau's water tower.) Mariotte, relevantly, "went into considerably greater detail about the expense of the water jets and the amount of water needed to supply them." According to him, account had to be taken of the rate of flow, the width of the nozzles, the friction on the pipe walls, and the air resistance, "all conditions that only geometry can evaluate."[15] He advocated increasing the diameter of the canalizations when the water was flowing faster so that the diameters of these pipes would be comparable with the square root of the rates of flow, and he calculated these rates of flow as a function of the height of the reservoirs. Mariotte returned to the question of water jets in his *Traité du mouvement d'eau* (1686), and he may have had the water engineers of Versailles in mind when he set the following problem: "Given the average height of a reservoir and a jet at an oblique angle, calculate where it will meet the horizontal plane."[16]

Mariotte also did some work on air, and his research developed that of Galileo, Torricelli, and Pascal on atmospheric pressure. "We have only known about air for a short time," he observed in 1679; he described this gas as more condensed in its lower strata and "more expanded" as it rose. He added that the gas was blue but "this color could only become apparent where it was very thick."[17] This work on air, its thickness and its color, is so important in relation to the seventeenth-century landscape artists who were known and appreciated by Louis XIV and Le Nôtre that we shall return to this question when we discuss the aesthetic of Le Nôtre. For the moment, however, we shall simply observe that hydrostatics was one of the favorite areas of research for seventeenth-century scientists and one in which the physics of the day acknowledged the supremacy of geometry. This was not the case in all areas and particularly in the life-sciences, where dissenting voices, notably that of La Quintinie, could be heard.

CHAPTER EIGHT

The World of Plants and the Silent Progress of the Life Sciences

ORDER AND VARIETY were the two ruling principles in the vegetal decoration at Versailles; on the Grande Terrasse, close to the château, flowers displayed their bright colors in the parterres; in the Petit Parc they were confined to the inside of the bosquets, which used palisaded trees as a frame; in the Grand Parc, which extended faraway into the country, tall trees were the lords of the land, asserting their right to be there by virtue of prior possession. Trianon was a world apart, where flowers reigned supreme either in the parterres or in the orange trees planted in open ground and protected in the winter.

Great care was given to the planting of the parterres; they were marked out with lines according to conventional methods later described by Dézallier d'Argenville; the floral decoration followed, according to geometrical patterns that took colors, shapes, and sizes into account. All available means of transport were used to bring the flowers in. The king loved the effect of bright colors, and even when he was far from Versailles, he thought about its flowers. After Colmar had been taken, he wrote to Colbert from Nancy, "I am expecting to find many late and early flowers, since my brother has told me that the garden was not so full of them as usual and that Le Bouteux was keeping some back, and I believe it is for that reason. Keep that in mind."[1]

Michel Le Bouteux, the flower gardener with whom Le Nôtre regularly collaborated along with Colinot, stored flowers in greenhouses before using them to decorate the parterres with pots, but many were also supplied to him directly and often from far-flung places. Colbert, knowing what pleased the king, noted in the *Ordres et règlements pour les bâtiments de Versailles* (Orders and regulations for the buildings of Versailles) in 1664, "Visit Trianon frequently; check that Le Bouteux has flowers for the king throughout the winter."[2] The indefatigable minister took care to ensure regular deliveries from Provence. In his correspondence with Arnoul, the intendant des Galères (Intendant of the galley fleet) in Marseilles, we find recommendations and orders that prove how much care he took with these supplies: "You will find enclosed a memorandum of the flowers required for the royal gardens, which must be sent in July of this year, except for the tuberoses, needed for Trianon, which can be sent next year."[3] In 1670, he ordered jonquils, tulips, tuberoses, narcissi, and hyacinths. He also had flowers sent from Holland and set up a royal garden in Toulon to ensure regular supplies. In that connection, he sent Bodard, the intendant des Galères in charge of the project, a letter that demonstrates his ever-present concern to get the precise measure of everything and obtain the best results: "Have a plan made straightaway, showing the orientation and exact measurements, and send me at the same time a memorandum detailing exactly how many flowers it contains at present and how many can be grown annually, so that the requirements of the royal houses can be fully met."[4]

Of course, this only applied to the flowers that were not grown on the spot because, in good years such as 1686 and 1687, the nurseries in Versailles produced up to 250,000 pots of flowers. This meant that new and efficient methods for growing had to be developed, notably for pot plants, and the skills of Dutch gardeners were called upon, despite the wars between France and the United Provinces. The brothers Dambresne, who were in charge of growing tulips from 1669 to 1682, are always referred to in the *Comptes des Bâtiments du Roi* as "Flemish gardeners."

Where were these flowers planted? In the parterres, where they brought color to the enroulements of the borders, and in the bosquets, where they brightened the backdrop of trees and trellises. In the *Comptes des Bâtiments du Roi* a payment is recorded to Le Bouteux of 600 livres for "festoons, bouquets, and floral ornaments for the decoration of the Salle du Festin et du Bal" provided for the fêtes of 1668; in 1671 payments were made to Louis Barbier and Antoine Deslauriers for honeysuckle and "plants and flowers" supplied for the bosquet and the allées of the Etoile.[5]

But the floral decoration of the parterres was on a much bigger scale than in the bosquets, and that was what was immediately striking when one entered the gardens. Saint-Simon said that Le Nôtre did not consider it important since he thought that the parterres were only there for the benefit of the nursemaids who saw them from the upper stories where they were confined. It is indeed very likely that Le Nôtre's tastes were more inclined to the play of water and the grand structural effects where his command of the landscape was so dazzling. Even so, he was also admired for his design of the parterres. Tessin bears this out in his *Relation*: "The Parterre [de la Terrasse] is utterly beautiful and demonstrates the genius of Monsieur Le Nôter [*sic*]; I have drawn it and the turf in the beds and the enroulements look very attractive."[6] Flowers arrived by the cartload at Trianon. According to the *Comptes des Bâtiments du Roi*, Henry Julienne was paid more than 1,600 livres in 1686 for "20,050 double jonquil bulbs and one hundred livres and a half weight of double anemones, bought in different places," while Pierre Trutry received only 183 livres for "2,300 Saint-Claude cyclamen bulbs and 1,700 lilies that he fetched from Dauphiné, Auvergne, and Savoie for the Trianon garden."[7] We have some idea of what the floral decoration of the Trianon parterres looked like thanks to a statement indicating different plots and varieties. We also know from Saint-Simon that the scent of the tuberoses at Trianon was sometimes so strong as to be unpleasant (Fig. 19).

The flowers were therefore the most brilliant, highly scented, and luxurious element of the garden vegetation. They gave charm and beauty to the parterres de broderie: this term is so apt that clothes were inspired by floral embroidery. But the background vegetation itself was made up of trees and shrubs brought to Versailles in massive quantities. The *Ordres et règlements pour les bâtiments de Versailles* signed by Colbert in 1674 give us an idea of the kind of work that held pride of place in the gardens during the years when they took on the appearance that was preserved until the first replanting in 1775–76. The gardeners had no lack of precise instructions before setting to work.

> Remove the bad soil from the allée between Saturn and Apollo; dig trenches to plant box there.
> Construct the side path from the Fontaine de Saturne to the Allée des Tilleuls and plant it with maple.
> Replant the side path with maple, if there is none there.
> Dig trenches and fill them with good soil in the allée between the wall and the Ile Royale and plant limes there to replace the ones that are dead.
> Plant elms and palisades along the walls of the orangerie.[8]

Fig. 19. The geometrical design of the Parterre Sud. Photograph by Jean-Baptiste Leroux. The baroque took the enroulements of parterres to a degree of perfection hitherto unknown. This resulted from the generalization of the long perspective in garden design. The axes of the gardens were lengthened, and the parterres were turned into rectangles with more space to accommodate enroulements that combined the elegance of geometric forms with the lively colors of flowers, as was also the case in ceramics and in dressmaking.

In his study of the replanting of the gardens of Versailles under Louis XVI, Pierre Francastel has used the archives to show which trees were in place from the beginning and how they were replaced.[9] The squares later to become the frame of the bosquets were essentially planted with oaks, thinly interspersed with chestnut, beech, ash, hornbeam, and wild cherry trees. Most of the trees in rows were elms or chestnuts. Yew and spruce could be found around the perimeter of the bosquets. The *Comptes des Bâtiments du Roi* shows that large quantities of trees, and sometimes sizable ones, were brought from the Ile-de-France and Normandy, but young trees were also sometimes taken out to be replanted in straight rows. La Quintinie was lavish with advice on the subject: "This is why the people taking out the trees must be extremely careful to keep them straight and remove them gently: large holes are needed for this or the trees will be sure to split or break a good root." Once they had been taken out, the trees were to be replanted "a good foot deep" so that the wind would not destabilize them.[10] The gardeners of Versailles followed this advice to the letter; in 1686 Jean Frason was paid 200 livres for the

"800 holes, 3 feet wide by 2 feet deep, which he is digging in the bosquets of the Petit Parc to plant sycamores."[11]

However, the trees that were moved in the Petit Parc and the Grand Parc were soon joined by a host of others. Tens of thousands of small elms were brought in from the 1660s onward, along with small hornbeam, horse chestnuts, and "ypréaux," or large-leaved elms from the Ypres area and bought in Flanders by the receveur général des finances d'Artois (Receiver general in charge of tax collection for Artois). In 1669, 1,700 walnut trees were planted. In the *Comptes des Bâtiments du Roi,* we find records of payments made to the gardeners Marin Trumel, Henry Dupuis,[12] and Macé Fouché, as well as payments for "trees, elms, limes, and others, supplied for the avenues and châteaux of Versailles and Vincennes" and for "several shrubs from the Vaux-le-Vicomte nurseries." In addition to these trees, which were to be planted in rows and for the background vegetation of the bosquets, appeared large quantities of wicker poles used to "arm" the trees and "palisade" the shrubs, as well as firs, yews, and "picea" (spruce), which were planted in the Fontaine du Dragon and the demi-lune of the Grande Allée.

Species are not always specified in these orders, but Dézallier d'Argenville, who was living in the area around Paris and writing in the years immediately after Le Nôtre's death, would doubtless have met with the latter's approval when he said that the "oak is better suited to forests than to allées" and "the elm is thought very acceptable in allées and bosquets," "the 'ypréau' in grand allées." Similarly, "limes in the bosquets," he claims, "can have all kinds of shapes," Indian chestnut "is suitable for the allées," "beech or 'fouteau'[13] for the palisades," and "acacia, which was at one time used in the allées and arbors, has a pleasant scent but is otherwise of scant interest."[14] All these trees are indigenous to Europe, and resinous varieties do not figure prominently among them.

The Grand Parc, as the woods used for hunting with dogs were called at the time, was the object of what Thierry Mariage has described as "redevelopment on a truly regional scale." He continues,

> The Grand Parc at Versailles, stretching as far as Trappes, Bois-d'Arcy, Villepreux, and Rennemoulin, took in 34 farms and also the villages of Buc, Saint-Cyr, and de Bailly, as well as the Forêt de Marly and the Bois de Satory. Translating this into present-day measurements, the Grand Parc covered 15,000 hectares (approximately 37,067 acres) as opposed to 765 (1,890) today. . . . A study of the *Comptes des Bâtiments du Roi* allows

us to identify an important period for planting between 1668 and 1672 and to establish that roughly 130,000 trees were brought in.[15]

This major reforestation did not slow down. Ernest de Ganay, once again according to the *Comptes des Bâtiments du Roi*, tells us that in the autumn of 1686 alone, within a month and a half, "1,585 thousand small hornbeams, 148 thousand goat willows, 9 thousand maples and hazels, 8,400 elms, 255 sycamores, and 85 thousand small two-year-old elms were transported to Versailles from Lyon and Rouen. In 1688, 25,000 trees were brought in from the Artois area."[16]

By covering the geometrical surfaces and volumes of the parterres, bosquets, slopes, and glacis with vegetation, the flowers, shrubs, and trees brought living color to the gardens. The variety of shapes and hues that wind, rain, and the changing seasons give to the face of nature added to the life provided by movement of water. In them was created a sense of poetic mystery that the mechanical sciences could not express in geometrical terms. La Quintinie was clearly aware of this.

> Philosophers and chemists produce grand dissertations to seek to establish which are the best manures, and this is done with the same precision as mathematicians apply to decide what is needed to draw a straight line, etc. The public is greatly obliged to these gentlemen whose curiosity and powers of observation lead them to probe the secrets of nature in such depth; I hope that we shall gain greatly from it, but in the meantime until they succeed, I think that as far as I and those who approve of what I write are concerned, we cannot do better than to continue acting as I already do, that is, in a pure, simple, and unsophisticated way, in the knowledge, moreover, that the fertility of the soil does not consist, so to speak, of an indivisible point.[17]

One must allow for La Quintinie's sense of humor here, picking up on the definitions used by the geometers, in this case of the famous "indivisible point" which, as we saw earlier, legal experts such as Cardin Le Bret had used to vindicate mathematically the sovereignty of the king. But under the cloak of this good-natured banter, he nonetheless put his finger on one of the difficulties encountered by mainstream science at that time. How could phenomena as simple as the changes wrought by the growth of plants and animals be explained? If one said, as Descartes did in the conclusion to his *Traité de l'homme*

(Treatise on man), "After that, I desire you to consider that all the functions I have attributed to this machine, such as the digestion of meat, the beating of the heart and arteries, the nourishing and growth of limbs, respiration, waking and sleeping. . . . I desire you to consider, I repeat, that in this machine these functions are a natural and unique consequence of the arrangement of the organs—no more no less than the movements made by a clock or other automaton follow from its counterweights and wheels,"[18] then one was highly likely to reach the same conclusion as Tauvry, one of Descartes's disciples: "To apply physics correctly to the human body, I exclude from it all unrelated concepts; namely all the faculties, and I think of it as a static, hydraulic, and pneumatic machine in which the bones are the supports and levers, the muscles the ropes, the heart and lungs the pump, the blood vessels the canals where fluids circulate constantly."[19]

It was precisely the statics of the machine, whether human or vegetal, that posed a problem. La Quintinie could see clearly that sap circulates toward the ends of branches and roots; from that perspective he was one of the "circulateurs," or supporters of a circulatory system, whose opponents were so well described by Molière in *Le malade imaginaire*. But on the basis of sound empirical observation, he did not think that the sap "circulated constantly," like water in a pump. Vegetal growth seemed to him a marvel that was "infinitely difficult to understand and explain": that is why in his book he describes in loving detail the operations of nature, sometimes using culinary metaphors (trees, for example, "slowly cook" their fruit, protecting it with their leaves) that show an intuitive and poetic approach.

He shows roots generating the sap from a mixture of water and soil, then when spring warmth comes, making its way along the channels in the bark to emerge into the open as buds, while at the same time working underground to make the roots grow longer: "the sap, therefore, swelling so that it breaks through the bark containing it, then flows out of all the exits it is capable of creating; and from the liquid form it had before it broke through, it becomes solid when it emerges into the soil just as it does into the air: in the soil, it takes the being, form, and nature of roots, just as in the air the sap in the branches becomes leaves, fruits, and other branches, etc."[20]

Thus, the sap circulates, but it is transformed, changing its nature. When it becomes a leaf, a flower, or a root, it changes from a liquid to a solid state, undergoing, "so to speak, a metamorphosis." This is a far cry from the way a machine functions. To explain what he describes as "a never-ending miracle of nature," La Quintinie does not accept a mechanistic account, which would explain the form and nature of leaves and fruits by the shape of the pores through which the sap passes, and he forestalls the objections of his opponents, who claim that they are awaiting the invention of "good glasses or microscopes" to discover the shape of these pores, by saying that his hope is for suitable instruments to one day discover "the gravitational power of roots" for which there is no mechanical explanation.

This is a scientific universe that foreshadows the vitalism of the following century, one that would find its voice in the work of Linnaeus, Buffon, and Bernardin de Saint-Pierre. It is of them that we are often reminded when La Quintinie tries to describe in words and images his fascination with the inexhaustible fertility of the natural world. Was he alone in trying to establish experiential truths that did not readily fit with the physics dominant in every technical area? Undoubtedly not. The opinions voiced in the king's potager were echoed in the Académie des sciences, particularly in Claude Perrault's work on anatomy, and it is an example of the rich intellectual life of Versailles in that period.

Before we conclude this chapter on the empire of the geometers by returning to the work of Claude and Charles Perrault, which will lead naturally to the next section on the arts, let us take one last look at La Quintinie's *Instruction* where we see him at work in drawing a particularly interesting parallel, that between grafts and water jets. La Quintinie's reputation for carrying out grafts on fruit trees was so great that Louis XIV came in person to the potager to take lessons from him and get some practical experience (Fig. 20).[21] Grafting was the source of one of the metamorphoses that so amazed La Quintinie: by using grafts, the trunk of a quince tree could be crowned by branches of a pear tree, simply as a result of the passage of sap through scions. On this subject, too, some mechanical scientists were simplistic enough to explain this phenomenon by comparing the scion to the adjutage of a water jet, but an adjutage in which differently arranged openings, or pores, would produce pears in one case and apples in another. As one might expect, anything about water jets attracted attention at Versailles, but La Quintinie was prepared to take up the gauntlet, saying that "the mystery of grafting is undoubtedly too shrouded in obscurity for that to be an adequate explanation." His argument is very characteristic of the way in which he rebuts any mechanistic explanation.

If it is in use for a long time, an adjutage wears out, and eventually breaks down altogether; but our scion, by contrast, gets stronger the more it performs its function. Every adjutage can only produce a particular form of

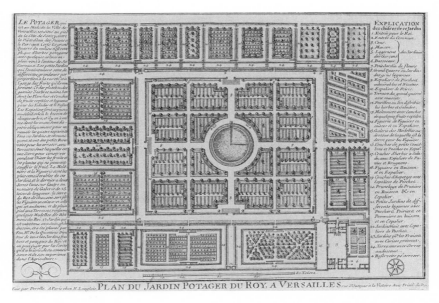

Fig. 20. The King's potager. Plan by Adam Perelle, ca. 1690. Musée du Château de Versailles.

jet; but every scion produces an infinite variety of effects, all separate and very different, namely bark, wood, leaves, flowers, fruits, etc.; and these fruits are themselves different in their color, shape, taste, flesh, seeds, etc. Consequently, you might say that our scion, which produces an infinite number of other scions, would produce an infinite number of adjutages, which cannot possibly be an appropriate comparison for the ordinary adjutages of a fountain, since they cannot reproduce.[22]

When La Quintinie's son published the *Instruction* in 1690, two years after his father's death, Charles Perrault wrote an idyll that appeared at the front of the volume. It evokes certain themes that are developed in the book and even some of the same images, particularly one comparing roots with mouths that "draw in food and form liquor." At that time, Perrault had lost the privileged position he had held under Colbert, who had died seven years earlier. Louvois had indicated to him that his services were no longer required, but he was still a member of the Académie française and was possibly beginning to collect the popular tales for which his name is known today and in which the mysteries and metamorphoses of nature also figure so prominently.

Moreover, the scientific legacy inherited from his brother Claude, who had just died, mattered to him a great deal. Now, as we have seen, the latter's role in the Académie des sciences was closely linked to its actual foundation. Keen to promote collaboration between the "geometers" and the "physicists," he made his reputation primarily among the latter through his work on anatomy. A doctor by training, he had developed a theory of hearing in which the concept of elasticity was central. This sufficiently demonstrates that rigidly mechanistic theories did not appeal to him, and although, like all scientists of the period, he was influenced by Cartesian physics, he no longer accepted that animals could be considered machines.[23]

In this respect he shared Christiaan Huygens's view that work on anatomy should be carried out "following the plan outlined by Verulam,"[24] that is, the Baconian method. Bacon was the leading light of the empiricists, among whose number were some of the most remarkable scientists of the Royal Society of London, in particular Boyle, Sydenham, and Newton, who were engaged in a wholesale critique of Cartesianism and what they called the geometers' method. Chemistry was beginning to emerge as an influential science; the language of geometry was inappropriate to serve its ends because, in the eye of the chemist, the composition of bodies was more important than their form. Boyle took as a given all the work that had been done on the weight of air; what interested him was its composition. He had seen from his own work that a solid could metamorphose into a gas through the action of a liquid, and since gas was formless, geometry could not be much help in explaining that process. This is why he reformulated Galileo's dictum, saying that nature was not a book written in the language of mathematics but in the language of corpuscles.[25]

La Quintinie's work, even if it is modest, at least in tone, shows just how rich intellectual life at Versailles was, even though it was not uncontroversial at a time when the quarrel of the Ancients and the Moderns was dividing artists and men of letters over aesthetic questions that were also important for gardens.

PART III

An Open-Air Palace
Gardens and the Arts

You are familiar with Le Nôtre's style, are you not?
—Madame de Sévigné

CHAPTER NINE

Gardens and Culture at Court

IN *LA PROMENADE de Versailles*, Mlle. de Scudéry, whose highly mannered novels were very popular in the seventeenth century, takes three characters on a visit to the gardens and acts as their guide. Her guests are Télamon, Glycère, and a member of their family, a "beautiful stranger" whose mysterious identity adds a romantic note to the pleasure of discovering the gardens. She describes their arrival on the Grande Terrasse as they come out of the vestibule as follows:

> But in that place, after passing through the corridor, the beautiful stranger, Glycère, and Télamon gave a great cry of admiration at the beauty of the view. And indeed from that vantage point, one can see several great parterres with round bassins and jets, and beyond those parterres, jets and fountains of water, a canal four hundred toises long and sixteen wide, which in defiance of Nature and its situation, runs straight up to the top of a hillock, and to the right and left woods seem to bow down as if to leave in clear sight the distant view beyond. I had difficulty in persuading this amiable company to move away from such a charming place.[1]

The "great cry of admiration" from Mlle. de Scudéry's characters expresses the feelings of everyone who visited or lived in the château. If the court was the cynosure of all eyes, it was because it gathered together in a setting that was the envy of all Europe. Hence the key role of the gardens. Since the quarters that housed the two thousand permanent guests of the king were not spectacularly comfortable or spacious, their occupants preferred the great open spaces in the galleries and salons of the château or, of course, in the gardens. In the gardens a courtier could see the king and be seen by him, greet him, present compliments, and possibly be summoned to accompany him on his walk. These public places represented the majesty of the king and nothing was too fine for them. The courtiers were constantly refining their dress, their language, the courtesy of their exchanges, and even the way they walked so that they were in harmony with the setting that had been devised for them. A sense of the aesthetic was taken for granted at Versailles, and it was more prudent to cultivate one's own or, failing that, to rely on generally acknowledged models, because this was the only way to conform to the established standards in a closed society where derision was a lethal weapon.

Le Nôtre's gardens were designed to dazzle visitors from all over the world, from Mlle. de Scudéry's friends to the doge of Venice, from William of Orange's envoy to the Siamese ambassadors. The king and those in power used the gardens as a means of honoring important guests. Christiaan Huygens relates how when he arrived at Versailles, the fact that Charles Perrault was with him was enough to warrant a full display of the fountains playing. But most of all, the gardens satisfied the rigorous scrutiny of a court that could appreciate the munificence of the prince. And the prince who in turn welcomed them as participants in what he termed a "société de plaisirs" knew how to share with them the sophisticated pleasures of palace life, but in the open air. He had succeeded in making Versailles a cultural center whose luster spread well beyond the frontiers of France. Paris kept its prime position in the eyes of foreigners and of the French themselves, but everyone knew that Versailles was the artistic capital of France and had been since the early years of Louis XIV's reign. Voltaire observes, with some astonishment, "The court became the center for all the pleasures and a model for other courts. The king took pride in giving fêtes that put those of Vaux in the shade. It seemed as though it was nature's delight to have France generate all the greatest artists in every sphere and bring all the most beautiful and comely men and women to her court."[2]

This center of excellence attracted all the talents—otherwise, why would Molière have gone there?—and the decor of the château and gardens was the living, concrete image of what the world then saw as the ideal setting. All who went to Versailles were aware of this, and writers outdid one another with superlatives describing the glories of the spectacle before them. The following lines from La Fontaine echo the admiring cries of Mlle. de Scud-éry's heroes:

> Phébus brille à l'envi du monarque français;
> On ne sait bien souvent à qui donner sa voix;
> Tous deux sont pleins d'éclat et rayonnant de gloire.
> Ah! Si j'étais aidé des filles de mémoire
> De quels traits j'ornerais cette comparaison!
> Versailles ce serait le palais d'Apollon;
> Les belles de Versailles passeraient pour les Heures;
> Mais peignons seulement ces charmantes demeures.[3]

> [Phoebus shines forth to rival the French king;
> To choose between them is no easy task:
> The splendor of both is brilliant and dazzling.
> Ah! Were I inspired by the Muses
> Such fine comparisons could I evoke.
> Apollo's palace would describe Versailles,
> The Hours, the lovely ladies of its court;
> But let us only paint these charming haunts.]

"These charming haunts"—Apollo's palace was indeed the palace of the god of the arts, a god surrounded by the Muses. It was a place where music, po-etry, and dance would charm all the senses or, in a word, a kind of Olympus where gods and goddesses, "all the most beautiful and comely men and women," in Voltaire's words, came together in an ideal spot. The king himself exemplified this ideal society. This is what André Félibien had to say about the portrait Le Brun had painted of him:

> That bearing and stature, so grand, noble, and natural, which we admire and respect so much in Your Majesty and with which the Ancients were wont to depict their demi-gods, are so well captured in this portrait that no one could fail to recognize you, and such as you appear, when lead-ing your armies, you inspire fresh ardor in the spirits of those who have the honor to follow you.
>
> It is not an accident that the beauty of the body has always been seen as the outward sign of the beauty of the soul and that the proportion and

symmetry of the parts from which that exterior beauty is formed seem to bear witness to the concord and internal harmony that make up the generous soul. That is why the beauty of the body has been said to be more than a well-proportioned arrangement of a series of different parts and is rather a kind of glow emanating from the beauty of the soul, which shines forth and bathes the body in its grace, an incarnation of the excellence of the inner man.[4]

Since high heels were responsible for the "bearing and stature, so grand, noble, and natural," it is easy to make fun of Félibien's description, but that is to miss the main point. What matters is the desire to glorify the king so as to glorify at the same time the dream of perfection that he embodies. For nothing is more tenuous or more tenacious than a dream, and it is as difficult to comprehend its mysterious nature as it is to understand its power. The dreams of seventeenth-century courtiers, like our own, belong to their particular culture, and a culture is made up of many different things—inherited traditions, emotional climates, consensual ideas accepted or not—and it stimulates in many the desire to represent and express themselves that it is difficult to analyze and break down a web of such complexity. For Félibien and the world of the court, the king's "external" beauty comes from the "proportion" and "symmetry" of his physical being, his "interior" beauty from the "concord" and "harmony" of his moral being.

Proportion, symmetry, concord, harmony—these four words give no hint of patriotic fervor or uplifting emotion. Proportion brings to mind measures and their relationships, symmetry evokes a formal parity, while concord and harmony suggest the compatibility of sounds and their consonance. These are all abstract notions, and we find it difficult now to understand that the physical and moral beauty of a prince could be described in those terms. We seem to be back in the world of the geometers where figures and measurement are sovereign and emotions have no place. It seems to us that there is a contradiction—and Romanticism is doubtless responsible for this—between the felicitous but rigorous organization of forms, whether in the body of the king, in the design of gardens and buildings, in the plot of classical tragedies, and in the almost complacent abandon evoked by the "sweet transports" and the "raptures of love" so often heard in the ornamented arias of baroque operas. This contradiction becomes even more marked when we see this facile sentimentality decked in all the mists of illusion in the paintings of Albani and Cotelle, much liked by Le Nôtre and the king, in which figures, floating on clouds, smile at cherubs cavorting in the heavens. Despite this, the king, whose eyes glistened with tears as he listened to the "tender" Racine, would describe enthusiastically the geometric beauty of the trench dug outside Saint-Quentin. And the court, who thrilled to the account of the misfortunes of the Grand Cyrus[5] and craved dramas packed with metamorphoses onstage, were equally admiring of the austere elegance of the Grand Trianon.

In the eyes of the court and the king, Le Nôtre was the greatest gardener of the age, and that is why visitors to Versailles saw the gardens as the ultimate expression of the life, grandeur, and truth of natural forms. Their admiration was made up of the blend of emotions and implicit judgments that we call a sense of the beautiful. Some of these judgments and emotions are easy to understand: the vast size of the place, the sumptuous materials used, the carefully orchestrated display of the fountains, and the plantings invariably make an instant impression on any visitor. But beauty is something else, and if we are to appreciate it fully, we have to make an imaginative effort to recapture the past and give the words "proportion," "symmetry," "concord," and "harmony" the affective charge they had at the time. Once that effort has been made, it will be possible to show how the abstract criteria used to define beauty were reconciled with the taste for illusion and sentiment that come together in the literature and painting of the period. In that context, Le Nôtre's style will appear to be an all-encompassing expression of humanity's vision of nature at a time when garden design in France was particularly rich.

That said, we must be clear about exactly what Le Nôtre contributed to gardens like Chantilly, Sceaux, and Versailles. Le Nôtre has a considerable reputation but he is not well-known, as an international conference commemorating the tercentenary of his death showed. Only a few of his designs and hardly any of his writings have survived.[6] We know little of the way he worked, except that he acted as the leader of a team. In Versailles, this team included members as eminent as the king, who had his own opinions about gardens, and Le Brun and Jules Hardouin-Mansart, who contributed ex officio to the architectural and sculptural elements of the parterres and bosquets. However, no one disputed that the work of Le Nôtre was fundamental to the whole conception of the gardens; he designed the way they would look by creating the contours, putting in a hydraulic network, and selecting the plantings, and he was recognized as a great artist. He enjoyed the confidence and friendship of Louis XIV, who knew how to pick his entourage. He was very much in demand and was often obliged to make excuses for being late or missing appointments, even with Le Grand Condé. He would not have had such an illustrious reputation if he had not been acknowledged as a "skillful" (*habile*) man who had a certain "genius" (*génie*), to quote the terms frequently used at the time to describe the skill and imaginative invention of artists. In a letter to her daughter, describing the château of Clagny built for the king's mistress Madame de Montespan at the height of her favor, Madame de Sévigné has left us an eloquent tribute to the high regard in which Le Nôtre was held.

> You cannot imagine how triumphant Madame de Montespan was, surrounded by her twelve hundred workmen: the palace of Apollidon and the gardens of Armide pale by comparison. You are familiar with Le Nôtre's style, are you not? He has left in place a small, dark wood that creates a very good effect; there is a small grove of orange trees in large containers with alleys where you can walk in the shade; and to hide the containers, there are palisades on each side, tall enough to lean on and resplendent with tuberoses, roses, varieties of jasmine, and carnations. It is undoubtedly the most beautiful, the most astonishing, and the most enchanting new idea imaginable; it is a delightful grove.[7]

People of culture were therefore in agreement on what was meant by "Le Nôtre's style," and it is indeed a phrase like that which gives us some idea of its complexity. Madame de Sévigné mentions Armide and Apollidon, who were the heroes of *Amadis of Gaul* and Tasso's *Jerusalem Delivered*, epic romances in which magicians and sorceresses wield their power via a wealth of metamorphoses. This is a long way from the rational world of the geometers, and it is as though the gardens designed by Le Nôtre had contrived to enchant us and persuade us rationally at the same time. They enchant us by creating whole worlds, cocooned by trellises and palisades where the imagination holds sway; they persuade us by demonstrating that their structure follows logically from a particular kind of architecture and site. Le Nôtre's "style" was a harmonious blend of esplanades and intimate settings, strong light and deep shade, open landscape and secret sous-bois—in short, wide perspectives and bosquets that he created with supreme success in Versailles. In this context, a rash critical judgment might mention his genius in the modern sense of the word, and this would be true if by "genius" one is to understand the exceptional ability to synthesize. But to appreciate the full extent of the synthesis, you have to uncover its different elements and the means by which they are brought together. In the case of a true artist, that is a lifetime's work.

CHAPTER TEN

Le Nôtre

An Independent Genius

ANDRÉ LE NÔTRE was born near the Tuileries Gardens where his father, Jean Le Nôtre, was in charge of designing the parterres. His future career was never in any doubt since he belonged to a well-known dynasty. The Le Nôtre family was as well-known in the gardening world as the Mansart family in architecture or the Couperins in music. The young André must have shown obvious gifts and talents in many different areas because he was encouraged, perhaps by his family, to make frequent visits to the atelier of Simon Vouet where, among other young painters, he met Le Brun. His father was probably quite content for him to go as a neighbor to get his training with an acknowledged master who had opened a small academy in the galleries of the Louvre, as it was generally recognized that knowledge of painting was useful to gardeners. In his *Traité du jardinage selon les raisons de la nature et de l'art,* Boyceau explains that an understanding of beauty in garden design can be gained "from architects and others who know about portraiture and good geometers," and that "an initial training in such sciences" is just as necessary "for the construction of a garden as a knowledge of soils and plants." He is quite explicit: "if a gardener knows nothing about drawing, he cannot create or judge ornamentation."[1] This advice could very well have been taken by the Le Nôtre family, who knew Boyceau—Louis XIII had appointed him intendant of the royal gardens—and it is probable that André Le Nôtre worked with him on the Luxembourg gardens. Boyceau's influence could have proved crucial since he was rightly considered to be an intellectual. The precision of his thinking and his analytical sharpness—characteristics that make his *Traité* a major work—must have been appreciated in the world of the great Paris gardeners.

When Le Nôtre approached Simon Vouet to help him train as a painter, he chose the most qualified and competent man in Paris. According to Jacques Thuillier, Vouet knew how to "welcome young people with a vocation, recognize talent, instill rather than teach the mysteries of art, and let everyone follow their own bent."[2] Moreover, he had learned a great deal in Rome, where he had lived for fourteen years (1612–26) during a time when artists benefited from an exceptionally rich intellectual atmosphere. Many different currents of opinion intermingled there: admirers of Caravaggio sought to create dramatic contrasts of light and shade, and members of the Bologna school were more inclined to prefer the harmony produced by a solid academic construct. Even more important for garden design, numerous landscape artists worked there. Some were Italian, such as Annibale Carracci, and others had come from northern Europe; these ultramontanes from beyond the Alps included great artists such as Bril, Poussin, and Claude Lorrain. Like so many others before them, these painters had come south primarily because Italy seemed to have been the source of all the arts since the Renaissance (both Richelieu and Colbert admitted this but made every effort to wrest that honor away for France), but also because the great Venetians—Giorgione and Titian—had shown them all the possibilities offered by the rich colors they could use to paint the Roman *campagna*. In the countryside around Rome, with its lakes, wooded hills, statues that were sometimes still standing, ancient ruins, and an exceptional purity of light, any artist who wanted to paint "classical" or "pastoral" landscapes found a plethora of themes. So, in Rome, Vouet was able to encounter what we would now call the major trends in contemporary painting. After his return to Paris, he was able to pass on to his pupils the insight into European art that he had gained: Le Nôtre is proof of this, since his collection included paintings by Albani, Poussin, Claude Lorrain, and Bril. All were landscape artists, all representatives of the powerful Italo-Franco-Flemish movement that had been formed in Rome when he was making his first foray into the world of gardens.

When Boyceau advised young gardeners to learn about painting, he was not necessarily expecting them to train as landscape artists like Le Nôtre under Vouet. Boyceau had in mind the outline of the parterres and the perspectives created by the view of the parterres and allées from the house, as well as the contours of the gardens when they were not on level ground. But an embarrassment of riches is no bad thing: Le Nôtre was learning about landscape when his practice brought him into contact with architects. We know from Jules Hardouin-Mansart's funeral oration that his uncle François Mansart "had given insights to" Le Nôtre. Hardouin-Mansart says no more than that, but even so the claim seems likely to be true. In the 1630s the two men worked for Gaston d'Orléans, and in the 1640s Mansart built the château and gardens of Evry-Petit-Bourg, near Fontainebleau, where Le Nôtre was at the time.

At this point we can see the full expression of Le Nôtre's personality as an artist, arising from his training and his tastes. As is always the case with creative geniuses whose work speaks for them—Shakespeare and Rembrandt are examples—we have to start with the work itself and a few scant biographical documents as a means to get to know him. Among the latter, his collections of paintings, bronzes, and medals give us valuable clues, since Le Nôtre, like Louis XIV, had a keen visual awareness, and he is best understood through images. Let us begin with portraits of the man himself.

During his stay in Rome in 1679, Carlo Maratta painted his portrait. Le Nôtre was then sixty-six, but his face and robust stature give the impression of health, calm, and even a certain majesty (Fig. 21). His cross of the order of Saint-Lazare brings a touch of bright red to the lace of his cravat. He wears his decoration the way some Ingres figures wear their Legion of Honor, showing that he is aware of the honor the king has paid him. This was one of his personal rules: he valued the respect that he was shown, but he never put himself forward and, above all, scrupulously observed the social rules, exactly as they were, perhaps thinking that they had never done him any harm. When he was ennobled, he chose three snails and a white cabbage for his coat of arms, making the point, somewhat humorously, that honors did not go to his head. Saint-Simon saw no malice in this, but appreciated it immensely, as the portrait he drew of him shows.

This modesty was reflected in the way Le Nôtre lived and in his legendary bonhomie. This was not pretense, since he liked simplicity and the openness of children. Bachaumont tells us that as a young child he went to visit the famous gardener who was by then an old man, and Le Nôtre kept him amused by drawing little men that looked like Callot engravings.[3] He had not lost his touch and still drew with firm, lively strokes of the pen that we see in his designs for cascades and bosquets. The child and the old man found common ground in these imaginative games where the lines play tricks with reality and then suddenly hold it captive as if by chance. All his life Le Nôtre liked these deft touches. On the back of the sketch of a new design for the avenue de Picardie in Versailles[4] we can see that he has done an

Fig. 21. Carlo Maratta, *André Le Nôtre, Designer of the King's Gardens*, 1679–80. Musée du Château de Versailles.

amusing sketch of a large person under a big hat with a toddler trotting along beside him.

This playfulness, which probably helps explain why he was such good company, and his disarming good nature, which preempted unpleasantness and jealousy, concealed real force of character. That was clear on a number of occasions, particularly during his visit to Italy. On his way across the Alps he stopped at Pignerol, the fortress where Fouquet was under house arrest. Le Nôtre spent some time with him, showing that he had not forgotten Vaux-le-Vicomte, where he had begun his great career. In doing so he ran the risk of incurring the king's displeasure, but his reputation protected him and he was able to take such a risk. During this same visit to Italy, he was commissioned by Colbert to draft a report on the Académie de France in Rome. This establishment, which had been the minister's personal creation, ensured that young French artists could "copy all the most beautiful examples of painting and sculpture that Rome could offer" so as to provide inspiration for their work after they had returned to France. Colbert wrote to Le Nôtre in Rome,

> I am pleased to learn from your letter that Rome affords you the sight of beauties that can embellish and ornament the king's palaces, and I should be glad if you would write frequently to me as long as you are in Rome.
>
> Make it your business, too, to discover everything concerning our academy so that you can advise us on your return of everything that should be done to ensure its success.
>
> You are right to say that genius and taste are divine gifts and that it is very difficult for men to acquire them. But though these academies cannot provide us with great men, they are nonetheless still useful in improving the skills of our craftsmen and ensuring that they are better than they ever were before in France."[5]

This is a key letter, providing us with an insight into how Le Nôtre was seen by other people, especially a great minister. And, to this great minister, who had founded four academies, Le Nôtre dared to say that institutions could not replace natural talent. This is completely in line with what he memorably said to another great man, the prince of Condé: "I shall continue to elevate my mind to embellish the parterres, fountains, and cascades of your great garden at Chantilly, Your Highness, as your most humble and obedient servant, Le Nostre."[6]

This phrase sums up Le Nôtre's whole personality, both in his deference to one of the great men of France and his quiet confidence in his own creative genius. If he can "seek inspiration" to create beautiful parterres, cascades, and fountains, it is because his designs are matchless. Le Grand Condé was well aware of this, since Le Nôtre was often obliged to cancel his visits to Chantilly because he was in such great demand elsewhere. He had become a veritable luminary, and the greatest in the land; even the crowned heads of Europe vied for his designs. Colbert, Louvois, Pontchartrain, Madame de Maintenon, and William of Orange all used his services or sought his advice. He was to landscape design what Bernini was to architecture and what Rubens had been to painting. This is not to say that he considered himself above what the academies taught or thought his genius so great that he had no need to observe or learn from others. He knew the debt he owed to his predecessors, but since he left no explicit record of it, we have to look into his collections to discover the nature of his tastes and the stamp of his creative imagination.

His collections, which have been studied by Stéphane Collucio, are, like his artistic training, strongly influenced by painting. He possessed no treatises on the art of garden design and, surprisingly, the few books he owned were mostly on English history. On the face of it, this apparent indifference to garden design is astonishing; but it is understandable. What authors would he have read? Olivier de Serres and Claude Mollet were from another era: they were Renaissance men and even the terms they used would no longer have been current. Those nearer his own age, such as Boyceau and André Mollet, were known to him personally, and having seen them at work, he had nothing to gain from their writings. He collected what he found useful and he did the same with painters as with gardens, passing up the writings of Mollet and Boyceau, just as he did Le Brun's or Mignard's paintings, which he had seen often enough in Versailles.

By contrast, his collection of paintings contained many works from the Roman school, whose importance he had learned to appreciate from Vouet. There were five Poussins, including large landscapes, such as *Moïse sauvé des eaux* (Moses saved from the water) and *Moïse frappant le rocher* (Moses striking the rock for water); three by Claude Lorrain, including *Port de mer au soleil couchant* (Seaport at sunset) and *Fête villageoise* (The village fête); canvases by Bril and Jan Breughel the Elder; and a Perrier, *Acis et Galatée* (Acis and Galatea). He seems to have had a predilection for Nicolas Poussin, whom he had met at the Tuileries: he commissioned a painting from him, *La femme adultère* (Christ and the woman taken in adultery), and he was probably pleased when the terms designed by that great artist for Vaux-le-Vicomte were bought by the king from Madame Fouquet and brought to the gardens of Versailles. They are still there today, in the Dauphin and Girandole bosquets.

Together with the many bronzes in his collection, these statues demonstrate Le Nôtre's appreciation of sculpture. It seems likely that he was particularly interested in the execution of relief, low-angled effects of light and the transition between projecting parts and the rest. His interest in medals may perhaps also be explained in the same way. The English physician Martin Lister, who on a visit to Le Nôtre had seen four cupboards filled with medals (among which were three hundred from William of Orange), commented enthusiastically, "These are without doubt the finest materials I have ever seen, with which to trace a history of medals."[7] Le Nôtre seems to have combined in this collection his interest in history and his lively artistic curiosity about anything that involved working with different surfaces. Du Breuil, in his *Perspective pratique*, drew the attention of engravers to the study of perspective: "An engraver on copper should be no less aware of [perspective] than the painter, since he does with his burin what the latter does with his paintbrush: perspective will teach him where he should etch sharply and where he should be more muted."[8] Le Nôtre's liking for contours is always apparent, with a sense of what must be "more muted" and what must stand out clearly, and in addition to their historic interest, the medals may have held the same appeal for him as the bronzes. He was a collector, but it was as an artist that he built up his collections, since he turned to the works of art that he loved in order to develop his technical skills and provide artistic inspiration. It was at Vaux-le-Vicomte that he first had the opportunity to give his skills and imagination full rein.

When Fouquet offered to take him on, Le Nôtre was known primarily as a designer of parterres. It was in this capacity that he had worked on the Luxembourg gardens, but working with Boyceau had trained him to deal with the aesthetic problems of the long perspective that Mansart had used so boldly at Evry, as well as at Maisons and Balleroy. Thierry Mariage has demonstrated the close structural links between the gardens of Evry-Petit-Bourg and Vaux-le-Vicomte, particularly as regards a great central axis intersected by two perpendicular axes.[9] It is no surprise that Mansart continued the central axis of the château into the gardens and out as far as the horizon; we saw how Descartes's "marvelous spyglass" brought the long perspective into the way nature was represented. But Le Nôtre had his own reasons, specific to garden design and more strictly aesthetic, for following in Mansart's footsteps. These had been provided by Boyceau, with whom he had worked on the Luxembourg gardens. The latter, writing in his *Traité du jardinage selon les raisons de la nature et de l'art* about long perspective, which he found "very fine," just like geometric forms, had said, "Square shapes are the most widely used in gardens, whether as a perfect square or as a rectangle, though in the latter there are great differences. But it is in these shapes that we find the straight lines that form the fine, long allées with a pleasing perspective, since, as they stretch into the distance, vision fades, making things smaller, as they converge, and this makes them more attractive."[10]

Boyceau had gone even further than this: he had provided a scientific and aesthetic rationale for the great central axis, explaining that gardens could not be beautiful if they were not symmetrical.

> All these things, however beautiful and choice, will be found wanting and less pleasing if they are not placed symmetrically and evenly, since Nature also observes this principle in her most perfect forms. The breadth and height of trees are made up of similarly proportioned branches; their leaves have two similar sides and their flowers, arranged in one or several sections, conform so well that we can do no better than try to follow that great mistress in that respect as in the other details that we have discussed.[11]

Just as the leaf is divided in two by its largest vein, gardens are divided by a central axis. Since they are a representation of nature, they have to follow the arrangement that nature follows in everything, which we find in branches of trees and flower petals. Boyceau's aesthetic endowed the baroque garden with a principle deriving directly from the nature of its own raison d'être. Le Nôtre would not forget that, but his training as a painter quickly enabled him to go beyond this precious lesson. Indeed, he grasped the fact that the great central axis led the eye out into the heart of the landscape and that the geometrical shapes of the parterres, slopes, and steps needed to blend as if by their very nature with the surrounding countryside. Adopting long perspective was to recognize that the structure of the garden was only one part of the whole. The painter's vision would from then on extend the scope of the garden architect's design.

When he arrived at Vaux, Le Nôtre found that he was being offered the chance to create a garden of this type. The view from the partly built château looked out toward a small wooded hill, at the foot of which meandered the River Anqueuil. All around stretched the plain and its broad horizon. He set to work and the structure of the gardens soon took shape. First, there was a central axis, perpendicularly intersected by two secondary axes. The first of these was formed by the line of the canalized river, and the second ran between the latter and the château. Then, at the end of that axis, the shape of the hill was changed to allow a grotto and to draw the eye toward the horizon along massive slopes placed at an angle and leading to the allée that opened up into the woods. That was how he contrived to weld the garden to the landscape, knowing that the vegetation he would plant around the parterres would blend into the nearby woods, which rolled away to the horizon in a distant bluish haze. This was what appealed to the eye of the landscape artist that Le Nôtre felt himself to be. The landscapes of the Roman countryside so dear to him would stand him in good stead, allowing him to re-create in his gardens, under the northern skies of the Ile-de-France, the calm and majestic grandeur of a Poussin or a Claude Lorrain. It is easy to understand how excited he must have been by his design and how his first venture proved to be a masterstroke.

If what Mansart had taught him was not forgotten in Vaux–le-Vicomte, neither were the lessons he had learned from André Mollet, at least where the parterres were concerned. Making full use of the long perspective, Mollet suggested that the transition from art to nature should be gradual. He positioned the parterres de broderie close to the house so that the eye would be drawn first to the parterres de gazon before traveling toward the end of the garden or the surrounding countryside. As he had written in his *Jardin de plaisir,*

> Then on the rear façade of the said house the parterres en broderie should be constructed, close to it, so that they can easily be seen and contemplated from the windows, without being obscured by trees, palisades, or any other high object that might prevent the eye from seeing the whole vista. After the parterres de broderie will come the parterres or *compartiments de gazon* and the bosquets, allées, [and] palisades (low or high as befits their situation), arranged so that the said allées always end with a statue or fountains.

Knowing that space was limited, but seeking to preserve the effects of the long perspective, Mollet stipulated, "At the end of these allées, there will be fine perspectives, painted on canvas, so that they can be removed from the effects of bad weather when we choose."[12]

Le Nôtre evidently did not need this sort of device for Vaux-le-Vicomte, but he did accept that the parterres should be arranged to allow for the long perspective and meet the need for the eye to be drawn smoothly into the distance. That said, it was obvious as early as the 1650s that the parterres were not his greatest concern; Saint-Simon was correct when he suggested that the parterres were largely there to amuse the nursemaids, who could see them from the windows because they were forced to stay inside the château. What mattered to Le Nôtre was the need to establish his command of space by extending his control to the most distant horizons. As the marquis of Dangeau judiciously remarked, "he could not abide a restricted view."[13]

The extent of Le Nôtre's contribution to advances in garden design can be appreciated by comparing the Boyceau and Mollet treatises, which appeared when Le Nôtre was a young man, with the Dézallier d'Argenville treatise, published nine years after his death. In the first chapter of *La théorie et la pratique du jardinage*, Dézallier d'Argenville refers to the "magnificent gardens" of Versailles, Saint-Cloud, Meudon, Sceaux, and Chantilly. But it is in the second chapter that he shows how much he owes Le Nôtre. He discusses the siting of gardens, differentiating the hillside proper, often a steep and dangerous location, the lower slopes, which were always good for the health and easy for the management of water, and the plain, where construction was easy because terraces and glacis were not needed. He continues, "The plain has the advantage of fine, naturally occurring level ground and air that is even purer than on the lower slopes of a mountain. Everywhere you look there are vast expanses of countryside, crisscrossed with rivers, pools, and streams, beautiful meadows and hills covered with woods and buildings, which form a pleasing background and give an invaluable natural perspective."[14]

He returns to this point when he explains the four basic essentials that have to be considered in the design of a garden: outlook, soil type, sources of water, and location. About location he says,

> A view and a fine outlook over beautiful countryside are needed for a
> good location: even though the latter is, in fact, less essential than the
> other three, it is one of the most pleasing features. . . . I found nothing
> more diverting and agreeable in a garden than a fine view, looking out
> over beautiful countryside. I cannot express how delightful it is at the
> end of an allée or the top of a terrace to come upon an open vista
> stretching for five or six leagues all around and filled with villages,
> woods, rivers, hillsides, meadows, and all kinds of different features that
> make up a more beautiful landscape; these are things you must see for
> yourself to appreciate their beauty.[15]

The first edition of Dézallier d'Argenville's book was written a few years after Le Nôtre's death, and when you read a passage like this, you immediately think, "Le Nôtre had a hand in that!" He was the one who made gardeners aware of the beauties of landscape. What can be seen at Vaux-le-Vicomte is also evident in all the other great gardens he designed. At Chantilly, he deliberately left to one side the old château because architecturally no part of the structure could serve as the beginning of a central axis; he created a tangent instead. But the tangent was not on level ground, and he turned this to an advantage by terracing a large esplanade that looks out over a landscape where the light from the clear surfaces of water is reflected everywhere over the dark mass of the neighboring forests. So his answer to the problem was different from the solution he found at Vaux, and, in a surprising anticipation of the picturesque, it led him to make the buildings an independent element in the landscape. At Saint-Germain, when the collapse of the grottoes meant that the terraces designed by Mollet and Dupérac had to be taken down, he designed the famous promenade, which overlooks the Seine valley and follows the line of the forest. That bold stroke created an axis starting at the château from which, as you walk along, your eye is drawn instinctively toward the bright light of the open horizon on one side and into the dark mass of the forest on the other. At Saint-Cloud, he found yet another solution, this time similar to the one at Sceaux. The unevenness of the terrain led Le Nôtre to use several axial arrangements: Julien Gracq, in his *Carnets du grand chemin* (Notebooks of the open road), describes it as "the château that has burst apart in the forest, showering its living fragments everywhere," and the surrounding landscape can be seen from a variety of different angles according to the lie of the land.

At Versailles, the site was indeed unique. The château, modest though it was, happened to be situated above a wide, open valley that stretched far into the distance toward the west. The line of the great central axis, therefore, ran to the furthest horizon without any need for human intervention. By constructing the esplanade around the buildings, it was possible to look out over a large, gently sloping expanse that led down to the *pièce d'eau des Cygnes*, as the Bassin d'Apollon was then called. This large space was a very suitable site for bosquets: you could go into them, as into a wood, or walk along allées that gave views out to fountains. Vaux had this feature only along the sides of the gardens, toward the Grille d'Eaux or the Confessional, whereas in Versailles the possibilities seemed boundless and, thus, worthy of a monarch: this probably explains why Le Nôtre and Louis XIV were so enthusiastic about it. From the Grande Terrasse, your eyes swept over a whole panorama, a natural stage set. Le Nôtre saw the opportunity here to give full rein to his talent: he would design the parterres, where he had already shown what he could do; he would integrate the gardens into the landscape, something he had achieved at Vaux;

and above all—at that time a new venture for him—he would construct the bosquets, which would become central to the whole project, a project that would make history if only because of its size, which was unprecedented.

Everything had to be carried forward simultaneously: the earthworks, digging out the water conduits, the decoration, the fountains, and the bosquets—all with a view to creating two very different types of effect: the bosquets kept you in enclosed spaces, whereas the terraces and the allées opened up views that enticed you to survey in lordly fashion the open space below. Nothing could have been more difficult than to harmonize the conflicting elements in this *concordia discors*, but Le Nôtre's fertile artistic temperament and his awareness of the main currents of thought in the intellectual life of the period enabled him to reconcile the rigorously geometric clarity of the different elements of the garden with the poetic intimacy of the bosquets. For him, as for most of his contemporaries, each of these two different forms of beauty set the other off to advantage. We shall now try to see why this should be so.

CHAPTER ELEVEN

Le Nôtre's Aesthetic

To ARTISTS OF the Renaissance and of the baroque period, geometrical figures—at Vaux-le-Vicomte there was a statue of Geometry by Anguier—had their own intrinsic beauty. If you wanted to "think of nobler things" and "elevate your mind," as Le Nôtre said in a letter to the prince of Condé, you had to withdraw from the everyday world of appearances to enter the realm of Beauty, and geometry was the science best suited to the quest for what Roger de Piles called "the essence of beauty": it employed pure, linear figures, products of human reason, and these figures were archetypes that allowed patterns to be imposed on the myriad forms of the natural world.[1] Mlle. de Scudéry's heroes were right: they exclaimed in surprise at the luminescent circles of the round bassins set in the landscape like large mirrors; they considered the Grand Canal superb, as its straight banks disappeared into the depths of space "in defiance of nature." These circles and this rectangle touched them personally and, like Le Nôtre himself, they would have endorsed the view of the English architect Christopher Wren: "Geometrical Figures are more naturally beautiful than other irregular ones; in this all consent as to a Law of Nature. Of geometrical Figures, the Square and the Circle are most beautiful; next, the Parallelogram and the Oval."[2]

It is understandable that an architect who was also one of the great contemporary astronomers of the time should have proposed a link between aesthetics and the sciences. In a world whose image, as we have seen, was largely constructed through geometrical and mechanistic means, the power of simple figures was exceptional, since in combination with one another they could explain the most complex phenomena. In short, they endowed reason with imagination. Descartes also used them for the same purposes as did Wren. Thus, in the *Discours de la méthode*, he shows clearly why a geometrically planned town is beautiful, which incidentally explains Louis XIV's aesthetic appreciation of the trench dug outside Saint-Quentin.

> So we can see that the buildings, which a single architect has undertaken and completed, are usually more beautiful and better ordered than those which several have tried to modify and improve, using old walls, built for a different purpose. Thus those ancient towns, which were originally only villages and over time have become large cities; they are generally so ill-disposed [*mal compassées*] without those uniform squares that an engineer can design as he pleases on level ground, that, although taking their buildings individually, there is as much or more art in them than in the others, yet when you consider the way they are laid out, with small and large buildings randomly situated, and as a result streets of different lengths and with bends in them, it would seem that it is chance, rather than the choice of men using their reason, that has so arranged them.[3]

To be beautiful means to be ordered or "compassé" (drawn with compasses) and consciously designed by men "using their reason." According to Descartes, the best artist is the engineer. Le Nôtre would not have disputed this: after all, he also had to use earthworks to organize his space. However, he would have found the argument a bit thin: for though geometry gave a language to forms, it did not give them a syntax, let alone a style. Artists since the Renaissance had been debating the nature of that syntax. After the image of the world had become geometric and linear perspective had been invented, the representation of space was rationally constructed. But making space homogeneous and subject to human reason, and articulating forms and colors in a way that was demonstrably logical was not the sole end of art. It was not enough for geometry to give forms their allotted place: these forms had to be combined to create beauty. Once their plans had been properly drawn and their designs well constructed, artists and writers used proportion, symmetry, and harmony to give their creations the consonance of shape and color on which artistic beauty is wholly dependent. When he chose his words to describe the king's beauty, André Félibien was following a well-established tradition. Earlier, Alberti had made the beauty of symmetry depend on a central axis, which Nature herself had decreed essential: "Nature herself gave animals two ears, two eyes, and two nostrils, but in the middle of these there is a single, wide, and generous mouth."[4]

Two centuries later as we have already seen, Boyceau had also advanced the hypothesis that symmetry was natural when he described the structure of leaves and trees. That said, we must remember that symmetry was often interpreted in the etymological sense of "corresponding, not identical, parts." The Saint-Germain promenade follows an axis but passes between forest and valley, thus establishing contrasting symmetry. Similarly in Versailles, the north-south axis in front of the château has a closed structure at one end (the Bassin de Neptune) and an open one at the other (the Pièce d'Eau des Suisses).

With regard to proportion, the tradition is even older. Vitruvius was often cited for art and architecture and Aristotle for the written word. The Renaissance, by reviving forgotten texts, increasing the number of translations, organizing debates in the academies, and above all by publishing numerous treatises, had used printing to make aesthetic questions central to social problems.[5] Renaissance thinkers, convinced that they had rediscovered Athens and Rome, had advanced the idea that everything produced in the Middle Ages was badly executed, distorted, and unacceptably overembellished. When, at Racine's suggestion, Louis XIV tried to read Amyot's translation of Plutarch, he exclaimed, "But it's gaulois!"; in other words, anything that was not limpid, clearly articulated, and elegantly structured belonged to the Dark Ages. Here again, mathematical calculation had a role to play. Vitruvius had written, "Nature has, in fact, designed the human body according to the following norms: the face from the top of the forehead to the roots of the hair is a tenth of its height, as is the open hand from the wrist joint to the joint of the middle finger; the head from the chin to the top of the cranium is one-eighth; from the top of the chest, measured from the base of the neck to the root of the hair, is one-sixth; from the middle of the chest to the top of the head, a quarter."[6]

There was clearly a regular pattern to these fractions, establishing a harmonious relationship between the limbs, head, and trunk. Since all the parts of the body could be measured by the same standard, it was possible to establish a relationship between the human figure and simple geometric forms. Da Vinci demonstrated this by drawing a naked man, arms outstretched, completely enclosed in a circle and in a square. The artists of the Renaissance and the baroque period adopted these aesthetic criteria, which began to be challenged only at the end of the seventeenth century by the Moderns, as they were called. It was largely thanks to this group, led by the Perrault brothers, that tastes gradually evolved and the value of styles, such as the Gothic and Chinese, which owed nothing to Greco-Roman antiquity, was once again acknowledged.[7] But the average art lover, however, did not share that view. The orthodox preference was for the harmonious proportions of regular, geometric style: this is understandable in the light of the role geometry played in how the world was constructed and represented. For Télamon or Glycère, there was perfect harmony between the proportions of the château, the parterres, the round bassins and the terraces, and the statues decorating them. The gods of antiquity were perfectly at home in these places, which had been designed so that the human body could chime harmoniously with the architecture.

This imaginative renewal of antiquity can also be explained by the way in which taste changed. Despite instructions from the eighteenth session of the Council of Trent and a policy seeking to combat the Reformation by controlling images and decorating baroque churches with countless scenes of martyrdom, the pagan gods continued to appeal to the contemporary imagination. The clergy itself led the way, since the popes who were most anxious to foster the worship of saints were the very ones who built up collections of antique statues, a paradox that is explicable if one remembers that baroque church architecture owed more to the pagan temples of ancient Rome than to Gothic cathedrals. The Jesuits were under no illusions about it. They gave Latin culture a prominent place in the curriculum because they rightly saw that it was the best way to educate young people who were to play a key social role, in either political or cultural life. The academies followed suit in the intellectual and scientific world, as Perrault's 1673 translation of Vitruvius demonstrates.

This explains why the words "proportion," "symmetry," "concord," and "harmony" figure so often in the writings of architects and gardeners during the Renaissance and the baroque period. André Mollet, whom Le Nôtre knew well since his godmother, Anne Martigny, had a been born a Mollet and generations of the family had been at the Tuileries, said in his *Jardin de plaisir*, "We shall give some details of the following drawings so that they may be executed in the proper manner, each in the necessary proportions."[8] He invariably links these proportions, for reasons explained in the last chapter, to criteria of mathematical measurements. Mindful of his Scandinavian readers because of his post at Queen Christina's court, he carefully converts the figures and specifies that for a parterre of forty-two toises square, the plates-bandes should be six feet wide, and for a parterre of twenty-eight toises square, they should be reduced to a width of five feet. Generally speaking, his other drawings follow the same rules. However, these rules are not strictly laid down: they are more a set of guidelines than formulae. In the baroque age, the tendency was toward more freedom in the establishment of proportions.

Nicolas Poussin is similarly cautious in the conclusions he draws from his measurements of the Belvedere *Antinous*. He says, for instance, about the measurements for the front: "From the join of the throat (A) to the end of the clavicle where it joins the acronion and the arm bone (B), measures a head"; about the measurements for the side, "The length of the foot is the same as the distance between the sole of the foot and the calf, and from the calf to the top of the knee."[9] This does not imply that the head and foot are the same size, but simply that the sizes of the head and torso are related, as are those of the foot and the leg.

We are fortunate to have a drawing by the Swedish architect Tessin, who visited the gardens of Meudon where he carefully measured the Parterre de la Grotte as though he were trying to fathom the mysteries of Le Nôtre's art. From his plan, it can be seen that the diameter of the circles that decorate the four corners is equal to half the width of the great enroulements at midpoint on the sides. Moreover, the center of these circles and the center of the spiral enroulements are on the same axis, the line of which is indicated by a broken strip of turf. One may then conclude that in this parterre, the coherence of the design comes from the arrangement of figures—these correspond sometimes in reverse, as is the case with the great enroulements—and from a harmonious blend of simple and complex figures that imposes a geometrical shape on the vegetation. However, one cannot go beyond that. These proportions are not subject to the same mathematical rigor as we find in the Renaissance in, for example, the botanical gardens of Padua or in the representation of the island of Cythera given in the *Hypnerotomachia Poliphili*.

This is understandable, for in the baroque period artists had acquired a sense of the immensity of space. Proportions still had an important part to play but implicitly, rather like the basso continuo in music, which is always present but not so obtrusive as to inhibit the composer's freedom.

Garden designers needed this flexibility, since the relationship between perspective and proportion created greater problems for them than it did for painters. To judge the beauty of a painting, the soundness of its composition, the proper distribution of light and shade, and the harmony of its colors, you had to position yourself at a precise point. Pascal defined this memorably: "It is thus with paintings seen from too far away or too close. There is only one indivisible point that is the proper place. The others are all either too faraway, too close, too high, or too low. In painting, perspective can make sure this is correct. But who can do that for the truth or morality?"[10]

Reading that text, so admirably clear and rigorous, one is tempted to ask, "And who can do that for gardens?" A garden is not a painting, since as one walks around, the point of perspective shifts. Louis XIV, who was aware of this problem, advised that viewpoints should be created in places that were particularly suitable to enjoy the outlook: "You must stop at the top of the steps. . . . Then you must go straight to the top of Latona and pause."[11] Le Nôtre, on the other hand, could not be satisfied with an interrupted view of his open spaces, and the interplay of perspective and proportion posed problems for him that he solved by following Boyceau's guidelines and introducing important innovations.

In the 1630s Boyceau had been the first to see that the introduction of the long perspective into garden design meant that "raised bodies," as he called them, had a very clear part to play. If you placed the vanishing point on the horizon this meant that you saw the gardens from an angle almost touching the ground. Thus, any trees and buildings appeared correspondingly elevated. Therefore, the view from above, which was so common in the Renaissance, was abandoned in favor of the view that suited the long perspective "tending to a point" on the horizon. This led gardeners in the baroque era to put palisades along their allées: this doubled the effect, since the gradual reduction in the height of the walls of greenery visually echoed the corresponding reduction in the width of the allées. But these "raised bodies" would impact the interplay of proportion, and with his usual rigor Boyceau was the first to observe this: "The width of the allées must be in proportion to their length and also to the height, differentiating in this respect an enclosed from an open space, so as to create there a pleasing grace (*grâce*), the correct measure for which may be extended or reduced."[12]

In other words the relative proportions must work on both the horizontal and vertical planes but need not be absolutely precise. Boyceau's use of the word "grâce" is very revealing since it had (and still has in modern French) the etymological meaning of "granted favor." This is what differentiates it from "beauté," allowing La Fontaine to say in his poem "Adonis" that "grâce" was "more beautiful still than beauty." Grace, then, is something extra that cannot be explained; that "something" which changes everything because it loosens the straitjacket of strict proportions (Figs. 22 and 23).

Le Nôtre also organized his open spaces so that the interplay of relative proportions conferred grace on the whole landscape. The lie of the land at Versailles allowed him to do this in two ways. The view could be enjoyed from specific, particularly well-placed points. In the center of the Galerie des

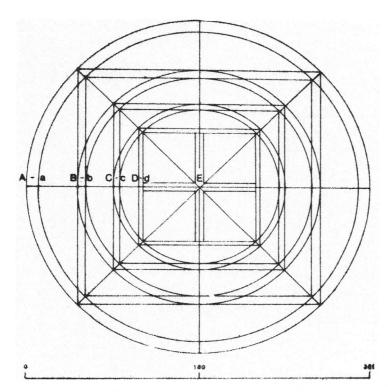

Fig. 22. *The Botanic Garden in Padua.* Mathematics and proportions in a Renaissance garden. E. M. Terween-Dionisius, "Date and Design of the Botanic Garden in Padua," *Journal of Garden History* 14 (1994): 213.

Glaces, for example, the gardens could be seen stretching along the central axis, like the auditorium and the stage as seen from the royal box in the theater, where the "indivisible point" of political sovereignty was made visible to all. A similar effect, also due to the way proportions worked within the perspective, is created by the view of the two north parterres from the Salon de la Guerre. The Bassins des Couronnes are not in the center of the parterres, and the two allées leading to them at an angle produce an effect of foreshortened perspective, making them appear longer than they really are. There is nothing comparable on the other side, in the Parterres du Midi. Everything suggests that Le Nôtre found two separate solutions to the problem: on the Midi side, the space is completely open, leading the eye up over the orangerie straight to the Pièce d'Eau des Suisses; by contrast, on the north side, the foreshortened

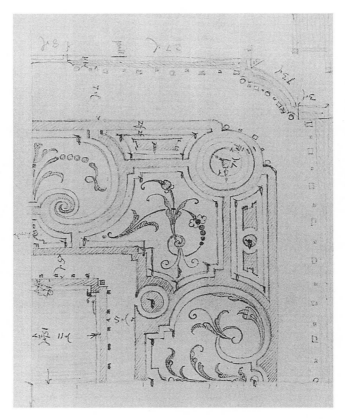

Fig. 23. Nicodème Tessin, *Measures of Le Nôtre's Parterre at Meudon*. Harmony and proportions in a baroque garden. Reproduced by permission of Nationalmuseum, Stockholm. At Padua, the alleys' width is determined mathematically. The same ratio ($\sqrt{2}$) is applied as one moves away from the center of the circle (E): $C - c = D - d \times \sqrt{2}$, $B - b = C - c \times \sqrt{2}$ etc. Le Nôtre's use of proportions is free from mathematic fetishism. Harmony is what matters, and he balances the regularity of his bordures by the freedom of his enroulements.

perspective sets the walls of greenery back from the two bosquets, the Arc de Triomphe and the Trois Fontaines, then draws the eye more rapidly toward the sloping Allée d'Eau. The viewer's gaze is channeled all the more—and Le Nôtre's supreme skill is evident in this kind of invention—because the Bassin de la Pyramide, built at the entrance of that same allée on a trapezoidal surface, creates the effect of a funnel. The effect he was seeking to produce can be seen very clearly in Etienne Allegrain's painting *Promenade de Louis XIV en vue du parterre du Nord* (Promenade of Louis XIV looking to the Parterre du Nord). From all these viewpoints, one can see how well proportions and perspective are married together, both horizontally, when you look at the parterres or water mirrors, and vertically, when the different heights of topiary, statues, fountains, palisades, and the blue line of the horizon combine in harmonious layers.

But the aesthetic pleasure afforded by the open spaces of Versailles does not stop there, because they are designed so that the forms keep changing as you continue your walk. If you simply climb up or down the orangerie steps or the inclines of the Bassin de Latone, the way that the angles open and close without any alteration in the proportions gives pure intellectual pleasure, since the bassins and the parterres form ovals and parallelograms, whose height seems to change at the same time as a whole part of the gardens. As you walk along, new harmonies appear in the gardens at every step, bestowing a kind of power over nature since, Orpheus-like, you enjoy aesthetically the order that you impose on it. Your walk is not simply a means of getting from one point to another; it is mankind at one with the world.

This sense of harmony is so real, and Le Nôtre makes you experience it in a whole range of different ways. Sometimes he shows you a serene, orderly expanse of landscape, with nature wholly under control. Then he springs a surprise, an apparent threat to that order, which is then restored. This happens as you climb the Latona steps or the Cent Marches, when you see the sharp, horizontal lines of the parallel steps etched against the sky and then, suddenly, the decorative trophies and chimney pots along the line of the château rooftop appear. Their amortizements seem to rise independently from the ground until, in due course, the façade below appears and the illusion vanishes. The surprise and visual shock come from the sudden appearance of a whole palace, so close by but hidden from view until that moment. Then the illusion reinforces the power of reason, since the harmony of the gardens you have walked through is crowned by the harmony of the buildings.

Once again, it is human reason that controls the optical devices by which perspective is foreshortened or lengthened to make objects seem closer or farther away, as if the power of optics could allow man to change the face of nature as he pleases and confirm the influence of the intellect over appearances. Just as the scientist's telescope can reveal mountains, valleys, and a whole landscape with its shadows and depths on the apparently smooth surface of the moon, so the artist, with an arrangement of converging and diverging lines, can change the appearance of reality, despite the fact that it seems to be definitively fixed. Moving the perspective point is therefore necessary to achieve correct measurements in gardens.

At Vaux-le-Vicomte the parterres de broderie are shorter than the turf parterres that follow them. At Versailles the bosquets are longer the further away they are from the château: between the transversal axes created by the Allées des Saisons, they are square, then afterward they become rectangular. Similarly, knowing that the south side of the gardens does not run parallel to the north, Le Nôtre put diagonals in the Bosquet de l'Ile Royale and then used these diagonals again to radiate out above the Bassin du Miroir. In that way, by adapting to the terrain, he was able to avoid a tediously bilateral symmetry. This solid construction is built around the great central axis, which is itself vigorously underscored by the Tapis Vert and the two allées that come after it. Proportion played an important part here, since once it had been decided to lengthen the Grand Canal in 1671, the Tapis Vert was immediately made wider. But this additional length was itself put into perspective, as you look out from the Grande Terrasse, by a very effective optical trick. At the west end of the Grand Canal, the Bassin de Gally is a rectangle of 195 meters by almost 400, while, on the other hand, the Bassin de la Tête, as it is known, forms at the opposite end a square with sides roughly 125 meters long. If the two bassins had been the same size, perspective would have made the one farther away look much smaller. By using this device, they appear the same size, but only when you see them from the château; if you walk down toward the Bassin d'Apollon and then along the Grand Canal, you can see the Bassin de Gally getting longer and gradually assuming its true shape as you get closer. Thanks to that optical device, the outer edges of the gardens seem to recede as you try to reach them, and this creates in a real physical sense the same impression of infinity as a simple optical illusion produces from the terrace.

Open Spaces: The Use of Perspective and Proportions

Light and Shade

The combination of optical tricks of perspective and effects of light figure among the great innovative features of the baroque garden. The treatises of the "Perspectivists" are an important factor in their success, since they linked the work of scientists and the research done by artists, who had often trained as geometers. Most of these treatises were written in countries where the scientific movement was at its height: France, Italy, and Holland (at the beginning of the seventeenth century, Vredeman de Vries published *Perspectivae* and *Variae architecturae formae*, which includes garden designs). It is in the first two countries that shadow begins to be used to give perspective an expressive power, linked to the existence of a strong source of light. While Galileo and the painter Ludovico Cigoli were engaged in a lengthy correspondence about how to measure the shadows cast by the mountains of the moon so as to make a relief map of it,[13] Caravaggio was reaching the end of his short career, and his work sent a shock wave through European art by showing the dramatic impact of a sharp contrast between light and shade. In France, Salomon de Caus, whose *Perspective avec la raison des ombres et des miroirs* has already been mentioned, was known as the creator of the Hortus Palatinus at Heidelberg, and everything he had to say about the sun was certainly consonant with the taste of Louis XIV and Le Nôtre: "When the sun casts its light, it is certain that shadow will be created where its rays cannot reach, and even though the sun is of immense size and (in the view of some) is one hundred and sixty-six times as large as the Earth's globe, so it is that this size is only a point in relation to the rays that it casts into infinity, not only over the Earth, but all around it, since it is certain that even the stars above the sun are lit by its rays."[14]

But light is inseparable from the shadows it casts, and it was "the force of the shadows," as it was then known, from the sun that threw objects into relief. In his *Perspective pratique*, Jean Du Breuil wrote, "It is through shadow that objects acquire the power to make appearances seem real to us."[15] Boyceau and Mollet do not mention this, probably considering that it was common knowledge, and particularly applicable to painting, but Salomon de Caus had done so on their behalf, and Du Breuil illustrated what he said by using examples from gardens.

Shadow could, indeed, bring out the effect of vanishing perspective in an allée. Boyceau had shown that in an allée bordered by palisades, the lines tend toward a point in both the horizontal and two vertical planes; anyone could see that the effect of the shade was to accentuate this gradual narrowing by projecting onto the light ground a dark surface, which also diminished as it reached the vanishing point. A comparable effect could be obtained by shrubs, which had been clipped and planted at regular intervals along an allée. The shadows they cast on the ground turned according to the position of the sun, tending to become longer or shorter but without losing a recognizable shape: a cone stayed conical, and a cube and a round shape lengthened but still kept their familiar shape, thus demonstrating, if necessary, that geometric forms remain constant. And so a whole pattern of shadows was cast, replicating on the ground of the allées and esplanades the pattern of the parterres and "raised bodies." In addition to that—and all the baroque gardeners used this additional resource—the intricate shape in which a cone of vegetation had been cut allowed a shadow to be cast on the ground while smaller ones moved independently on the surface of the shrub itself.

In Versailles, Le Nôtre was able to exploit the "force of shadows" to the full, since, in fine weather at least, it was always available because the central east-west axis follows the path of the sun. There is ample time for the network of dark lines, turning slowly on the ground, to close or open angles and to shorten or elongate shapes. But the great vertical blocks of the shadows themselves make a visual impact that is perhaps even stronger. By emphasizing the contrast between the palisades in full light and those in shadow, they ensure that the palisades really do function as "raised bodies": the sharply outlined masses of greenery that result bring out most effectively the structure of the allées and bosquets. The same distinction is obtained in the rows of statues, whose symmetry is highlighted by the play of similarities and contrasts: some of them are bathed in the dazzling brilliance of their marble, while others are silhouetted in gray shadow against the dark green of the trees.

The "force of shadows" also brings out the majestically harmonious contours of the gardens. When he created Vaux-le-Vicomte, Le Nôtre had already shown his outstanding ability to organize large volumes of space, which gave him complete control over the site. In Versailles, the works carried out in the first fifteen years of Louis XIV's reign gave the gardens their definitive form: on three sides of the Grande Terrasse the sloping surfaces of the Allée d'Eau; the steps of Latone followed by the Tapis Vert; and the Cent Marches. These inclines are sometimes seen from the side, as is the case, for example, at the Cent Marches or the inclines of Latone when looked at from the bassins or the Lézards: they then form long diagonals down to ground level, creating the effect of a wedge in the solid, vertical surfaces between the dominant horizontals. The full brilliance of the setting sun can sometimes catch these long triangles, so that the light flooding the façade of the palace extends into the gardens. At other times of the day, the sun leaves part of them in the shade, striking a somber note in the exuberant ensemble of the fountains and parterres.

Sometimes this play of light and shade is even more complex, when the curve of the contours reveals the elegant shape of a vertugadin. The Bassin du Miroir is a particularly good example, when the sloping turf forms a majestic crescent that tapers off into the Allée d'Hiver. The curve is so vast that the light and shade no longer create a balanced structure of well-defined forms but instead blend harmoniously so that gradation from one extreme to the other is imperceptible. The eye follows (or rather is drawn gently along) the lines that move apart as they stretch into the distance, to meet again at the edge of the fountain, sweeping a broad green band out and back against the dark background of the bosquet. In the calm water of the bassin, the reflection of this double movement intensifies the delightful effect, while just beneath the surface ripple the inverted images of the statues of Apollo and Diana, the tutelary gods watching over this kind of miracle.

Mirrors

The play of light and shade, for which the gardens of the Sun King are renowned, would be much less abundant if the effects were not enhanced by water. As you look out at the view from the Grande Terrasse, the sky curves around and soars above your head like a vast tent of light, but this sweep of light is also reflected on the ground by the horizontal surfaces of the water mirrors. Your eye follows in the distance the flowing stream of light from the Grand Canal, which brings you back toward the château, past the Bassin d'Apollon, the Bassin de Latone, and the two mirrors of the Parterre d'Eau. The same effect is repeated if you follow the north-south axis from the Bassin de Neptune to the Pièce d'Eau des Suisses. The splashes of light against the greenery or in the open areas of the gardens bring them alive and lift them by lighting them from below. They are magic surfaces, mirroring statues and trees ("marble and leaf," as Pierre-André Lablaude puts it), stone façades, clouds, and the ever-changing light of the sky. Without their water mirrors, the gardens of Versailles would not be what they are; they would be a faceless mask.

The importance of mirrors, particularly in relation to their use in telescopes and spyglasses, has already been discussed. The works of Descartes, Stevin, and Snellius were much read and quoted in treatises on perspective, which made the link between art and optics. No artist of the period would have denied these links. But art went beyond demonstrable truths, and even if the use of mirrors to put shade into perspective was part of their métier, and even if they placed a mirror on the floor of a church before decorating the dome with saints and martyrs, who looked down on the world from the heavens, painters knew that correct drawing was not the be-all and end-all of a work of art. For them, as for the scientists in the academies, the mirror was a means of acquiring knowledge that changed both the way they saw the world and the way they represented it.

In *Las Meninas*, Diego Velázquez—who had a fine collection of treatises on perspective—represented the king and queen of Spain and the young Infanta, Margarita, surrounded by people in his employ; he himself also figured, brush in hand, at the rear of the canvas. The monarchs, the principal figures in the scene, appear only in a mirror placed on the wall facing them. The viewer, who is positioned where they are standing, knows what they can see: from left to right, the painter who has stopped work to look at them, their own image in the mirror, their children and the servants who are turning toward them, a dog wrapped up in its own thoughts, and farther back, behind this group, a majordomo, deferentially opening the door to a corridor, down which they are looking. All eyes converge on the royal couple, but only they see the whole scene. Velázquez was, thus, using a mirror to express one of the main tenets of absolutism, which Louis XIV and Bossuet often reiterated in their writings: only the prince can understand the whole situation, since his preeminence allows him to be all-seeing. So, in *Las Meninas*, using mirrors is doubly meaningful: it enables space to be rigorously constructed and to reveal a political truth.

Many other examples of this exist, notably in the work of Georges de La Tour, where mirrors get the better of appearances while being supposed to reflect only their image. *La Madeleine repentante*, whom he painted several times, sits in front of a mirror, but she is looking away from it, since her thoughts take her beyond the vanity of seeing her youth and beauty. Even so, the mirror does serve a purpose: the light of a candle and the darkness that surrounds the flame are reflected in it. In this way, it increases the space where shadows linger, bringing the thoughts of the young girl back to what her meditation on death is really about, and making her aware, perhaps for the first time, of the conflict between the nothingness that threatens to engulf her and the light that she can reach if she is strong enough to change her ways. Here again, the mirror is an instrument of revelation, but this time it is moral reality that is brought to light.

Turning to the landscape artists of the time, it is clear that mirrors give them a means of expression, which seems essential for several reasons. First of all, because they use water mirrors, which are the handiwork of Nature herself and offer her the chance to gaze on her own image with no apparent artifice. Second, because these mirrors produce a partial central axis, creating symmetry between part of the landscape and its reverse image, a symmetry that can be suddenly disrupted when a piece of uneven ground or the shadow of a tree breaks the surface of the water. Third, because this surface of water reflects light from the sky and serves as a secondary source of light. Finally, and most important, because a mirror always seems to contemplate the scene it reflects (Fig. 24). It introduces a meditative note into the ensemble of forms and colors, and if it is true that Nature sees her own reflection, the viewer, on the other hand, can discover not just the image of the landscape but also the expression of the painter's artistic sensibility. According to Roger de Piles, "[the landscape artist] is free to use everything that can be seen on water, earth, or air; because anything that art or nature can produce may contribute to the composition of his paintings. So if painting is a form of creation, it is more particularly so in the case of landscape painting."[16]

The great landscape artists admired by Le Nôtre were thus able to use water mirrors to lend their art a power of expression that reinforces that of shade. In *Les funérailles de Phocion* (Phocion's funeral), Poussin places a shining stretch of water between the cortege at the front of the composition and the hills on the horizon, on which appear temples and houses. Phocion is traveling for the last time along the road where life goes on around him, but the water is still and is the only element in the picture, other than the slow pace of the two pallbearers, which strikes the funereal and triumphant note that the painter seeks to evoke. Here, too, the mirror allows us a revealing insight. The contrast between the misfortune of a just man and the impassive face of Nature confers grandeur on the tragic nature of human destiny. In the midst of that impassivity, the calm surface of the water offers an image of meditative silence, which the viewer and the painter share. The waters of the Nile have a similar function in another painting by Poussin, *Moïse tiré des eaux* [Moses saved from the waters], which was in Le Nôtre's collection for a long time until he presented it to the king. But, in this instance, the viewer meditates on the fragility of the greatest of destinies and on the strength of human compassion. Around the group of people emotionally moved by the rescue, you see the river everywhere. This vast mirror reflects different images that all evoke the solemnity of such a great moment in human history; some passersby are watching the scene; others, as is always the case, take no notice; a time-worn pyramid rises toward a sky that is broad and darkly serene, lit on the horizon as if by a divine omen (Fig. 25).

Le Nôtre was not, of course, seeking to create that kind of moral or religious effect at Versailles, but he had a sense of the awe-inspiring and he held up to Nature the mirrors that best reflected her grandeur. To do so, he used

Fig. 24. Water mirrors in Jean Du Breuil, *La perspective pratique*. Du Breuil shows how a mirror seems to attract objects standing at a distance from its banks. The reflected images of the trees and of the house find their place on the water by complying with the laws of reflection and perspective, as in a painting.

Fig. 25. Nicolas Poussin, *Moïse Saved from the Waters*, ca. 1670. Photograph by Arnaudet. Musée du Louvre, Paris. Réunion des Musées Nationaux/Art Resource, NY.

the reflecting surfaces in the bassins to diversify the sources of light, as all the contemporary landscape painters did. In one of his early poems, Racine describes the brilliance of a great expanse of water catching the sun's rays, and with surprising foresight he made the étangs of Port-Royal distant—if ill-fated—forerunners of the mirrors he would later admire at Versailles.

> Déjà, je vois sous ce rivage
> La terre, jointe avec les cieux,
> Faire un chaos délicieux,
> Et de l'onde et de leur image.
> Je vois le grand astre du jour
> Rouler, dans ce flottant séjour,
> Le char de la lumière;
> Et sans offenser de ses feux

La fraîcheur coutumière
Dorer son cristal lumineux.

Je vois les tilleuls et les chênes,
Ces géants de cent bras armés,
Ainsi que d'eux-mêmes charmés,
Y mirer leurs têtes hautaines;
Je vois aussi leurs grands rameaux
Si bien tracer dans les eaux
Leur mobile peinture,
Qu'on ne sait si l'onde, en tremblant,
Fait trembler leur verdure,
Ou plutôt l'air même et le vent.[17]

[I see already on this shore
The earth, together with the sky,
Mingling the waters with heaven's image
In magical disorder.
Across its watery home,
I see the great day-star
Drive its chariot of light;
Its inoffensive blaze leaving
The customary coolness quite unscathed
And gilding its shining crystal.

I see the lime trees and the oaks,
Giants with a hundred fighting arms,
As if entranced with their own image
Mirror their lofty heads therein;
I see their great branches, too,
Paint their shimmering portrait
So clearly in the waters
That we do not know if that water, trembling,
Stirs their green leaves
Or if it is the air itself and the wind.]

In this poem, Racine is describing the course of the "chariot of light" across the surface of a great expanse of water. But Le Nôtre did not always seek to create that type of effect: in Versailles, as elsewhere, he varied the size and the shape of his mirrors. The Grand Canal and the Pièce d'Eau des Suisses do not serve the same ends as the Bassin de Neptune or the Fontaine du Dragon, and it is easier to explain the function of the different mirrors by starting with the smaller ones.

In the Bassins des Saisons, which are of medium size and situated where allées meet, the structure of the gardens is the most important thing. An intersection is a place where there are perspectives leading in four different directions. When you reach this special spot you feel drawn to discover new spaces. The palisades that guide your steps open out to reveal distant parts, as yet undiscovered, with different effects of light. So it is important that this focal point should be marked out, since it governs the way in which the promenade is "directed," in the sense that critics used the term, to define the art of maintaining the interest of the reader or viewer.

As you approach one of the main intersections, you see opening up an elliptical bassin, in the center of which is a sculpture group evoking a season. From the Bassin de Bacchus (Autumn), you can see at right angles; in the distance, Summer and Winter mark two other high points of what appears to be a large square defining the structure of the gardens. The intellectual pleasure of occupying a key position in a vast composition of buildings and gardens is compounded by a pleasure of a quite different kind, born of the reflections from the water surface. The water acts, in fact, like a well of light, so that the surrounding trees are lit from beneath like scenery on a stage with footlights, except that their brightness is ever-changing. Like the water mirror in landscape paintings, it is subject to fortuitous changes; as you get closer, the reflection of the "great branches" in Racine's poem disrupts the increasing intensity of light and its color changes from gray or blue to green. Moreover, the dancing reflections in the water seem to make you move faster. The upside-down trees quickly supplant one another and you can see the trees of the next allée before you have left the one leading into it. For a moment, appearances deceive you until reality takes over again, once you start walking through the palisades in the allée ahead.

In the larger bassins, such as the Bassin de Neptune, the logic is quite different. Designed to close the perspective along the north-south axis, this bassin is below the Bassin du Dragon and the Allée d'Eau, which leads back to the château. Its shape is dictated by its position, fanning out from the foot of a supporting wall, along the top of which are vases with water spouts. In Louis XIV's time, the sculpture groups representing Neptune, Oceanus, and Proteus had not yet been erected, and three groups of eight water jets, also arranged in a fan, fused together horizontally. The effect that Le Nôtre was trying to create was clearer then than it is now. Standing at the north end of the bassin, as did Jean Cotelle to paint it, you saw first before you a mirror of calm water, then came the water, ruffled by the horizontal jets, which seemed to be tumbling down toward you, and finally the diaphanous curtain from the water spouts, through which you could see the Allée d'Eau leading up to the château between the two bosquets. This whole spectacle was topped by the column of water from the Bassin du Dragon, which rose to a height of twenty-seven meters. The sight was a truly splendid water display. The size of the bassin, the fact that all the water from the north parterres flows into it like a sea, and even the presence of a steep, high supporting wall, its shadow falling over part of the bassin, lent the scene a mysterious grandeur bearing the divine stamp of Neptune.

Fountains

The effect sought by the Dragon fountain is quite different, since the water jet gushing from the monster's jaws suggests the power of his breath and, by extension, the even greater strength of Apollo, who is slaying him. Since the bassin is much smaller than that of Neptune, as you walk around it you can see the composition of the sculpture group, which seems to be broken up in the water, coming together again. The monster, in the center, is in the throes of death, while cupids, confidently astride swans, are riding away after surrounding him closely and lightheartedly showering him with arrows; they are escorted by leaping dolphins with water jets gushing from their open mouths and nostrils. It looks like a dangerous merry-go-round where even the most skillful can only be a pale imitation of Apollo, who is the real dragon slayer, captured by the sculptors in the full force of his demonic fury. The sculpture group, designed by Gaspard and Balthasar Marsy, was initially restored in the eighteenth century, then again in 1889 when it was partially redesigned; in this new avatar, the dragon is a rather fanciful creature, closer to Gustave Doré's *tarrasques*[18] than to baroque monsters, but the sense of movement has not been lost and that is the most important thing. Cotelle's painting shows this, clearly foregrounding the monster pierced through the heart by one of Apollo's arrows, while the terrified onlookers flee and the gods look on with Olympian detachment at the final moment of an unsurprising victory.

In these tumbling waters baroque art fantasy reaches its apex, but the effect is just as striking when the fountains are not playing and, in the eerie silence of early morning, wisps of mist swirl around the writhing monster. This is similar in spirit to the idea behind the Bassin d'Apollon and the Bosquet de l'Encelade. The powerful and universally understood political symbolism of the statues glorifies the lord and master of the gardens. The Bassin d'Apollon is a particularly good example of this. At first sight, it is surprising that Apollo's chariot rises from the water on the west side of the château, crossing the path of the sun rather than following in its wake. However, when the rays of the early morning sun flood Tuby's famous sculpture group, you see at once that this is when the gold of the statues is at its brightest and the horses, monsters, and sea gods, tearing themselves away from the waters, raise up the light most strongly to the skies above. The water soars upward, too. It streams out on every side, a jubilant expression of awakening nature and the latent energy of the yoked team. A jet rises high above the figure of the god, reminding us, as do the trumpeting tritons, of the miracle that is the dawn of light in a sleeping world.

One of the great beauties of the open spaces in Versailles is the ceaseless play of water and light in the architecture of the vegetation. When the fountains are still, the waters reflect the color and the depth of the sky so that the decor of château, trees, and gods seems poised between the infinity above and the infinity beneath (Fig. 26). When they are playing, the adjutage chosen changes the shape of the jets so the water can go from a vaporous mist to a liquid mass, or from a smooth sheet to bold little plumes dancing in the wind. La Fontaine captures this scene perfectly in *Les amours de Psyché et de Cupidon.* He first describes walking down the Tapis Vert, then goes on to the Bassin d'Apollon and the Grand Canal, which are, as he says, the two "seas" in which Apollo starts his course.

> On descend vers deux mers d'une forme nouvelle:
> L'une est un rond à pans, l'autre est un long canal,
> Miroirs où l'on n'a point épargné le cristal.

> [You descend toward two seas with a new and different shape
> One is round with side parts, the other a long canal,
> Mirrors where the crystal superabounds.]

Then, turning to Apollo himself, he describes the water spurting from his torch, turning into "crystalline atoms" and rising like a column of light.

Fig. 26. Palisades along the Grand Canal on a misty day. Jean-Baptiste Leroux's photograph captures the powerful effects of projected shadows that seem to plunge into the water. Pierre-Denis Martin used the same effects in his *Vue du Bassin d'Apollon*.

Au milieu du premier, Phébus sortant de l'onde,
A quitté de Thétys la demeure profonde:
En rayons infinis l'eau sort de son flambeau;
On voit presqu'en vapeur se résoudre cette eau;
Telle la chaux exhale une blanche fumée.
D'atomes de cristal une nue est formée;
Et lorsque le soleil se trouve vis-à-vis,
Son éclat l'enrichit des couleurs de l'iris.

[Amid the first (sea), Phoebus rising from the waters
Has left Thetis's dark domain;
In myriad streams the water flows from his torch
To dissolve almost into a vaporous film,
Like a mist of white lime.
A cloud of crystalline atoms takes shape;
And when it meets the sun
Its brilliance glows still brighter with a rainbow-colored luster.][19]

The poet's intuition here has captured one of the greatest successes of the bassins in Versailles: the relationship between sculpture and the use of water. Water intensifies the purity of geometric forms, and the statues suggest the violence and even the disorder in situations of crisis, whether they represent a Titan in torment, a monster in its death throes, or the chariot of a god, torn from the waters and soaring toward the sun. The arts of the sculptor and the hydraulic engineer combine to harmonize the movement of both water and statues so that the former seems to continue the movement of the latter, as if trying to express the life flow in the veins of every living thing.

Recalling what Descartes says in his description of the animal spirits circulating throughout the body to convey orders from the brain to the limbs, it is clear that he, too, understood in his own way, as a philosopher, the relationship between fountains and the contemporary concept of the life force in nature.

> As the animal spirits flow, thus, into the cavities of the brain, they pass from there into the pores of its substance, and from these pores into the nerves. There, according to whether they actually enter them or merely tend toward it, more in some, less in others, they have the force to change the shape of the muscles that contain these nerves, and by that means to move all the limbs. In the same way, in the grottoes and fountains of the royal gardens, you may have observed that the force with which water is expelled from its source is alone sufficient to move various machines, and even to make them play instruments or speak a few words, according to the way in which the pipes have been arranged.[20]

That said, there is obviously a considerable difference between the part played by water in the machines he mentions and the role of water in the Versailles bassins, and this is a good indicator of the progress made by garden design in half a century.

Descartes, writing at the time of Louis XIII, probably had in mind treatises like *Les raisons des forces mouvantes* by Salomon de Caus or the gardens of Saint-Germain where the grottoes were famous for their machines. By the time of Louis XIV, these effects seemed either too trivial or too mannerist for contemporary taste. Water was no longer expected to move automata but to lend an increased expressive power to statues. Art was preferable to artifice, but the human or animal forms still had to be seen as part of the continuum of moving forces that brought nature to life, and from this perspective the statues play the same part in bosquets as they do in open spaces.

Water Mirrors

But before we plunge into the enclosed world of the bosquets (and as a complete contrast), a last visit to the Grande Terrasse will allow us to compare the three greatest water mirrors: the Parterre d'Eau, the Pièce d'Eau des Suisses, and the Grand Canal.

The Parterre d'Eau brings life to a large open space, and to do this it has to reflect the greatest possible area of open space. From the château, it looks like a double source of light, blue or pearl-gray depending on the color of the sky, its sheen rising from the Grande Terrasse, and its effect is particularly striking in the Galerie des Glaces where the light from the parterre meets the light from the whole landscape reflected in the mirrors. From the terrace, the two water mirrors stretch beneath the grand avant-corps of the façade, so that its vast expanse can be seen upside down against the background of the sky, an image that incidentally is never static, since it can be ruffled by the slightest breath of wind. The effect is even more dramatic when night is falling on the gardens: the roles are then reversed, and it is the lights from the château that dance and sparkle in the water of the parterre. We do not know whether Le Nôtre was responsible for the parterre in its present form, but it is difficult to believe that he was not part of the team that designed it. But we do know that before the two elongated bassins, which are there today, there was a third quadrilobe bassin on the Grande Terrasse designed by Le Brun, which had replaced the parterre de broderie created by Boyceau in the time of Louis XIII. "A quatrefoil of bassins surrounds a central pièce d'eau, with a pattern of boxwood broderies around the rim and with bronze vases and marble statues placed alternately around the edge."[21]

Pierre-André Lablaude gives us an accurate idea of how beautiful this water parterre must have been. But the only notion that we have of its elegance today comes from contemporary illustrations and the reference that Achille Duchêne makes to it in the 1910 water parterre in Blenheim where, interestingly, the delicate effects of the Versailles-inspired water mirror are seen against the background of Capability Brown's eighteenth-century landscaped lake. So true is it that the landscape architect, like any other, can create astonishing effects by juxtaposing different styles. When the terrace was built, so much basic work was involved (earthworks, installation of pipes, controls for the fountains) that, even if the design of the first Parterre d'Eau was not his, Le Nôtre must have been consulted when it was created. Given that the second parterre, which we can see today, fits better into the perspective of the great central axis, leading the eye more freely toward the horizon, and that the statues, too, are arranged so as to show to advantage the brilliance of the wide stretches of water, Le Nôtre, despite being over sixty at the time, must have had a hand in these important changes or, at least, could not have disapproved of them.

We may not be sure of Le Nôtre's role in the design of the Parterre d'Eau, but there is no doubt that his name is directly linked to the Grand Canal and the Pièce d'Eau des Suisses. These are the biggest water mirrors in the gardens, and they are key to the overall structure, since one is at the end of the east-west axis and the other at the end of the transverse one, north-south. However, their shape is as different as their orientation. The former is about twice as long and half as wide as the latter, and if geography could exist in the imagination, the first might be compared to the Atlantic, the second to the Mediterranean. The Pièce d'Eau des Suisses continues, in fact, the Parterre de l'Orangerie, the warmest part of the gardens by a stretch of calm water, more like a lake than a bassin. Piganiol de la Force makes this point in his *Description de Versailles*, noting that it is 350 toises long and 120 wide and that "its shape suggests more an étang than a bassin."[22] It is wide enough to catch the sunlight for a long period as it rises to its height and to reflect it back toward the orangerie and the Grande Terrasse. It is like an inland sea warming the atmosphere.

The Grand Canal, on the other hand, stretches faraway toward the west, and the sun seems to follow it rather than cross over it. It catches the sun for long periods, but not steadily, since the dominant winds often mean that the ocean breezes blow across it. You need to have seen the Grand Canal in bad weather to realize how much the winds bring it alive, not just because they ruffle the water but because when they blow toward the château, the water is dappled with light. The canal is the first thing you see when you reach the Grande Terrasse, even when you catch sight of the gardens through the vestibule windows from the Cour de Marbre. It is also the last thing you see as you leave the château.

The Grand Canal is probably the most spectacularly successful water mirror of all the baroque gardens in France, the crowning achievement, at Versailles, of an already long-established tradition. The first water mirror in Fontainebleau in the early seventeenth century was imitated soon afterward in Courances, Saint-Cloud, Maisons, and Tanlay, gardens designed by François Mansart and Pierre Le Muet.[23] Arguably, they represent an original contribution by France to the history of the baroque garden, even if Holland and England have also had their part to play in highlighting the value of light and long perspective in gardens. If Le Nôtre did not find Italian gardens to his liking—at least, that is what his nephew claimed—perhaps we might account for this by the rarity of canals, which can be explained by the rugged nature of the peninsula and its meager water supply, or by the ingenuity of gardeners in damp countries of northern Europe who made a virtue of necessity and used the problem of drainage to create long stretches of water that also served an aesthetic purpose. In France, Germany, England, and Holland, these long water mirrors, which allowed the vanishing point to be placed on the horizon, established a calm, grandiose version of the baroque, whereas in Italy, the vanishing point was drawn upward into the sky, as in the Villa Aldobrandini or the Villa Garzoni, for example, which meant that the introduction of the long perspective into gardens was more dramatic.

Everything seems to indicate, therefore, that in Versailles Le Nôtre exploited to the full the potential of a new determining factor in the structure of gardens. He used it to transform a marsh into a huge reservoir of clear water and a source of light, both of which suited the Sun King's political intentions very well; he also used it to bring together all the efforts that were being made to survey, measure, and draw up maps so that the whole landscape would be a mosaic of forms created by representing nature as inspired by contemporary optics. The Grand Canal, therefore, rapidly emerged as a key element in the structure of the gardens. Opened up in 1667 and enlarged in 1671, it fixed the extent to which the Tapis Vert could be widened and as a result determined their overall dimensions. It also acted as an optical link between the landscape of the Ile-de-France at one end and the Bassin d'Apollon at the other. And the Bassin d'Apollon appeared from the start as a key feature around which everything revolves: the ascent toward the Bassin de Latone and the château, the open perspective to the west, and the transversal axis, separating the world of the bosquets from the Grand Parc.

This axis, even though it is hidden by the bosquets if you are standing on the Grande Terrasse, still has a visual presence because as your gaze travels down the Tapis Vert to move back up the horizontal surface of the Grand Canal, you get the impression of a fold in the landscape. This can be explained by the phenomenon of inertia. The eye which has been following the sloping plane of the Tapis Vert tries to continue moving down below the Bassin d'Apollon; when it cannot do so, it rebounds and glides on toward the horizon as if it could go on to infinity. This is why Mlle. de Scudéry's heroes, like twenty-first-century visitors, have the impression that the canal stretches away into the landscape "despite the situation of the place and despite Nature." But why would one have wanted a surface of calm water to give the impression of forcing Nature, while it is staying level and immobile? The dual nature of the Grand Canal, both axis and mirror, is involved here.

As an axis, still seen from the château, it is shaped like a long rectangle intersected by three transverse branches. The nearest is elliptical while the two others appear rectangular. In fact, as we have already seen, the first is a regular octagon—"a circle with side pieces," as La Fontaine puts it—126 meters across, the second an irregular octagon, built on the scale of the transverse canal that leads to Trianon, and this sets it in a square with sides measuring 195 meters, and the third is a very long, irregular octagon, broadly recalling the shape of the second, but twice as long. Everything is calculated so that from the château the transverse branches look the same and you do not appreciate their true shape until you see them close-up. In his study of the Parc de Sceaux, Georges Farhat describes this effect as anamorphosis, by analogy with the play of perspective used by painters—Holbein in *The Ambassadors* or Emmanuel Maignan in his fresco for the cloister of La Trinité-des-Monts—when they elongate forms in part of their paintings so that they are only recognizable when seen from a particular angle.[24] Whether Le Nôtre resorted to this kind of optical artifice is open to question. He certainly made use of optical devices but devices are not conceits and the very size of royal gardens probably precluded, in his opinion, the use of quaint effects intended for cabinets of curiosities. In the case of the Grand Canal, what he wished to achieve was a kind of foreshortening that brought the limits of the gardens nearer to those who saw them from the château and which, once the eye had reached this limit, caused it to run with accelerated speed to the vanishing point on the horizon.

As a water mirror, the Grand Canal has an essential function. Le Nôtre was very conscious of the fact that his gardens were designed on flat ground but that they are best seen from the château as a panorama, and therefore on a vertical plane. Unlike the painter, he does not create spatial depth but takes it as given and constructs his panorama by laying it out below the horizon. That can clearly be seen in one of his designs held in Stockholm (Fig. 27). In it, he crosses the vertical and the horizontal planes to suggest the correspondence between the figures drawn on the paper and what one sees when they are laid out on the ground. Similarly, in Versailles he creates the effect of a fold, as he did at the pivotal point of the Bassin d'Apollon, to "lock" the Grand Canal between the horizon and the lowest point of the gardens, thereby restoring its central

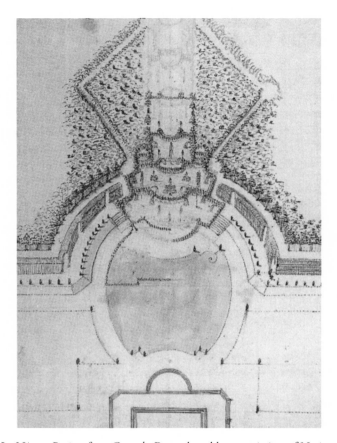

Fig. 27. Le Nôtre, *Project for a Cascade*. Reproduced by permission of Nationalmuseum, Stockholm. This drawing shows Le Nôtre's empirical rendering of the third dimension while drawing up a plan. He suggests the height of embankments, trees, and palisades by their shadows. His bold, lively strokes make his plan come to life.

axis at the place where it becomes a water mirror. This masterstroke enables him to create variety within continuity, bringing a long stream of light to the furthest part of the gardens, which might otherwise have seemed monotonous coming after the lively world of the bosquets. In the big open spaces, he thus combines the effects of perspective and light, demonstrating clearly his debt to contemporary landscape artists. His pioneering role in this area has already been discussed in relation to the links between Boyceau, Mollet, and Dézallier d'Argenville, and it is in Versailles, or more precisely thanks to the Grand

Canal, that one can best appreciate how he has opened up gardens to the land-scape. This cornerstone of his design has allowed him to add the effects of color to those of light and perspective.

Aerial Perspective and Landscape

Le Nôtre can be said to have started from what Boyceau said about open al-lées, namely that they had to be wide enough to "see the air coming from above."[25] On the Grand Canal, the palisades were far enough away from the water to make as much space for the air as could be wished. Le Nôtre knew and admired the landscape painters whose use of aerial perspective was uniquely effective in suggesting the presence of a mass of air between the horizon and the viewer looking at a landscape. There is an obvious link be-tween the scientific studies, discussed in the previous chapter, on the weight of air and its blue color which, to quote Mariotte, "can only appear if there is great density."[26]

One may reasonably conjecture from this that, a generation before Le Nôtre, the theoreticians had made the link between long perspective and the existence of a background in gardens. Had this not been the case, André Mol-let would not have discussed painted perspectives: these theoreticians had in a sense opened the garden up to landscape, but in an abstract way. It fell to Le Nôtre to take this approach to its logical conclusion and reveal its full poten-tial through the Grand Canal, whose orientation served his purpose ad-mirably. The rays of the setting sun at its western end pierced through the atmosphere, creating the phenomena that had been scientifically analyzed by Mariotte and Picard and described as follows by Roger de Piles in his treatise:

> In terms of painting, the sky is that part of the ether that we see above
> us, but it is also, more particularly, the layer of the air that we breathe
> and where clouds and storms are formed. Its color is a blue that becomes
> lighter as it approaches the earth because of the presence of vapors between
> us and the horizon, and these, being shot through with light, transmit it to
> objects more or less intensely according to their degree of proximity.

It must merely be observed that since this light is yellow or red in the evening as the sun is setting, these same objects take on not just the light but the color, too. Hence, since the yellow light, mixing with the blue of the sky, is naturally colored, it changes the blue, turning it a shade of green that is darker or lighter according to the intensity of the yellow light.[27]

This implicit reference to the backgrounds of Claude Lorrain or the atmospheric effects of painters such as Paul Bril or Albert Cuyp recalls Dézallier d'Argenville's comments on Claude's paintings when he describes "the resplendent crimson on the horizon," and the "air setting all the surrounding objects ablaze with light,"[28] thus proving that aerial perspective had reached the world of the gardens as a result of the way Le Nôtre had brought the landscape into them (Figs. 28 and 29).

From this point of view, the Grand Canal is unique. In Vaux-le-Vicomte or Sceaux, you can come upon the canal unexpectedly. In Chantilly, it intensifies the solemn atmosphere of the place with the incessant sounds of the cascade, where the waters, as Bossuet memorably said in his funeral oration for the prince of Condé, "are silent neither by day nor by night." In Versailles, the canal has a completely different role to play. By continuing the central axis beyond the Bassin d'Apollon, it controls geometrically the transition from the bosquets to the horizon and imperceptibly adds the gradation of colors used by the landscape artists to the tapering effect of linear perspective. The parallel with Claude is very clear here. If you have seen the sun rise over the Bassin d'Apollon, you must also see it set in summer over the end of the Grand Canal. The blazing disc of the setting sun serves as a point of perspective and also floods the whole of nature with Dézallier d'Argenville's "resplendent crimson." It appears to be the pivotal point around which the whole landscape is laid out, and this is true for two separate reasons: in a geometrical sense, insofar as all the different volumes are constructed in relation to it, and in an optical sense since it is both light and color. All the shadows seem to converge on it, while the last rays stretch out toward the château and linger over the bassins, a final stream of light splashing the bassins of the Lézards and of Latone.

Enclosed Spaces: The Realm of the Bosquets

The Intellectual Atmosphere of the Bosquets

The painterly eye, so obvious in the gradations of color, which abound in the Grand Canal, is equally apparent everywhere in the open spaces of the Versailles gardens, whether in the flower borders of the parterres, the gold, bronze, or

Fig. 28. The Bassin de Latone and the great perspective at sunset. A comparison of Jean-Baptiste Leroux's photograph with Claude Lorrain's *Port de mer au soleil couchant* shows how, at sunset, the Grand Canal combines visual and aerial perspective. The solar globe is the source of light from which all colors proceed; it is also the vanishing point leading the eye to infinity.

Fig. 29. Claude Lorrain, *Port de mer au soleil couchant*, 1639. Musée du Louvre, Paris. Réunion des Musées Nationaux/Art Resource, NY.

marble of the statues, or in the contrast between the ocher surfaces of the allées and the different shades of green that distinguish the grass from the trees.

However, if this applies to the esplanades and the terraces, it applies even more to the bosquets. As soon as you are inside, the dominant tones of green, blue, or gray, which you see in a panoramic view of the gardens, are enhanced with complex variations. This then is a world where the geometer is ever-present of course, but often eclipsed by the set designer, the poet, or the storyteller. In other words, geometry gives way to imagination and the pleasures that men and women (for the latter were very important in Versailles) expected when they entered places expressly designed to delight the senses.

It would probably be going too far to represent the bosquets as a female domain, given over to entertainment and the pleasures of society life, and contrast them with the male world of the engineer, the strategist, or the politician as represented by the open spaces. However, some facts speak for themselves.

It was Madame de Montespan who made the Bosquet du Marais what it was—a fairy-tale world that art had wrested from nature, just as Louis XIV had wrested Versailles from a quagmire. It was a delightful idea and flattering to the king. The reeds, which were part of the original landscape, remained, but the stagnant water was transformed into an enchanting spectacle of a thousand jets, spurting from this unpromising terrain and fusing into a translucent curtain above a bassin. Around this bassin, small circular cabinets formed recesses, as described by Félibien.

> In the middle of each recess stands a large oval table of white marble, twelve feet long and supported by a pedestal and consoles of jasper marble. On each table is a gilt-bronze basket, filled with simple flowers from which a large jet of water springs up and then falls back into it, so that the table does not get wet. So when you are eating, you have the pleasure of seeing the fountain play in the midst of all the dishes, without water touching them or causing you the least discomfort.[29]

A keen sense of the decorative is behind such refinements, and the king was appreciative of this feminine touch. Through Madame de Sévigné we know how he personally escorted ladies who had attracted his notice around the gardens: "Madame de La Fayette was yesterday at Versailles, where she was well received, indeed very well in that the king took her into his carriage with the ladies and took pleasure in showing her all the beauties of Versailles, like any private individual whom one visits in the country. He spoke only to her, and received with great pleasure and courtesy her compliments on the marvelous beauties that he showed her."[30]

Alongside the serene geometry of the open spaces, the bosquets were a universe where sentiment mattered more than science and where illusion enjoyed a special status. Madame de La Fayette, the author of *La princesse de Clèves*, would certainly have been aware of the allusions here and there to the France of long ago, and the king, as he escorted her around, also knew the classics of courtly literature. In the gardens that we see today, only the structure of the vegetation survives in some of the bosquets preferred by the ladies of the period: we must describe them in the same way as those that have been restored and can be seen in their pristine glory.

It is in the bosquets that the court culture and the complexity of its intellectual life can best be recaptured. This life was divided between the triumph of science, as portrayed by the academies, and the thousand and one undercurrents that preserved a link with the past, to "the France of long ago" and the pleasures of the imagination that novels of courtly love, theater, ballet, fêtes, and over-refined affectation equated with court life. As Montesquieu puts it, "One finds at court a delicacy of taste in everything, which is produced by continuous use of the luxuries procured by a great fortune."[31]

The "delicacy of taste" to which he refers could not be produced by a culture entirely controlled by the decisions of the prince. Even though it had its
affectations—placing Benserade on a par with La Fontaine, Mlle. de Scudéry,
and Madame de La Fayette—or even failed to recognize the talents of some of
the great contemporary writers, that culture was underpinned by a consensus
of opinion, which has often been endorsed by historians. We must, therefore,
rediscover the basis of this consensus if we are to understand how "the style of
Le Nôtre" suited the construction of an ideal environment, and how this ideal
relates in certain respects to the *paysage héroïque* (heroic landscape) and the
paysage champêtre (rural landscape) as defined by Roger de Piles in his *Cours
de peinture par principes*. The *style héroïque* was for him "a composition of objects which in their particular style draw from art and nature what each can
produce that is great and extraordinary."

He continues,

> The sites are wholly pleasing and wholly surprising; man-made objects
> are solely temples and pyramids, ancient sepulchres and altars conse
> crated to the gods or pavilions of a regular design; and if Nature is not
> represented as chance has us see her every day, she at least appears as we
> imagine she should be. This style is a pleasing illusion and a kind of
> enchantment when produced by an artist of real genius who is right-
> thinking, like Poussin who used it so expressively.

As for the *style champêtre*, he defined it as follows: "The style champêtre is a
representation of landscape that seems not so much cultivated as left to the
vagaries of untamed nature. She can be seen in all her simplicity, without artifice or false enhancement; but Nature, when left free, knows much more skillfully how to adorn herself with all her ornaments than when constrained by
art."[32] Of course, Le Nôtre's style adapted all that to garden design and emphasized the pleasures of the present rather than the dreams of antiquity. But,
it certainly represented Nature "as one imagines she should be," "as a kind of
enchantment." It is also at least probable that, left to himself, he would have
allowed the "style champêtre" a greater role than it eventually had in Versailles. We shall return to that question later.

Initially, in French gardens, the bosquet was inspired by the Italian *bosco*. It
purported to be a wild place where the trees were kept in the "state of nature,"

in the sense that the ancients understood of nature unsullied by humanity. In Versailles the early bosquets were created when the allées were opened up, and seen from the outside they have preserved something of their primitive appearance. They seem to be impenetrable and can be entered only along paths leading off at an angle that arouse your curiosity and give no hint of what you are about to see. When Jean-Baptiste Martin le Vieux painted the Bassin de Neptune, he showed clearly the interior of the Bosquet de l'Arc de Triomphe and the Bosquet des Trois Fontaines as genuine clearings surrounded by thick woods. Piganiol de la Force, in his *Nouvelle description des châteaux et parcs de Versailles et de Marly*, defines them as "small woods of different shapes, planted symmetrically, and with small compartmented allées" (Fig. 30).[33]

All the bosquets were decorated with statues, monuments, and fountains, each with its own theme. Since the mythological figures in the bosquets were sometimes the same as the ones in the large open spaces, it is through the classical gods that the common cultural elements in the two realms of the gardens are most clearly apparent.

The Statues

It might seem surprising that the Olympian gods should have ranked so highly in a place where the lofty outline of the royal chapel dominated the skyline and where reminders of the king's piety were ubiquitous in court ceremonies. However, educated people had a double culture: they were well aware that moral questions went with religion, while arts, pleasures, and to a great extent knowledge lay with Greco-Roman antiquity. The feeling for nature reflected this dichotomy. Protestants and Jansenists sought to limit the dominance of the pagan gods over the art world; this is evident in the efforts they made to christianize the gardens by disconnecting them from the ancient mythology (Bernard Palissy, Olivier de Serres, and Port-Royal are famous examples); but the court did not live in a saintly fashion, and the Olympian gods were seen as symbols, used in art to represent the forces of nature and human passions. Education, particularly the teaching of the Jesuits, made use of pagan divinities to embody allegories, and allegories were attractive because they sharpened the wits while at the same time allowing pleasure to be felt from understanding an abstract idea by means of a beautiful image.

In addition, the culture of classical antiquity allowed nature to be represented intellectually in a way that corresponded with the thinking of

Fig. 30. Jean-Baptiste Martin le Vieux, *Vue perspective du château de Versailles depuis le Bassin de Neptune*, ca. 1693. Musée du Château de Versailles. This view shows clearly the visual shocks that the bosquets are meant to produce. Seen from the outside, they look like small woods. The visitor experiences mixed feelings of curiosity and apprehension as he enters them by an oblique alley where he feels he is being misled. Then, suddenly, a splendid spectacle, grandiose and almost supernatural, bursts into view. The baroque aesthetic always favored effects of this kind.

contemporary science. Geometry and arithmetic had both been born in Greece and both were held in high esteem by the academies. The Greeks and Romans had used science and art to investigate nature and they remained supreme in those domains. The king's cultural policy owed much to the classics and he could appeal to them to lead his struggle against the religious zealots in the early days of his reign. In the bosquets you still find something of the atmosphere that Nocret captures in his painting *L'assemblée des dieux*. The king is represented as Apollo, the queen as Juno, Monsieur the king's brother as the Flambeau of Aurora, Madame his wife as Flora, his daughter La Grande Mademoiselle as Diana the huntress, Anne of Austria as Cybele the mother of the gods, and the royal children as cupids. The queen of England, Monsieur's mother-in-law, is offering him coral and pearls, treasures found deep in the perilous ocean where her fleets sailed, which entitles her to hold Neptune's trident in her hand.

This explains why a whole iconographic program had been envisaged by Colbert's Grande Commande, commissioning the decor for the Parterre d'Eau designed by Le Brun. Around the quadrilobe basin, which was in place from the early 1670s to 1683, were placed figures representing the Four Seasons, the Four Elements, the Four Humors, the Four Continents, the Four Poems, and the Four Times of Day. These twenty-four allegorical figures were positioned on the Grande Terrasse where the four cardinal points that determine the layout of the buildings and gardens can be seen most clearly. The systematic rigor they gave to the iconographic program of the gardens was lost when the decoration of the Parterre d'Eau in its present form took as its theme the rivers of France. The statues intended for Le Brun's bassin were then scattered in the relatively haphazard way that we see today: Africa and Europe with Earth and Night on their left, and Spring between Daybreak and the Lyric Poem.[34]

After the ambitious program of the Grande Commande had been abandoned, Le Brun's bassin was replaced by the two water mirrors that we have today, and this has made the role of the Grande Terrasse as an intersection between the two axes much more apparent, since the highest section of the north-south axis has been opened up and the east-west axis begins beneath the main body of the château. Aesthetics have triumphed over metaphysics, and there is no reason to complain today when we can see the rivers of France, calm and powerful, lying along the edge of the bassins, more in harmony with the children and nymphs around them by whom they are fêted. Strength and grace are thus united on the esplanade from where the whole panorama of the gardens opens out, and undoubtedly in this way the statues are more closely allied to the landscape than to their symbolic meaning. But surely, enclosing the world within a quaternary arrangement, in which the order of the seasons controlled literary genres and the continents corresponded with the humors, and placing that group on the terrace from which the king controlled nature, was a risk. Could it not turn Louis XIV into a second Nero and Versailles into his Domus Aurea? Might it not disturb the balance between Christian and pagan culture that he wanted to maintain? Whatever the reasons that finally led the king to reorganize the iconographic program of the Grande Terrasse, priority was given to landscape architecture over the consistency of a closed mythological system which, in any case, probably looked *dépassé*.

The statues and vases positioned along the allées below the palisades and trellises demonstrate this priority. Their role is difficult to achieve: they have to be sufficiently unobtrusive to point up, as a series of white marks against the dark green of the foliage, the receding perspectives, the inflexion of the bends, and the angle of the long diagonals. This is particularly clear on the Grande Terrasse, on the Fer à Cheval de Latone, on the whole length of the Tapis Vert, and on the esplanade of the Bassin d'Apollon—in other words, all along the central axis where the statues escort you, tempting you to stop and hear the tales of their dealings with the gods from their marble lips. Some are copied from classical antiquity, but all show how contemporary French sculptors, all linked to the academy, have equaled the highest achievements in Europe, including Italy. Statues by Houzeau, Granier, Roger, Mazeline, Cornu, le Perdrix, and Jouvenet are on a par with the better-known Tuby, Lespangnandelle, and the Marsy brothers. They can also rival those of classical antiquity, and several of the copies are magnificent chefs d'oeuvre in their own right, as, for example, *Ariane endormie* (Ariadne asleep), at the entrance to the Allée de l'Orangerie, near the south parterre, or *Vénus à la coquille* (Venus with the shell), the Coysevox copy of an antique statue (which was copied again for transport to the Louvre), or *Gladiateur mourant* (Dying gladiator), opposite it at the foot of the Rampe de Latone, a copy from an antique statue in Pergamon.

In the bosquets, the statues do not have the same function as in the big open spaces. Positioned in out-of-the-way spots, they seem more freely expressive. You have to go right up to them, and in the calm of the trees, they are eloquently discreet. As Rodin said to his friend Gsell, "Antique sculpture is best suited to foliage. . . . The Greeks loved nature so much that their works are in their element within it."[35]

If statues are in enclosed spaces, it is easier for true art lovers to contemplate and reflect on them at leisure, and in the Bosquet de la Girandole and the Bosquet du Grand Dauphin there are terms that will hold them there for a long time. Some are by Nicolas Poussin and were bought by Louis XIV from Mme. Fouquet after her husband had been imprisoned. The French painter's admiration for antiquity is clear: seeing the noble poses of Hercules, Pomona, and even Pan, it seems as though the painter has tried to capture all that is immortal in antique sculpture. The anecdote reported by Bellori is well-known. Poussin was in the ruins of ancient Rome with a foreigner who wanted to take "some rare vestige of antiquity" back home; wishing to oblige his companion, the painter bent down and picked up "in the grass, a little earth and gravel, with small pieces of marble and porphyry crushed almost to a powder," and he said, "Here you are, sir, take this for your museum, and say: this is ancient Rome."[36] And it is true that something of the grandeur of antique statuary has indeed come to Versailles by way of Vaux-le-Vicomte and the labyrinthine paths that great collectors devise for masterpieces.

In the end, the decision to abandon an overambitious iconographic program has given greater emphasis to themes linked to the life of nature, the exuberance of childhood, and youth in all its dazzling beauty. It is here that the statuary is at its best, especially in places where you have to search for it. Take, for example, *Bain des nymphes* by Girardon, Legros, and Le Hongre from a drawing by Le Brun. This is a magnificent piece, radiating youth and sensuality, but difficult to see because it is always in shadow; it is in every way a perfect illustration of what La Fontaine says about the Grand Canal.

Cherchons des mots choisis pour peindre son cristal.
Qu'il soit pur, transparent; que cette onde argentée
Loge en son moite sein la blanche Galatée
Jamais on n'a trouvé ses rives sans Zéphyrs;
Flore s'y rafraîchit au vent de leurs soupirs;
Les nymphes d'alentour souvent dans les nuits sombres
S'y vont baigner en troupe à la faveur de l'ombre.[37]

[Let us seek the choicest words to paint its crystal waters
May they be pure, transparent: let the silver waves
Fold in their embrace the fair nymph Galatea.
The gentle Zephyrs have never quit its banks,
Refreshing Flora with their sighing breeze;
And often in the dusky nights, the nymphs around
Meet there to bathe in friendly shade.]

In other sculpture groups less hidden, such as the Marmousets or the *Ile des enfants*, previously in Marly, the water contributes and adds complexity to the effects of the figures, falling in translucent curtains from the edge of the basins, splashing the little bodies frolicking on a child-sized island, while the water spits angrily under the barrage of drops.

The Fountains

If there is one thing that sets the realm of the bosquets apart, it is the more intimate and subtle experience it affords of the magical effects of water: when the grotto occupied the site of what is now the chapel, it contained a complex series of fountains. They were reminiscent of those in earlier grottoes, when visitors were dazzled by the machines that exemplified the extent of Renaissance curiosity about the emerging science of mechanics. In Versailles, these automata had disappeared, but the fountains were even more magnificent and now existed purely as a spectacle. The grotto, which was on the north side of the gardens (the same side as the Bassin de Neptune), evoked the resplendent mysteries of the underwater world. André Félibien has left an eloquent description of his amazement at the varied effects of the fountains, from bubbling cauldrons to mists of tiny droplets.

> When the waters from the reservoir, streaming from a thousand different outlets, gush forth everywhere and are virtually the only element filling the place, a whole river seems to flow from the urn of the god, which lies on its side in the central niche, as if at the entrance to a cave. Water boils out in the other niches where the horses of Apollo stand. The tritons and mermaids beside the arcades pour it into the large marble shells set against the pilasters. It tumbles from every possible place in the vaulted roof. Then, running counter to this cascade, from a jasper table in the center of the entry to the grotto, a large jet of water soars upward so fiercely that as it hits the rock at the top of the vault, it forms a great crystal mushroom in this place, and as the water falls it makes a circular, silvery curtain that comes apart only toward the very bottom. Then from the gravel that serves as the grotto floor and from a thousand invisible holes, as if from several springs, a multitude of water jets rise to hit the vault so hard that they fall back as forcefully as they rose up. Thus, with the waters showering everywhere from so many different places, it is

impossible to tell from which source they come. But what can be seen are myriad little globes of crystal amid a confused mass of drops and atoms of water, which seem to move in that place like the atoms of light visible in the rays of the sun. And since the pillars and the sides of the grotto are full of mirrors and all the different droplets are reflected over and over again, the splendor of this grotto is quite extraordinary, like several grottoes that together make a water palace of boundless size.[38]

This is a superb description of the magical effects of water and, incidentally, one that notes the role of mirrors in increasing the sense of space. We owe to La Fontaine, who also described the strange beauty of the grotto, one of the most vivid evocations of the way in which rocaille enhances water in all its forms.

Au haut de six piliers d'une égale structure,
Six masques de rocaille à grotesque figure,
Songes de l'art, démons bizarrement forgés,
Au-dessus d'une niche en face sont rangés.
De mille raretés la niche est toute pleine:
Un Triton d'un côté, de l'autre une Sirène,
Ont chacun une conque en leur mains de rocher;
Leur souffle pousse un jet qui va loin s'épancher.
Au haut de chaque niche un bassin répand l'onde;
Le masque la vomit de sa gorge profonde;
Elle retombe en nappe et compose un tissu
Qu'un autre bassin rend sitôt qu'il a reçu.
. . . .
Quand l'eau cesse et qu'on voit son cristal écoulé,
Le nacre et le corail en réparent l'absence:
Morceaux pétrifiés, coquillage, croissance,
Caprices infinis du hasard et des eaux,
Reparaissent aux yeux plus brillants et plus beaux.[39]

[Above six even, ordered pillars stand
Six masks of shell and rock grotesquely shaped
Imaginings of art, bizarre demonic forms
Perch high above them on a facing niche.
Inside it jostle myriad rarities:
A Triton and a mermaid, stand each side,

And in their hands a conch of rock they hold,
Hurling a jet of water as they breathe.
Above each niche, a basin spills the flow;
Spewed from within the mask's cavernous throat;
It cascades, as a curtain, falling into folds
Caught by another basin, and instantly let go.
. . . .
When water ceases and its crystal ebbs,
The nacreous shell and coral branch appear;
Petrified fragments that replace the streams,
These time-tossed whims of oceans and of chance
Emerge, their radiant beauty greater still.]

If you go to the bosquet known as the Salle de Bal, you will have some idea of
the rocaille described by La Fontaine and Félibien. It covers steps compartmented by facings of red Languedoc marble: curtains and eddies of water cascade down from the musicians' gallery, their sparkling brilliance intermingling
with the flickering lights of the tall gilt torchères, placed at ground level. This
is one of the bosquets that have been restored, and it gives you a real sense of
what court entertainment must have been, as well as allowing you to rediscover
one of the highlights of garden architecture in the baroque period. Sumptu-
ously extravagant materials and exquisite workmanship are combined here;
this is indeed the perfect place for dancing: music seems to tumble from the
trees above the gallery, inviting the dancers to create that living harmony of
sound, movement, and human forms, which is the essence of their art (Fig. 31).

The Bosquet de la Colonnade is another of these special places. From the
time it was built by Jules Hardouin-Mansart, this circular colonnade was considered one of the jewels of the gardens. Piganiol de la Force has described its
beauties. He observes that it consists in "eight columns of violet-colored breccia, twelve of Languedoc marble, and twelve of *bleu turquin* marble," noting
that the breccia is a "dirty" white (off-white, as we would now put it) with
separate bands, and the turquin "marbled with 'dirty' white, from the Genoa
coast. He continues: "Each column corresponds with a pilaster of Languedoc
marble. At the top of each is an architrave-cornice, which serves as the entab-
lature. The columns are linked by a semicircle of arches, their archivolts decorated with masks of nymphs, naiads, or sylvan gods. This work is topped with
a Corinthian cornice, above which is a plinth with bas-relief *postes*[40] ending in
a volute on which stand vases in white marble finishing in pine cones."[41]

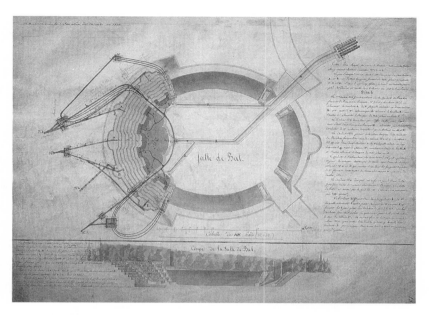

Fig. 31. The Salle de Bal, plan and cross-section. *Recueil des plans relatifs aux eaux des jardins et des bâtiments des châteaux de Versailles et des Trianon fait depuis 1809 jusqu'à 1830 par Dufour architecte du roi.* Plate 15. Archives, Service des fontaines, Versailles. Alexandre Dufour (1760–1835), who had worked for Napoleon at Fontainebleau among other places, was appointed architect to the king by Louis XVIII. As such, he was attached to Versailles from 1810 to 1835, and it was he who built the colonnaded pavilion at the southern extremity of the south wing also called "aile vieille." The pavilion still bears his name. Dufour was also in charge of the gardens. He drew up a complete plan of their hydraulic network. This wash drawing bearing manuscript annotations describes the circulation of water in the Salle de Bal, also called the Bosquet des Rocailles.

La Colonnade is always very impressive because of the color of the marbles and the delicacy of the arcades. There would seem to be an obvious link with the peristyle on the island of Cythera described in book 1, chapter 21 of Colonna's *Hypnerotomachia Poliphili:* "The columns stood two by two along the specially designed double plinth, and after a row of six columns, there was a square pillar topped with a ball of gilded copper; these columns were differently colored, with two of chalcedony, two of green jasper, and two of red jasper."[42] That said, if Hardouin-Mansart's Colonnade was inspired by Colonna's peristyle with regard to the colored marble and the columns placed "two by two," it is far superior in one respect—the twenty-eight marble basins with elegant jets of water, which rise in the air to fall back between the columns in a transparent curtain. Everything about the Colonnade—its circular shape, the perfect geometrical form according to contemporary architects, the delicate design of columns and water jets, and the blend of colors against the trellises and trees—creates a harmonious ensemble, an invitation, as it were, for music to unite with all the other arts. The court musicians did occasionally play there.

Visiting this bosquet in the twenty-first century gives you a striking impression of the different kinds of baroque sensibility. For in a setting that evokes the divine geometry of the Renaissance, you can see right at the center of the circle a sculpture group, *L'enlèvement de Proserpine* (Rape of Persephone), by Girardon after a drawing by Le Brun. It represents the mythological illustration of the passing of the seasons and the cycles of nature in a particularly disturbing way. The king must have wanted to give it pride of place: he had the sculptor, Girardon, present him with a model in bronze, and then three years passed before the marble sculpture group was put into place. There is a stark contrast between the brutality of the abduction scene and the ethereally harmonious colonnade with its feminine ionic capitals and delicate fountains. Pluto is bent on making off with his victim as fast as possible, knocking over a handmaiden who is trying to intervene and carrying off Persephone, who is calling despairingly for help. The scene captures the decisive moment when masculine force triumphs, something the marble conveys memorably in a soaring mass of lines, which swirl around and break as they collide.

The Encelade, another bosquet that has been restored to its former glory, contains another striking portrayal of violence, a Titan buried alive by Athena as a punishment for rebelling against the gods. A powerful jet of water gushes from his mouth as if his last breath is being crushed from his chest by the weight of stone and lava. Le Brun, who did the drawing from which the sculptor Gaspard Marsy and the rocaille worker Berthier worked, doubtless had in mind the garden of Castello and Ammannati's Antaeus, who seems to be breathing out a jet of water as Hercules lifts him off the ground. In the Encelade, the political symbolism is very clear and particularly appropriate given its proximity to the Bassin d'Apollon. The Sun King flies to the rescue of Latona while the rebel Titan plunges from the heavens into the lava. The bosquet is a stage set, reached by an allée where a sharp bend keeps a surprise hidden. When you enter, you come upon a circular gallery where trellises make a bower; as you make your way toward the great jet of water that you can see from the Allée d'Apollon, you are completely unprepared for the terrifying sight that meets your eyes. Cotelle depicts the effect: from the top of Olympus, Jupiter strikes the rebel with a thunderbolt, hurling down the giant whose struggles make the earth quake as he knocks over a table that the terrified onlookers have abandoned in their flight. The whole scene is reminiscent of the sudden, spectacular changes of scene that delighted contemporary theater audiences. It was the same in stage sets for ballets, an art form the king liked a great deal. The abbé Marolles explained that a ballet should have "a fictitious subject with captivating, unusual, and supernatural elements," and continued, "Whether the ballet is serious or comical, it should always include extraordinary things, with something of the supernatural about them."[43]

In the ballet *Hercule amoureux*, in which the king danced in 1662, the Vigaranis, who had replaced Fouquet's favorite, Torelli, exploit the full potential of machines to produce grandiose effects. During Act III, which takes place in a flower garden (ballets were often set in gardens), Venus, descending from her chariot, meets Hercules and makes a magic seat covered in herbs and flowers rise from the ground. A little later the spirits "locked within the seat" rise from it and "bring the statues in the garden to life." What was true of the ballets was also true of the theater and the fêtes that took place in the gardens, and it is remembered in all the descriptions of fêtes in Versailles.

The present-day visitor to Versailles may rejoice that the Trois Fontaines, the Encelade, and the Salle de Bal have been restored to their pristine glory. They give an idea of what the court liked in the way of promenades and spectacles. Yet some of the finest bosquets have disappeared and been replaced by more modest substitutes, and while we stroll in the places where they formerly stood we can conjure up a virtual image of their magnificence with the help of contemporary documents. One of them was the Marais, now replaced by the Bains d'Apollon; another was l'Ile Royale, now replaced by the Jardin du roi, but there were two more, both considered key features of the gardens, the Théâtre d'Eau and the Labyrinthe.

The Théâtre d'Eau was one of the most elaborate bosquets, a triumph of the partnership among architects, scenographers, and hydraulic engineers. Kenneth Woodbridge has called it "one of the most ingenious of the Versailles water spectacles," describing it as "a big round space, about 52 meters in diameter, divided into two; one part being an amphitheater with three tiers of turf seats, the other a stage, just over a meter high." He adds, "Three alleys converged on the stage, each with a canal falling in cascades whose water fell ultimately into basins surrounding the stage. On either side of the canals, round about the stage and in niches in the hedge surrounding the auditorium, were a multitude of fountains whose jets could be changed in five different ways: straight upward; curving to make berceaux, inward or outward; or circles in front or behind. Rock and shellwork into which the water fell added to the decorations."[44] The bosquet had one more major attraction: its structure. It had been designed by Carlo Vigarani, the famous scene designer who had come to Versailles following in Lulli's footsteps. Vigarani had treated the whole bosquet as a theater, but a theater in the Palladian spirit of the Teatro Olympico in Vicenza. The three converging alleys were a fine example of what was then called *perspective accélérée;* the alleys grew narrower and narrower as they led the eye away from the stage into the obscurity of the woods. The resulting optical effect was striking; the bosquet looked longer than it actually was and the contrast between the dark woods and the shining water was all the more impressive as the water jets could be made to operate in several directions. This was baroque aesthetics at its best: lavish, animated, and full of optical conceits (Fig. 32).

The Labyrinthe was an unusual concept, particularly well suited to the intriguing world of the bosquets. Originally designed in 1665 by Le Nôtre as a maze of allées, it was later decorated with statues of animals and lively fountains playing in rocaille bassins as an illustration of Aesop's Fables. A few lines by Benserade below the bassins served as a moral comment on the scene in question. Thanks to Cotelle, we have some lively paintings of the main sculpture and it is regrettable that the labyrinth was demolished under Louis XVI and replaced with the Bosquet de la Reine. Piganiol de la Force has given a useful description of it. He first describes the labyrinth as a "network of allées bordered with palisades where it is easy to get lost." He then gives a valuable indication of the colors involved: "At every turn, you see a fountain decorated with delicate rocaille, and representing very simply a fable, the subject of which is indicated by a four-line inscription in gold letters on a bronze plate, painted black" (Fig. 33).[45]

Piganiol then describes each animal group; a single fable will suffice to give an idea of how the bosquet might have looked. Here, for example, is how he describes the biggest sculpture group, which could be seen at the entrance immediately after the statue of Aesop on the left and Eros on the right.

>The Grand-Duke and the Birds
>Here, the Grand-Duke owl sits in the middle of a bassin de rocaille and a large number of birds, crowded into a trellised half dome with

architectural ornaments, pour water on him because they are annoyed
by his mournful cry and his ugly plumage.

Les oiseaux en plein jour voyant le duc paraître
Sur lui fondirent tous à son hideux aspect.
Quelque parfait qu'on puisse être
Qui n'a pas son coup de bec?

[When to the birds by day, the Grand-Duke owl appears,
They fall upon him by his looks repelled
However perfect one might be
From biting beaks, who has immunity?][46]

One can deduce from Piganiol's words ("A cockerel in the middle of the bassin
registers his protest with the water that he spouts forth") that the spouting
water is a visual representation of the birds' cries, a simple device similar to the
speech bubble in a cartoon.

We know the Labyrinthe had been devised to provide instruction for the
Dauphin. Perhaps that explains why Benserade's quatrain, not one of his most
inspired pieces, seemed suited to a pupil whose talents were not deemed outstanding. And then one begins to regret that La Fontaine was not invited to
have some of his verses engraved on the "bronze plate, painted black" that Piganiol mentions. But La Fontaine was not well regarded at court. His efforts
to defend Fouquet had displeased the king. Moreover, he had a taste for a libertine style and distanced himself from orthodox religion. The king did not
appreciate this at all from a political point of view, and that mattered to him
more than anything. As Marc Fumaroli has shown, this contentious stance
was compounded by La Fontaine's resistance to Colbert's cultural policy and
the wholesale recruitment of intellectuals into academies.[47] The fact remains
that the animals in the Labyrinthe suffer from these human quarrels, and the
language they were given is less ingeniously elegant than that of the fables.
Benserade did not possess the art of expressing things so exactly that the manner of saying them itself reinforced the truth of the message. But the idea of
bringing men and women to seek after wisdom in the depths of a wood was a
good one.

Charles Perrault took the hint and he gave his own version of the
Labyrinthe, which is far more interesting than Benserade's because it relies entirely on the strategies of the art of love.[48] To take but one example, this is the

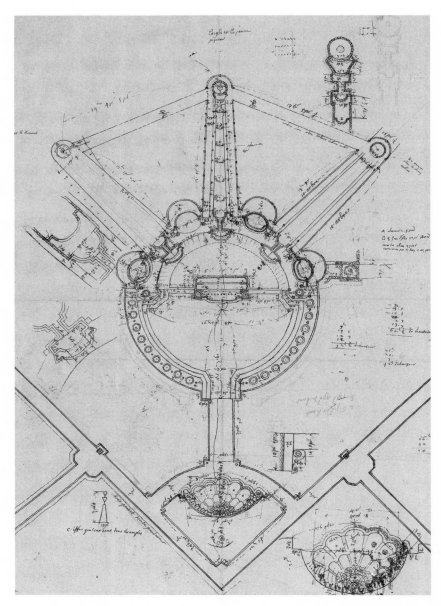

Fig. 32. The Théâtre d'Eau, by Carlo Vigarani. Plan of the structure and of the water circulation. Bibliothèque nationale de France, Estampes, Paris.

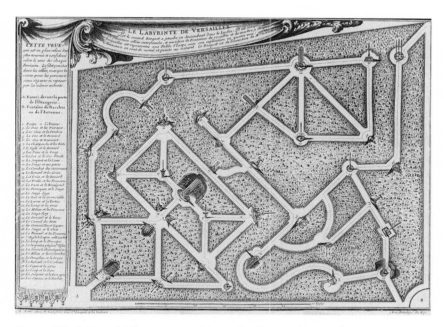

Fig. 33. *The Labyrinth*. Plan, ca. 1690. Musée du Château de Versailles. Statues of
Aesop and Love stand at the entrance to the labyrinth. The large trellis work serving
as a frame to the Battle of the Animals is just behind. The labyrinth's aim is to
allow the visitor to be led by his curiosity. While at one fountain he discovers
another in the distance. Sometimes he has to choose between two allées, but the
only rule is to avoid seeing the same thing twice. One thinks of Boileau's "Reason
has often but one way to proceed." What is strange about the labyrinth is that
Charles Perrault, its original designer, has presented his own interpretation of the
labyrinth in his *Recueil de divers ouvrages en vers et en prose* (1675). His verses, much
more spirited than Benserade's, are all about gallantry and the strategies of love.
Equally mysterious is the design of the allées, which has sometimes been described
(without any documentary evidence) as a combination of the letters composing Le
Nôtre's name.

dialogue between Aesop (by Tuby) and Love (by Le Gros), whose statues
stood at the entrance to the labyrinth:
   Benserade gave them two lines each:

   L'Amour
   Oui, je peux désormais fermer les yeux et rire;
   Avec ce peloton je saurai me conduire.

Esope
Amour, ce faible fil pourrait bien t'égarer;
Au moindre choc il peut casser.

[Love
Now I can close my eyes and smile at life;
With this thread in hand I cannot lose my way.

Aesop
Love, that thread is weak and could lead you astray;
The slightest shock is enough to break it.]

With typical elegance, Perrault proposes another dialogue.

Esope
Avec mes animaux pleins de ruse et d'adresse
Qui de vos moeurs font le vivant portrait,
Je voudrais bien enseigner la sagesse,
Mais mon voisin ne veut pas qu'on en ait.

L'Amour
Je veux qu'on aime et qu'on soit sage,
C'est être fou que n'aimer rien.
Chaque animal le dit en son langage;
Il ne faut que l'écouter bien.

[Aesop
With my animals, which are clever and crafty
And which give a true picture of your ways,
I would fain teach you to be wise,
But my neighbor does not wish you to be so.

Love
I wish you to love and yet to be wise,
To love nothing is madness.
All animals say so in their language;
Listen to them and you will know how to behave.]

Perrault's version was published in 1675 and the king cannot have been unaware of its existence. It may well be that he was amused by it and that he

gave his tacit permission to print a piece of poetry that finally suited both his taste for pleasure and his wish to promote elegant behavior at court.

Another mystery about the labyrinth that has never been solved is the design of its allées where curves are far less frequent than straight lines, a rather unusual disposition. It has been argued, without any proof, that Le Nôtre has used the letters of his name (LE NOSTRE) to make a visual joke signifying that a labyrinth is a place in which you lose not only your bearings but also your sense of identity. The mystery—one could even say the mysteries—of the labyrinth may be said to prefigure the later *Contes* by Charles Perrault, where the forest as it existed in ancient France is linked with a sense of the supernatural that his writings helped preserve.

We can understand why the supernatural should be there in its ancient form, and it is even more apparent when we see the bassins where the statues seem to have come down from Mount Olympus to join in the magic of the fountains. Greco-Roman mythology was well established at court. La Fontaine said of the princess of Conti, "I thought she had come down to us from Mount Olympus." And Guyonnet de Vertron, in his capacity as royal historiographer, said to Louis XIV, "All the gods are here today in your enchanted palace."[49]

In these circumstances, Ovid might seem the Latin poet best suited to bring the classical gods to the gardens. In his *Metamorphoses*, mythology is no longer obscure; the gods are made human, yet at the same time retain an element of the supernatural in their adventures, which would provide subjects for the amazing feats that Torelli's machine designers, and later those of the Vigaranis and Bérain, made possible with their machines. More than any other era, the baroque had a taste for the spectacular, for surprise and illusion in any shape or form; it delighted in any kind of arresting, visual shock. This was an age accustomed to looking at the world with eyes better equipped than ever before to see increasingly distant objects, to transform a point of light into a star or a translucent drop of water into a world teeming with tiny creatures, and it found changes in appearance endlessly fascinating. Pascal, who was always ready to condemn passing fads, used these wonders to demonstrate the unreliability of our knowledge: "From a distance, town or countryside is simply town or countryside, but as you draw closer, you see houses, trees, tiles, leaves, grass, ants, ants' legs, and so on to infinity. We call all of that countryside."[50]

But wonders delighted the age. They proved that modern society, thanks to the power of its machines, could make the enchanted world of the ancients tangible, and this was never more obvious than at Versailles, where the gardens themselves had emerged from former marshlands.

The Gardens and the Sister Arts

The great writers of the period perceived that the king's gardens provided an ideal stage, a chamber of echoes for the gods of antiquity. In his *Amphytrion*, Molière used the myth, which Ovid recounts in Book VI of the *Metamorphoses*, to draw a parallel between the relationship of Louis XIV with Madame de Montespan and that of Jupiter with Alcmene, the wife of the eponymous Theban general. In the well-known story, Alcmene, deceived by the master of the gods who had taken on the appearance of her husband, spent an innocently happy night with him and this led to a series of misunderstandings for the unfortunate general and his valet, Sosie. The name "Sosie" (double) says it all. We are not sure who are gods and who are men in this nocturnal imbroglio. Sosie (played by Molière) sums up the situation when he says to his master, "You, Monsieur, are double, like me."[51]

The denouement comes about when Jupiter appears "in a cloud, on his wing, armed with his thunderbolt, to the noise of thunder and lightning." That is how Cotelle shows him in his painting of the Bosquet de l'Encelade. When you see that bosquet, you cannot help but think that the court recognized the settings they liked and the mythological figures familiar to them since childhood.

Similarly, when Racine's *Iphigénie* was put on for the first time in the orangerie, the setting of the château was directly used. Félibien has given us a description of this memorable premiere.

> So the stage was erected at the end of the allée that leads to the orangerie. The decor represented a long tree-lined allée, with fountains and bassins here and there, and at intervals grottoes in rustic style, but delicately worked. On their entablature was a splendid balustrade, where flower-filled, porcelain vases were arranged; the basins of the fountains were white marble, supported by gilded tritons, and in these basins were others, higher up, carrying gold statues. At the back of the theater, this allée ended in tents that were similar to those over the orchestra and, beyond, was another long allée that was the Allée de l'Orangerie itself, with tall orange trees and pomegranates, interspersed with several porcelain vases filled with different flowers. Between each

tree and the next stood large candelabra and gold and silver gueridons, on which were crystal girandoles, lit by several candles. This allée ended in a marble portico; the pilasters supporting the cornices were of lapis lazuli and the door seemed to be gold plate. In this theater, against the backdrop that I have described, the royal company of actors played the tragedy of *Iphigénie*, sieur Racine's last play, which the court greeted with as much acclaim as all the other plays by this author.[52]

True, Racine declared in his preface that he had contrived to save Iphigénie from Calchas's knife "without recourse to a goddess or a machine." However, his final scene describes the way this denouement came about, and the audience in the sumptuous setting of the orangerie could imagine the marvels that the ballets and operas showed onstage. In the following passage, Ulysse, an attendant, describes the death of Eriphile, the second Iphigénie, when she decides to sacrifice herself.

> Furieuse elle vole, et sur l'autel prochain
> Prend le sacré couteau, le plonge dans son sein.
> A peine son sang coule et fait rougir la terre,
> Les dieux font sur l'autel entendre le tonnerre;
> Les vents agitent l'air d'heureux gémissements,
> Et la mer leur répond par ses mugissements.
> La rive au loin gémit, blanchissante d'écume
> La flamme du bûcher d'elle-même s'allume.
> Le ciel brille d'éclairs, s'entrouvre, et parmi nous
> Jette une sainte horreur qui nous rassure tous.
> Le soldat étonné dit que dans une nue
> Jusque sur le bûcher Diane est descendue.
> Et croit que s'élevant au travers de ses feux,
> Elle portait au ciel notre encens et nos vœux.

> [She flies in fury and from the altar by her hand
> The sacred knife she takes and strikes her heart.
> As drops of blood fall, reddening the ground
> Above the altar roars the thunder of the gods;
> The air is stirred with timely, soughing winds
> The ocean answers with its bellowing waves.

And far away the foam-flecked shores cry out.
Unbidden from the pyre the flame leaps up.
The brilliant lightning cleaves the sky in twain,
And fills us with a calming, holy fear.
The soldier, awestruck, claims that in a cloud
He saw Diana to the pyre descend,
And thinks that through the clouds she rose
Bearing to heaven our incense and our prayers.]

It is often said with some justification that the life of nature does not play a significant part in French classical tragedy and is only glimpsed occasionally in a metaphor or in narratives, such as the one by Théramène, or Le Cid, or the one by Ulysse that we have just cited. However, Racine sets part of *Esther* in a garden, and one collected edition of his plays has views of gardens as frontispieces to the tragedies. This is not surprising when one considers the structural similarities between the alexandrine in classical French verse and the role of the central axis in architecture. That structural parallel owes something to the importance given to the caesura by Malherbe and then Boileau (who in his *Art poétique* acknowledges his predecessor's contribution). This was their way of implicitly rejecting the loose prosody of the Renaissance poets who, in their view, neglected the art of "proper cadence." But what does proper cadence mean if not an endorsement of the effect of symmetry? Malherbe is a staunch defender of rich rhyme that repeats the same sound twice to give a solid binary basis for rhythm. Moreover, he enforces strict respect for the caesura, or in other words, he lengthens the sixth syllable to create an additional effect of symmetry: "Furieuse elle vole, et sur l'autel prochain / Prend le sacré couteau, le plonge dans son sein."[53] The caesura lengthens the word "vole" in the first line, as it lengthens "couteau" in the second. The actor can use that stress to increase the volume of his voice or vary the speed of his delivery, and the two syllables cannot be linked to the following one without upsetting the balanced structure of the line. In addition to the symmetry of the rhyme ("prochain" and "sein"), the caesura creates a further symmetry, which is rhythmic rather than phonic, to sustain the "proper cadence." By subdividing the line into two hemistiches, it creates an axis through the center of a series of alexandrines, the shape of which is kept regular by the rhyme. It is this that creates the solidity of the classical line, making it easy to remember and forcing mind and ear to restore meaning by reordering inversions, while respecting the symmetry. Just as in gardens, order is determined by a central vein. It is hardly surprising, therefore, that Racine's theater is more powerful in Versailles than elsewhere. As Voltaire said in *Le siècle de Louis XIV*, "The time when a duc de La Rochefoucauld, the author of the *Maximes*, would go to a play by Corneille after conversing with a Pascal or an Arnauld will remain unique in human history."[54]

He might have said the same thing of the memorable evening when the whole court was crowded among the trees and the vases of flowers to hear the music of Racine's verse float over the orangerie of Versailles. That performance was a feast for the mind and of the senses and is doubtless more durable than the 1662 Carrousel or the fêtes of the Ile Enchantée two years later; but cultural life at Versailles was made up of many different elements, and everything is important if you are seeking to restore to the bosquets something of the life they once had.[55] The account of the first day of the fêtes known as the Plaisirs de l'Ile Enchantée is attributed to Molière and in it, the orangerie is already linked with the world of the theater. About Versailles it says, "This is a château that could be called an enchanted palace, since refinements of art have so admirably complemented the efforts of nature to make it perfect. . . . Its symmetry, the richness of its furnishings, the beauty of its walkways, and infinite variety of its flowers and its orange trees make its surroundings worthy of this exceptional place."[56]

Such a place was entirely suited to suggest the palace of Alcina, the sorceress in Ariosto's *Orlando furioso*, which was very popular at court because it combined the romanesque with elements of the chevaleresque and the supernatural. This intellectual atmosphere owed more to the Moderns than to antiquity. Ariosto and the novels in the overrefined style of the salons were not considered worthy of inspiring sculptors, but they came into their own for anything ephemeral, such as fêtes, which brought to life the world of plumed knights, Moors, and feats of arms with its elaborate rhetoric and amorous intrigues. Louis XIV commissioned Lully to write an opera about the knight, *Amadis de Gaulle*, and it is not surprising that he chose *Orlando furioso* as the theme for one of his major fêtes. The Bassin d'Apollon was used to represent the place where the sorceresses held the bewitched knights prisoner: "In just a few days we festooned with gold a large circular area at the junction of four great allées between tall palisades with four porticoes, each thirty-five feet high and twenty-two across the opening. We also hung several paintings that showed the arms of His Majesty."[57]

These settings were designed by Carlo Vigarani, who created another spectacular surprise for the performance of *Georges Dandin* during the entertainment in honor of the peace of Aix-la-Chapelle in 1668. As Félibien noted, "[In the last act] the decor changes in an instant and it is hard to believe that so many real jets of water have disappeared, or that, instead of these cabinets and allées, all that can be seen in the theater are large rocks among trees, where several shepherds and shepherdesses are singing and playing all sorts of instruments."[58]

Versailles returned to the state of nature—that was the nightmare that the clever designer from Modena presented to delight the curiosity of the courtiers. He was also commissioned to design one of the most elaborate bosquets, the Théâtre d'Eau.

The combination of light and water in fêtes that took place after dark was even more spectacular; the elegant, geometric forms of fireworks, as well as water jets, opened into the sky. Fortunately, we have very accurate descriptions and engravings of these highly prized entertainments that have given us a clear picture of them. In 1668, after the performance of *Georges Dandin* and the ball that followed it, a firework display flooded the château and gardens with light. Félibien has described its dazzling effects.

> A thousand lights leaped up from the middle of the water, as if they had fiercely thrown off their fetters, bursting out all around the edges of the parterre. A thousand other lights, pouring from the mouths of lizards, crocodiles, frogs, and bronze animals on the edges of the fountains, seemed to rush to the assistance of the first ones; and sometimes individually, sometimes in groups, they plunged into the water under the statue of several serpents, apparently attacking it ferociously. As the combat raged with a deafening noise and an indescribable blaze of light, the two elements mingled together so completely that it was impossible to tell them apart. The spectacle lasted only long enough to fix in the mind a beautiful image of water and fire when they meet and make war.[59]

In this way, after the victory, the king made gunpowder heard and unleashed the tumult of war to celebrate the peace. This was understandable, bearing in mind that engineers like Belidor worked on both bombards and fireworks. But the same went for the gardens as for the interior of the château, where the Salon de la Paix faced the Salon de la Guerre. On some evenings when there was a fête, for example on the occasion celebrating the betrothal of the duke of Bourbon and Mlle. de Nantes on 23 July 1685, fire and water were united in the calm of the night when a sumptuous procession could be seen gliding down the Grand Canal. The marquis of Sourches described the spectacle as follows:

> Next His Majesty got into a carriage, and all the ladies followed in barouches that had been kept ready and waiting for them. He then boarded a ship on the canal and the whole glittering company sailed along it until ten o'clock at night in magnificent boats, which followed a yacht where, with drums and trumpets, the royal musicians sang and played tunes by Lully.
>
> At ten o'clock, the king disembarked below the Trianon: and, after they had gone up to the garden, they were served a munificent supper on four different tables set in the very cabinets that are at the end of the berceaux in the gardens. These were lit by a large number of crystal chandeliers. After supper, the king went back aboard and sailed to the end of the canal where the magnificent illuminations included fireworks. [At this point in the description, the marquis of Sourches interpolates a prosaic note: "These illuminations looked more expensive than they were, for they were normally made of earthenware pots filled with grease containing a candlewick, and large numbers of these were placed around in various patterns in places that were to be lit up. When they came to be lit, the effect was the most agreeable in the world. Other illuminations were done with lamps resembling ones that have oiled paper seals on which different figures were painted. Behind these figures were placed lighted earthenware pots; this made the figures glow brightly, and it was the most beautiful, magnificent form of illumination."] The whole château was similarly lit, as well as most of the beautiful parts of the garden: this made a magnificent and very pleasing sight from the boat in the canal where the king stayed until an hour after midnight.[60]

These splendid effects of water and light fueled the taste for the heroic and the grandiose on the Grand Canal and on the terrace at Trianon. Nevertheless, it was in the very same Trianon that Le Nôtre designed his last bosquet in an altogether different style, a style Roger de Piles would have called "champêtre" or "rustic."

The Secret World of Le Nôtre

We know that Hardouin-Mansart created the Bosquet de la Colonnade on the site of another bosquet designed by Le Nôtre, who had sought to create a very different effect, since it was called the Bosquet des Sources (Bosquet of the Springs). Le Nôtre had indeed used a small stream (still seen on what is known as the Du Bus plan of 1662) that flowed into the pièce d'eau that would later become the Bassin d'Apollon: he had created little "coulettes" [rivulets] of water among the trees to give the impression of a rural scene where the "genius loci" could be expressed. He was very different in that respect from Hardouin-Mansart. The latter was not particularly concerned with the natural character of the site and he often simplified—and made more severe—the lines of the bosquet by giving to architecture the priority that Le Nôtre accorded to the vegetal decoration. This was true of the Bosquet des Dômes and, above all, of the Montagne d'Eau.

Presumably Le Nôtre liked the bosquet he had designed, since he used the same idea again in Trianon, creating another Bosquet des Sources, which has also disappeared, probably because its natural, rustic style was fragile. But he has left a description of this second bosquet, which was in the corner made by the Galerie des Cotelle and the wing called Trianon-sous-Bois, and this fits with Tessin's testimony (Fig. 34). Here is what Le Nôtre had to say.

> The springs run along Galleries 10 and 11, and back along the apartment of Trianon-sous-Bois both lengthwise and across. In this space we have planted trees, standing apart from one another, enabling small canals to be created. These meander randomly, with falls in the empty spaces between the trees. Water jets are placed at irregular intervals. All the canals separate and come together as a result of the slope that the wood conceals. On each side of the wood are two rivulets that fall in small curtains with water jets twelve feet high. They end in two chasms and the water disappears into the ground. I cannot describe how lovely this place is. Its coolness allows the ladies to work, play games, and eat there, and it can be entered on the same level as the apartment. So from that apartment, you can go undercover to see the different beauties in the garden, the different allées, bosquets, woods in the whole garden, all undercover. I may say that, with the Tuileries, it is the only garden I know, and the most beautiful, where it is so easy to walk. I concede that others may have more beauty and grandeur, but this is the easiest.[61]

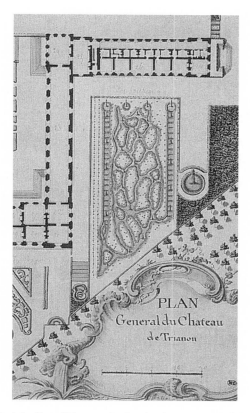

Fig. 34. *Plan général du Grand Trianon.* Jardin des Sources. Detail. Musée du Château de Versailles.

Le Nôtre's syntax is as charmingly unpredictable as his Jardin des Sources, but his description is eloquent. He has created a wooded water garden, cool and "easy," on the same level as the apartments. It may not have the "beauty and grandeur" of some others (to quote de Piles again: "left to herself, Nature knows what becomes her better than when art forces her hand"), but in the final analysis, he does find it the most beautiful. Thierry Mariage, who quotes this description in *L'univers de Le Nostre,* wonders whether "the aging Le Nôtre might actually have been won over by emerging naturalist tendencies."[62] The question is highly pertinent. One may recall in this context that Horace Walpole, one of the most subtle theoreticians of this movement also known as the "Landscape Movement," pointed out that the taste for a natural style partly originated in seventeenth-century courtly literature, notably in Honoré d'Urfé's novel *L'Astrée*.[63] That subtle and profound observation seems very well founded, remembering how popular the novel was throughout the century, particularly among the women to whom Le Nôtre refers in his description.

Everyone was familiar with *L'Astrée*. Its author was one of those provincial gentlemen who contrived to relate the perspective of their own part of the world to the amorous goings-on of shepherds and shepherdesses who oscillated, in an unfailingly genteel fashion, between joy and tears. This literary genre has always been popular when manners are becoming more refined, often thanks to the part played by women in high society. It suited the mood in France after the wars of religion, as it did in the court of Kyoto in the Heian period when the emperors were uniting the archipelago and making many links with the rich civilization of Tang Dynasty China. Honoré d'Urfé, a soldier who had stayed loyal to the Ligue, died fighting for the duke of Savoie. He steadfastly upheld a courtly image of ancient France—a "modern" theme—and the tender subtlety with which he portrayed love as the most important thing in life endeared him to women readers and influenced Mlle. de Scudéry, as well as the world of literary *préciosité* and psychological novels, such as *La princesse de Clèves*. At a time when Louis XIII and afterward Louis XIV prided themselves on having stamped out duels (as the Galerie des Glaces proves) and when the aristocracy sought to embody both military prowess and social sophistication, the emotional overtones of *L'Astrée* were so perfectly poised between the contradictory and the consistent that they inspired works of fiction that mirrored lived experience. Many aristocrats were particularly appreciative of this: they had to be at court to impress the king, but even so had not forgotten how attractive life in the provinces could be. It is difficult to describe the atmosphere of the bosquets without remembering d'Urfé's descriptions of the woods with the river Lignon meandering peacefully through them.

> Near the chamber was a hidden staircase leading down to a low gallery from which the garden could be reached across a drawbridge. In the garden were all possible treasures, whether fountains or parterres, allées or trees. Nothing that art could have contrived had been forgotten. Coming out of that place, one entered a large wood with different sorts of trees. There was a square of hazels, making such a charming maze that even though the elegantly winding paths became hopelessly confused and entangled, their shade was still delightful.[64]

More than a few of the ladies who enjoyed the Jardin des Sources must have remembered the literary associations that this emotional symbol of the forests of ancient France had for them. Perhaps when they reached the shade of the bosquets with a suitor (real or aspiring) they even said to themselves that at moments like that, etiquette no longer required them to follow paths dictated by geometry, as it did in the Parlement of Paris. Liberty prevailed, as did the caprices of nature, which had resumed its rightful sway. One might honestly wonder if, at the turn of century, the aging Le Nôtre was not promoting a new style, "elegant and winding" like the alleys described in *L'Astrée*. Looking back at d'Urfé, he was opening the way for the young Watteau.

PART IV

The Gardens of Versailles from Louis XV to the Present Day

History is a broad canvas.
　　—Victor Hugo

CHAPTER TWELVE

Louis XV

THE DEATH OF Louis XIV marked the end of an era. Everyone knew it, and there was good reason to believe that under the Regency, the splendor of Versailles would diminish. This fear seemed even more real since the crown prince, his great-grandson, was only five and the interregnum seemed likely to pose problems. The king's will was set aside by the Parlement; those closest to him were sidelined; the reins of power were in the hands of the Regent; Dubois was in charge of foreign affairs; and the future Louis XV had left for Paris to be educated. All these factors pointed to fundamental changes of political direction for the monarchy and in the corridors of power. Rumor had it, if Saint-Simon is to be believed, that Marly was to be destroyed.[1]

However, throughout the seven years of the Regency, the gardens of Versailles were as splendid as ever. The vegetation became even more luxuriant: in the bosquets "the atmosphere had already begun to feel more relaxed, softened by the less rigid nature of the arbors."[2] There was a feeling of opulence in the gardens, suggesting that they had reached maturity. A gardener always gambles on the future, and fifteen years after his death, Le Nôtre had clearly won his bet. Jules Hardouin-Mansart had also died, but his presence could still be felt in some of the bosquets, where he had left his mark both in Le Nôtre's lifetime and in the four years thereafter. In 1704 the Salle des Antiques, also known as the Galerie d'Eau, had become the Salle des Marronniers, the Salle du Conseil or Salle des Festins had changed into the Bosquet de l'Obélisque, and the Montagne d'Eau had become the Bosquet de l'Etoile. Almost invariably, Hardouin-Mansart had worked as an architect whose primary concerns were to simplify, reduce maintenance costs, and use stone rather than water.

The gardens had probably lost something of their mystery as a result, but gained instead a monumental elegance that was well suited to the softer outlines of the vegetation. That is how they appear in the Jacques Rigaud engravings, dating from the 1730s, and the pleasure that the young Louis XV took in the gardens when he returned to Versailles is easily understood.

He had been a child when he went away and, returning as an adolescent, he was delighted to rediscover childhood memories all around him. The lawyer Barbier has described the young king in his *Journal*, resting after a long day's hunting and embarrassing his (probably numerous) entourage by sitting on the floor of the Galerie des Glaces. He liked the gardens as much as the château. In an entry dated 4 September 1722, Barbier also noted,

> I saw our king yesterday at Versailles: he is hale and hearty, has a handsome, kindly face and a noble bearing. His appearance belies the gloomy, apathetic, stupid character that is attributed to him. I saw him walking in the gardens, his hat tucked under his arm, despite the cold wind. He is very handsome and will make a fine prince. I was very pleased to see him looking like this and I think that when he comes of age, he will impose his authority very successfully.[3]

Like his great-grandfather, whom he much admired, the young king enjoyed the outdoors and his marked love of hunting was soon apparent. The Grand Parc gave him ample opportunity to show his prowess by bagging impressive amounts of game. Moreover, he was a connoisseur of art and could not be indifferent to the beautiful setting his great forebear had provided for the exercise of royal power. He thus had three reasons for being committed to Versailles: his own pleasure, his obligations as king, and the simple fact that the upper echelons of the administration were firmly established in the château and the surrounding town. In less than a century, the village as it had been in the time of Louis XIII had become one of the ten most densely populated towns in the kingdom, and this rapid growth had been instrumental in establishing it as an administrative center.

So it was at Versailles that Louis XV's reign began, a reign that lasted fifty-nine years, almost as long as that of the Sun King himself. It came to an end at Versailles, too, but not before it had been troubled by the anticipatory rumblings of radical change. But Louis XV did not like radical change unless it suited him. He demolished the Appartement de Monseigneur, the Appartement des Bains, the Escalier des Ambassadeurs, and the Cabinet des Médailles because doing so allowed him to improve his daughters' accommodations; he commissioned Hubert de Cotte to build the Salon d'Hercule and Jacques Ange Gabriel the opera house, since he thought these essential to court life. While he did not change the places most closely linked to the memory of the king he admired, particularly the room where he had seen him die, he sought more and more frequently the calm intimacy of the small apartments he had built. Barbier commented, as someone well placed to know, that what was true for Versailles was true for all the royal residences: "In all the royal houses, there are small apartments for small, intimate suppers."[4] In his journal, the duke of Croÿ gives a brief but accurate description of these suppers. In December 1748 he notes, "The king sent a message by Maréchal d'Harcourt for me to come upstairs at 6 o'clock, and we had supper there in the small upper apartments, in the innermost part of the palace. There were only six of us with the king, who was charming in this small intimate setting, very easy in manner and even infinitely courteous."[5]

Louis XV was thirty-eight at the time, and it is unimaginable that his great-grandfather at the same age would have set aside the ritual of public life to dine with a select group of six people. From then on, the king's life was characterized by a taste for pleasures enjoyed in private, and not just the pleasures of the table; this brought out the sophisticated, secretive, darkly sybaritic side of his personality that would become more and more marked as he grew older. He did not have the same attentive concern, the same restless passion for the gardens that Louis XIV had had. He did not consider the natural mise-en-scène as essential for the exercise of sovereignty. He himself would not have initiated change in the architecture or atmosphere of a bosquet; he would not have altered the fountains and chivied everyone so that the new display could be enjoyed as soon as possible. The gardens were very costly. That he knew, and he was satisfied with doing only what was essential for maintenance in the Bosquet de l'Arc de Triomphe, the Bosquet des Trois Fontaines, and the Bosquet des Dômes. The subtle organization of space in the Théâtre d'Eau (now the Rond Vert) was allowed to disappear, and with it the fountains. However, the Bassin de Neptune was completed by the addition of sculpture groups that are still there: Lambert Sigisbert Adam's *Triomphe de Neptune*, Jean-Baptiste Lemoine's *Océan,* and Edme Bouchardon's *Protée.*

Even if he initiated few new developments in the gardens of the Petit Parc, Louis XV liked to walk there, and he used them to host fêtes. One of the most spectacular was held shortly before his death to celebrate the wedding of

Marie-Antoinette and the Dauphin. The duke of Croÿ, who was an attentive observer, has left a description of it whose accuracy is confirmed by an engraving done by Moreau the Younger in the same year as the marriage.

> In the gardens all the bosquets were decorated with special structures and hung with Chinese lanterns. A really superb sight was the series of illuminations from the head of the canal: a vast theater of triumphal arches, and girandoles and chandeliers intertwined. This, with the golden yews on the canal and the water covered with lit-up gondolas, created the best possible effect.

The organs, popular spectacles, and the illuminations in this vast garden paled into insignificance beside the fireworks. I took particular note of the twelfth and final display, a bouquet in the center of the sloping Tapis Vert. It consisted of 24,000 rockets, roads, and grenades, 25 large bombs, their rope mortars alone costing 300 livres, and a vast quantity of firecrackers, bullets, and sticks of bombs, creating a barrage of fire. The bombs, singly or linked together, being the most powerful, were designed to produce the most dramatic results, and since everything sloped down toward the canal, there was no risk to the château.[6]

Even though fêtes such as these were lavish, Louis XV did not seek the same prestige from them as had Louis XIV. He grasped the fact that they were politically useful, but he did not rejoice in it. He preferred opulence to formal splendor. He always acted as though he would never forget La Bruyère's maxim: "The only things a king cannot have are the sweet pleasures of a private life." These pleasures, which the Sun King had sought at Marly, Louis XV enjoyed every day in his small apartments and in the château Gabriel built for him at Trianon.

Even in the time of Louis XIV, Trianon had seemed the most intimate part of the great Versailles estate: it was surrounded by the flowers and orange trees opposite the main branch of the Grand Canal, which reflected toward the château the brilliance and warmth of the meridian sun. From everywhere in the château itself there were views across the parterres, which could be easily reached over level ground. But Louis XV preferred something more convenient and compact than this marble palace with its long wings. He worked with Gabriel to produce a palace at Trianon to suit his tastes, and the result proved most unusual. In this project, his preference for intimacy, convenience, and subtle refinement was evident, but there was also an undeniably fascinating note of rustic elegance and scientific curiosity.

He took his inspiration for this from the menagerie, built by Louis XIV at the north end of the horizontal branch of the Grand Canal, building opposite each another, as it were, a model farm and a botanic garden with a greenhouse incorporating all the most modern features. The king's intention was not to dazzle visitors with animals that had been brought from distant lands by the French ships that were constantly roving the seas; his motives were still political but of a different sort: he wanted to display and increase the rich natural resources of the country. As if to symbolize this, the new development was sited away from the great trapezoidal arrangement that Louis XIV and Le Nôtre had devised to make the marble Trianon a dependency of the château. In fact, you can see that the approach is a long, straight diagonal line, the Avenue de Trianon, which starts at the Bassin de Neptune, corresponding to the diagonal line from the foot of the Cent Marches to the Grille des Filles d'Honneur. Seen from the château, these two diagonal lines appear symmetrical, drawing the eye to the ends of the horizontal branch of the Grand Canal, where the asymmetry is offset by the marble Trianon.

Louis XV elected to situate his new development on the edge of Louis XIV's great ground plan and along a northeast/southwest axis, thereby ensuring its geographical independence: he tucked it into the Grand Parc in the same way that he tucked his small apartments into the main château, making every effort to ensure that the name of Petit Trianon would be appropriate. This provides us with a yardstick to measure the difference between the two reigns: the surface area of this Trianon was less than half that of Louis XIV's palace or Marly (Fig. 35). That said, there was nothing petty about a project in which were associated Madame de Pompadour, the king's official mistress since 1745, Gabriel, and the botanist Bernard de Jussieu. The building and gardens together covered approximately five acres, roughly one-third of which was given over to pleasure gardens, including the Pavillon (1748), the château (1762–68), and the Salon Frais (1751–53, restored 1983–84), which has survived. Only a few traces of the rest remain. The house where the gardener, Claude Richard, lived can still be seen, but the botanic garden has completely disappeared. It was demolished at the same time as the model farm, when Marie-Antoinette and Richard Mique put the site to a different use.

Madame de Pompadour died before the château was finished, but her influence is apparent in the intellectual atmosphere embodied by the Petit Trianon. Its "artistic elegance and life"[7] bears the stamp of an outstanding woman's personality. Fifteen years younger than the king, her intellectual capacities allowed her to mix with some of the Paris intelligentsia as well as artists

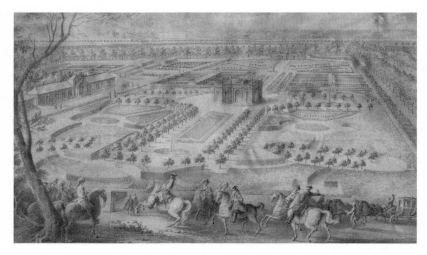

Fig. 35. Jacques André Portail, *Louis XV en vue des jardins de Trianon, de la ménagerie et des basses cours, du Pavillon français et du Portique de treillage*, ca. 1750. Musée du Château de Versailles. The château and the Salon Frais are still in progress. The domain strongly resembles a model farm.

(Bouchardon and Carle Van Loo), men of letters (Marmontel; Voltaire, whose play *Tancrède* is dedicated to her; Crébillon and Duclos), and philosophes, such as Helvétius, Diderot, and Quesnay, an economist of great reputation who was also her personal physician. As a result, she was familiar with what was going on in the world of learning and the arts, and we know, from what the king read, that he shared many of her interests. All this was significant in the choices Louis XV made and in the general tone of what went on in this domain. Here he could show that he was a man of his time, open to contemporary scientific trends in Europe.

Like Louis XIV, he was led by his personal preferences and political interest to keep track of these trends. But geometry and optics were no longer seen as the leading scientific disciplines whose infallible methodology reigned supreme over all the other fields of investigation. Newton and his followers called into question the geometers' method, which proved reductive since it did not accord sufficiently well with the meticulous observation of facts. They relied on life sciences, they kept meticulous records of their observations, and, using these records, which they called histories, they framed laws tentatively by the inductive method.

The time had come when, as Christiaan Huygens had said, the life sciences would impose new methods of investigation, ones that would not claim to dictate laws of nature instead of observing facts.[8] In that sense, La Quintinie had been ahead of his time when he made fun of the geometers who compared fruit-tree grafts to the adjutage of fountains.[9] In a naive and uncritical way, he forecast the changes that appeared shortly after his death. The eighteenth century was the century of Linnaeus, founder of modern botany, and of Buffon, whose *Histoire naturelle* is a vast overview of the world of animals and plants. Diderot, who, like Buffon, had access to Madame de Pompadour, stated that an object as defined by a geometer had no more reality than the conventions of card playing; his figures were rigid abstractions, and the set of rules by which he worked undermined his efforts to account for the operations of nature. He was a system builder, not a scientific observer.

Physiology, medicine, and the experimental study of living organisms had come into their own. This explains why the works of Locke, a philosopher who initially trained in medicine, were so successful. Quesnay was also a doctor, and his economic theories were metaphors drawn from his medical practice. He compared the circulation of wealth to the circulation of the blood and the nation with a living organism, and he gave substance to the idea that cultivation of the land by the "productive class" was the lifeblood that coursed through the other social classes. It was in Versailles that his famous *Tableau économique* was printed. It provided a flow chart of the economic life of the kingdom, explaining (with supporting statistics) the prime importance of agriculture. With that in mind, the Petit Trianon model estate could be interpreted as an interesting attempt to establish a link between the king and the peasants producing the wealth (in other words, the vast majority of the population), a relationship based in a scientific concept of economic life.

This hypothesis seems all the more persuasive in that the buildings in the farm and garden attached to the Petit Trianon clearly owed something to the Palladian style, which was then the height of fashion among the great English landowners. Undoubtedly, as Jean-Marie Pérouse de Montclos has demonstrated, the architecture of the Petit Trianon was inspired by the Hardouin-Mansart wing of Trianon-sous-Bois. But in the "Petit Château" and the Pavillon, Gabriel was also influenced by the famous Palladian "cube," based on the Villa Rotonda and used in England very often, with varying degrees of success at Chiswick, as well as Stourhead and Marble Hill. Gabriel's compromise allowed the development of a new style, opening up on all sides and providing comfortable, well-lit apartments. It was also a reminder that Palladio had gone back to classical roots by working in the great estates where the villa controlled agricultural production in the manner established by Roman agriculturalists. It was probably for all these reasons that the king, according to d'Argenson, was never so happy as "with plans and drawings on the table" and would boast about the style of the Pavillon to his visitors, saying that buildings should be erected "in that style."[10]

The pleasure garden that extended between the new château and the Grand Trianon was an original creation that marked the apparition of what may be called the rocaille style. It could also be called rococo, were it not for the fact that rococo is a term coined by the Romantics to make fun of their predecessors. This problem of terminology has its importance, the rocaille being the third stage of the regular style, which proceeded from the baroque as the baroque had proceeded from the Renaissance style.

The new garden was created around a central axis but the long perspective so dear to Le Nôtre was abandoned: a music pavilion interrupted it, creating a visual center radiating in four different directions; the alleys lost the proportions required by the long perspective (they became wider and their palisades were reduced in height); and everything was done to loosen the visual constraints of the baroque and to give the gardens a convivial, relaxed atmosphere where curves took the place of the rigid long lines so much in favor before. This preference for curves explains why the term "rocaille" came into existence in the eighteenth century, for rocaille ornaments, which had existed before, had always made use of rocks and shells to evoke the secret underground life of the earth, and the shells themselves were the very image of the curving shapes of the new style. At this point, it may be of interest to note that the rocaille held its own against the picturesque, which was then developing in England. In France it prospered until the 1770s, and its spread over Europe gave birth to dozens of gardens wrongly characterized as "in the style of Le Nôtre."

It is not surprising then that in his article "Jardin" for the *Encyclopédie*, de Jaucourt attacks the "absurd and mediocre" fashion for "winding allées" and deplores the ubiquitous "earthenware vases, Chinese figurines, bambochades,[11] and crudely executed sculptures in a similar vein." In his view, it was not because of their form that English gardens were beautiful but because of "the enchanting green of their lawns and *boulingrins*, the scent and sight of the rich variety of flowers, and the beneficent charms of nature, which are carefully but never elaborately adorned." The position taken in the *Encyclopédie* remained the same in the *Supplément,* published in 1775, in which the article "Jardin" still uses all the standard terminology: bosquets; palisades; pattes d'oie; pièces de broderie; salles vertes, and so forth.

Thus, Louis XV can be seen as an agriculturalist whose views were similar to those of de Jaucourt. He had a lively and genuine curiosity about scientific matters; botany captured his attention because significant progress was being made in that field—for example, the king corresponded with Linnaeus—and because it could have a direct impact on the way of life of the people.[12] Responsibility for organizing his garden was given to Bernard de Jussieu, who was one of the founders of a dynasty whose name remains associated with the development of botany from the early eighteenth to the mid-nineteenth century. Antoine, the eldest of the three Jussieu brothers, was born in 1686 and, like Guy de La Brosse, Louis XIII's doctor, and Fagon, one of Louis XIV's doctors, was both a doctor of medicine and professor in the Jardin Royal, which is now the Jardin des Plantes. The youngest, Joseph, born in 1704, took part in La Pérouse's expedition and was one of the first to explore South America. Bernard de Jussieu, in contrast, never left Europe. He was born in 1699 and followed Sébastien Vaillant as demonstrator in the Jardin du Roi. It was in that capacity that he was responsible for training his nephew, Antoine Laurent de Jussieu, the most celebrated botanist of the family, who made his name for his work on the classification of plants, *Genera plantarum* (1788), in which, although still influenced by Linnaeus, he proposed a more natural method of species classification. On that basis, Jean-Marc Drouin could claim that "the creation of the 'natural method' was essentially the work of the French botanists Bernard de Jussieu, Michel Adanson, and above all Antoine Laurent de Jussieu."[13]

Louis XV's advisor was, thus, one of the founders of a taxonomy based on the empirical observation of the plant world. Since we know from other sources that he had contacts with the world of medicine and pharmaceutical chemistry through his family network, we can infer that the gardens of Versailles were just as closely linked to scientific research in the eighteenth century as in the seventeenth century. Unfortunately, the precise nature of Bernard de Jussieu's role is difficult to establish, since he published nothing on his method, but he helped train Claude Richard, who lived on the spot and oversaw the planting of exotic trees, some of which still survive today.

CHAPTER THIRTEEN

Louis XVI and Marie-Antoinette

WHEN LOUIS XV died, ten years after Madame de Pompadour, Louis XVI and Marie-Antoinette took the future of the royal gardens in hand. There were considerable changes. The king took the radical steps that were needed and initiated the major replanting that his predecessor had never wanted to undertake. Many trees, already a hundred years old, were known to be vulnerable to storms; they had to be cut down and replaced. Then a difficult choice about the style of the replanting had to be made: in the end it was decided to preserve the form that the gardens had been given by Le Nôtre, Louis XIV, and Hardouin-Mansart. This was a wise decision, since replanting them in the increasingly fashionable English or Anglo-Chinese style would have meant breaking their organic link with the west front of the château and completely changing their structure and decoration.

The count of Angiviller, director of the Bâtiments du Roi, spoke at this time of "keeping the original layout" as a tribute to "the genius of the renowned Le Nôtre." Jean-Marie Morel, one of the century's best theoreticians, justified this decision in his *Théorie des jardins*, published in 1776; he suggested that since the gardens of Versailles were public in that they belonged to a royal residence, they should be "classified as symmetrical." The arguments that he put forward at this juncture were reiterated by Gabriel Thouin during the Romantic period.[1]

Two paintings by Hubert Robert are evidence of this major project. Some idea of the upheaval it caused in the gardens of the Sun King can be gleaned from the sight of the great trees cut down and the pit sawyers at work among the statues, with the château overlooking the whole scene as if it had sought

Fig. 36. Hubert Robert, *View of the Tapis Vert in 1775*. Musée du Château de Versailles.

refuge in its own history. Children play on a seesaw improvised from freshly sawn planks a few feet from the king, who has come to view the proceedings with the count of Angiviller. In these astonishing scenes, two centuries are caught side by side. In one, we see a moment of everyday life which, as we know, can change to suit any situation; in the other, we witness the disintegration of this great ideal landscape, which collapses as the trees come down. The stone of the buildings and the marble of the statues are left bereft, as the vegetation that sheltered them is destroyed. Even though this moment of helpless confusion heralds a new dawn, these two pictures are a sort of presentiment, prefiguring the great upheavals of the coming Revolution (Fig. 36).

From then on, the gardens were assured of a new lease on life, but there were nonetheless some concessions to contemporary taste. The labyrinth was demolished; this attractive maze disappeared and with it all the wit of Benserade and the fountains spouting from the beaks of his gossipy birds. It was replaced by the Bosquet de la Reine, a creation in the rocaille style that by then had won scientific support to sustain its claims to eminence. Low palisades and wide alleys, it was said, allowed for a better circulation of air, a sure way of keeping it free from "miasms."[2] Hubert Robert was given the task of redecorating the Bains d'Apollon and relocating the famous sculpture groups in the Grotte de Thétys, which had been destroyed almost a hundred years earlier.

These sculptures—*Les chevaux d'Apollon* by Guérin and the Marsy brothers, *Apollon servi par les nymphes* by Girardon and Regnaudin—which had been placed under canopies in the Bosquet des Dômes, seemed to be waiting for another grotto to house them. But there were grottoes and grottoes. For contemporaries of Colbert and the Perrault brothers, the term "grotto" still largely meant what it had in the Renaissance. It was a structure intended to evoke life underground and the walls were, therefore, decorated with congelations and rocaille. They sometimes contained machines that used the force of the water jets to create unusual effects such as whistling birds or automata playing out scenes from mythology. In his book *La raison des forces mouvantes,* Salomon de Caus has given some interesting illustrations of these wonders, which had been devised initially by mechanics from Alexandria, reproduced by the caliphs in Baghdad, and improved by Renaissance engineers. Louis XIV had been attracted to these curiosities. On one occasion, when he was staying in Saint-Germain, he had miniature grottoes, similar to the ones on the terraces of the great gardens nearby, built in the apartments of his favorites, Mlle. de La Vallière and Madame de Montespan, which adjoined his own. However, Louis XVI wearied of these wonders from another era and excluded automata from the grotto at Versailles. By contrast, he increased the number of water features: the cascades, bubbling fountains, jets, and curtains of water were a source of wonder admired by many visitors.

With the arrival of Hubert Robert, things changed once again. The fountains and the rocaille now seemed outmoded. A grotto had to be just that—a hole in the rock, a glimpse of the primitive world—and not a structure designed to display spectacular effects of water. The precious sculpture groups of the Bains d'Apollon were placed in the crevices of a sort of cliff, from which water seems to flow like a mountain spring. Hubert Robert was undoubtedly passionate about his work. Three drawings, now in the French national archives, show how he reworked the plans to create a much more irregular effect,[3] and he painted the *Bosquet des Bains d'Apollon* in 1803 to show the decoration as he had originally planned it when it was planted twenty years earlier (Fig. 37).

There is no doubt that Hubert Robert carried out the task given to him by d'Angiviller of "finding a way to change the location and appearance of the Bains d'Apollon so that they would be more picturesque as such beautiful artistic creations deserve to be."[4] The use of the word "picturesque" is noteworthy: a recent addition to the gardening world, it is used here in the Italian sense "in the manner of painters" and, by implication, not in the manner of

Fig. 37. Hubert Robert, *Bosquet des Bains d'Apollon*, 1803. Photograph by Jean-Baptiste Leroux. The Bains d'Apollon are shown as Robert meant them to be with full flowing waters. Cascades gush forth from mysterious grottoes in which remains of some primitive architecture can dimly be seen. It is reminiscent of Piranesi.

architects. The question is whether the statues gained from this change in their setting. Pierre Francastel says that much has been lost since they can now only be seen "from too far away and at too low down."[5] The prince of Ligne, in his *Coup d'oeil sur Beloeil et sur une grande partie des jardins d'Europe* (A glimpse of Beloeil and many European gardens), is even more critical: "I hope allowances will be made for the rock where the Bains d'Apollon are sited. I would find it magnificent in Fontainebleau or, perhaps, further away from the château.

Do not let paintings deceive you. It has the potential to be a splendid part of the garden. But the even the most beautiful of the horses and the finest marble figures look like pieces of bisqueware alongside the massive stone outcrops where they have been placed."[6] Today's visitors are inclined to share this feeling. The grotto, although beautiful, is ill suited to its statues, which are very different in style. The lovingly polished forms and even the poses of Apollo, his nymphs, and horses do not fit easily with this wild decor, which seems too rustic and too vast a setting for the treasures placed within it. Hubert Robert was more successful at the Petit Trianon because he was working with Richard Mique, Claude and Antoine Richard, and the queen in an atmosphere more conducive to the picturesque creations he liked so much.

Marie-Antoinette immediately felt at home in the Petit Trianon. Louis XVI had given it to her and she immediately allowed her many desires free rein. Her age had something to do with her liking for pleasure, since she was only eighteen when she became queen of France; but temperamentally, too, she was given to what her mother, the Empress Maria Theresa, called "a woeful extravagance in never applying herself."[7] Unfortunately this was true as far as botany was concerned: she redesigned Louis XV's estate and removed all the scientific constructions. Carried away by her discovery of the Anglo-Chinese style, the young queen asked Antoine Richard, the curator of the botanic garden, to come up with plans to reshape the garden in the latest fashion. The plans did not meet with her approval; the proposals submitted by the count of Caraman, who had created his own garden in his Paris townhouse, were quickly accepted.

The large greenhouse was demolished to make space for an étang. The work was supervised by Antoine Richard, who was still working there because of his exceptional knowledge of exotic plants, and by Richard Mique and Hubert Robert, who together landscaped the terrain around the étang in a rustic style: a rock; a grotto; a Temple d'Amour; an octagonal belvedere; a Montagne de l'Escargot; and a Pont des Rochers. A Chinese *jeu de bagues* was soon added and, from 1783, the different houses in the Hameau de la Reine were built, with a dairy, a mill, a barn, and little potagers. From a tower, called the Tour de la Pêcherie, there was a view right around this little village. The entire thing still has a charming elegance that impresses everyone who sees it, and visitors generally know enough about French history to be moved by the contrast between the utopian magic of this village and the fate of a young woman who fell rapidly from the highest position in the realm to misfortune and execution.

How did Marie-Antoinette come to be so passionately devoted to the creation of a hamlet? It seems probable that as soon as she arrived she was entranced by the heady intellectual atmosphere she found in France. When Louis XVI came to the throne, France was taking its revenge on Britain for the humiliating defeats of the Seven Years' War. The French were helping the emerging country of America gain its independence and were claiming to be the liberators of the insurgents. A climate of youth and generosity prevailed. In the upper echelons of politics, major changes brought Turgot to the Ministry of Justice and later the Treasury. The experiment was short-lived, but intellectually the time was ripe for the ideas of this brilliant man and they stirred up hopes that Necker would later turn to account.

Turgot was a chemist, linguist, and economist. In 1748 he had coined a neologism Jean-Jacques Rousseau used in his *Discours sur l'origine de l'inégalité.* Drawing on a property of gas, its expansibility, he had explained that men could be distinguished from animals insofar as they always sought to improve their conditions of life; they had, he said, an instinct for "perfectibility" that drove them to change the world, making it a better place for themselves. Building on this idea, Rousseau had traced the slow evolution of humanity over "multitudinous centuries," maintaining that since men lived under laws made by the rich and powerful, all their efforts were turned against themselves when they sought to improve laws that had been corrupted from the first. Only a beneficent and divine lawgiver could conceive of just laws, which would allow the instinct for perfectibility to work positively toward universal happiness.

The theories of the physiocrats were compatible with Rousseau's ideas insofar as they considered peasant farmers as a wealth-creating class but one without a political voice. Louis XV had perhaps shared the view held by certain philosophes that enlightened despotism could give the peasants their place, revolutionizing the economy. However, the young princess, who had little taste for learning, did not think so deeply: Marie-Antoinette probably was carried away by the popular enthusiasm for Rousseauist ideas, seeing them as a good opportunity to consolidate her position at court and challenge the formal manners with which she was ill at ease.

Perhaps she was also susceptible to the rhetorical outpourings of a movement that appealed to the heart as a way to win the mind. Europe's center of gravity was shifting eastward, and German-speaking civilization welcomed Rousseau's ideas because of his powerful emotional appeal and his love of music. France was discovering Gluck; Rousseau was Swiss; and Mique and Hubert Robert came from eastern France. Austria was well-known to botanists, because plants coming from the Middle East passed through Vienna, and

Marie-Antoinette, who had acquired her love of gardens in the town of her birth, sometimes called her hamlet Le Petit-Vienne.

Richard Mique had in the course of his career spent time in Lorraine.[8] He had been director-general of the Bâtiments du Roi of Poland. It was through Marie Leczinska that he came to Paris, where he settled in 1766, becoming chief architect to Louis XVI and Marie-Antoinette's contrôleur général des Bâtiments. Hubert Robert had been presented to the young royal couple in 1774 by the count of Angiviller, who had been partly responsible for the young prince's education, and the latter had just appointed him director of his Bâtiments: it was in this capacity that he had arranged for the king to meet the painter just before Versailles was replanted. Following the success of his two "Views," Robert was commissioned to undertake the alterations to the Bosquet des Bains d'Apollon. Thanks to Choiseul, who had employed members of his family, Robert's godparents held senior positions in the service of François de Lorraine and the latter had married Marie-Antoinette's mother, the Archduchess Maria Theresa.[9] There was an empathy among Marie-Antoinette, Mique, and Hubert Robert that resulted from the eastward shift in the focus of the Enlightenment.[10] Rousseau himself had close ties to prominent pietist currents of opinion in Germany, and when Goethe wrote his *Elective Affinities*, he drew on his many memories of Wörlitz, a landscape garden, in which important parts, such as the Neumark Garten, the Rousseau Island, the Elysium Garden, and the Damen-Platz, were constructed at the same time Marie-Antoinette was having her Hameau built (Fig. 38).

In addition, the concept of the perfectibility of the human species generated a whole array of images with a poetic quality that inspired artists. If mankind was invited to contemplate human history down "multitudinous centuries," the power exercised on the imagination by ruins was intensified, as was, perhaps even more markedly, the appeal of primitive huts and caves where our earliest ancestors had lived in the misery, but also the innocence, that went with poverty. Rocks, with their "indestructible, time-wearying mass," as the abbé Delille put it, anchored a garden poetically within time. This poetry found expression in the rustic caves, the mossy bridges, and the thatched roof, which were generally associated with mores as yet uncorrupted by civilization. That was the spirit in which Marie-Antoinette and her friends created a village setting so that the queen could live in the country closer to nature. According to Madame de Campan, "a dress of white percale, a gauze scarf, and a straw hat were the only ornaments of princesses. . . . The queen delighted in visiting the workshops of the village, watching the cows being milked and fishing in the lake."[11]

Fig. 38. Louis Nicolas de Lespinasse, *Vue du Temple de l'Amour à Trianon*, ca. 1780. Musée du Château de Versailles. Bouchardon's statue is hardly visible but the Château du Petit Trianon appears clearly on the left. Close to it is the Chinese roof of Marie-Antoinette's Jeu de Bagues. Further to the right, the Belvédère can be seen on a small elevation of ground.

This project and the habits that went with it probably did not meet with universal approbation. The duke of Croÿ recounts his first visit to Trianon with an irony that speaks louder than words.

> Richard and his son took me and I thought I was dreaming or had gone mad when I saw in the place where the great hothouse, the richest and most scientifically advanced in Europe, had stood, some quite high mountains, a great rock, and a stream. Never had a few acres of land changed so much and cost so dear. The queen was completing the construction of a large English garden in the grandest style, with great beauties, despite a mixture of Greek and Chinese styles which left me uneasy. Apart from that, the high mountain, fountains, the superb rotunda, the Palais de l'Amour, some of the finest Greek architecture, and turfed areas are at their very best. The bridges, the rocks, and some of the features seemed to me unsuccessful. The style was a hybrid that lovers of English gardens will have difficulty in accepting.[12]

He added to this criticism of the mixed English and Chinese style an interesting note on alpine botany that was at that time much appreciated, in part because of Rousseau and Haller.

> But what is superb is that Monsieur Richard, in accordance with his taste and talent, planted all sorts of rare species of tall tree; and since at that time I was reading with great interest the admirable Monsieur Besson's notebook on the Alps, which he describes from a naturalist's point of view, Monsieur Richard, who has made the journey specially, showed me growing there naturally all the trees and shrubs as they appear in stages in the Alps right up to the tree line. Pines are predominant, and magnificent larches, then as you climb, tall firs, then stunted firs with small leaves, then what Monsieur Besson and the local people call alder, though it is quite another species, albeit somewhat similar. Finally there is a small rose tree and a small climbing alpine juniper. With the trees that look like alders, these are the last. [13]

The Hameau de la Reine is so highly thought of today that it is tempting to complete the duke of Croÿ's description with another from one of Marie-Antoinette's pages, the count of Hezecques, who wrote his *Mémoires* after the Revolution and has given a more complete picture of the place.

> Opposite the château was a lawn and at the end of it a rock, shaded by pines, thujas, splendid larches, and a rustic bridge of the sort found in the Swiss mountains or the Valais cliffs. This wild, rustic perspective made the view from the third façade of the château even more charming, with the Temple de l'Amour discernible among the flowers and laurels. A magnificent Bouchardon sculpture represented the god of love in all his splendid adolescent beauty, cutting from a piece of wood the bow he uses to pierce human hearts. . . .
>   At the foot of a small valley, thickly shaded by trees, rose a massive, rustic outcrop of rock where the waters of a stream swirled and vanished. This stream twisted and turned a thousand ways in a flower-studded meadow and following its course as it wound about, you reached the entrance of a grotto, which was so dark that it took some time for your eyes, initially dazzled by the brightness, to see the objects within. This grotto was moss-lined and cooled by a stream, which ran through it. A bed, also of moss, looked invitingly restful. But, whether by chance or by

Fig. 39. The interior of the queen's grotto seen from the entrance. Claude-Louis Châtelet, *Vues et plans du Petit Trianon at Versailles*. Biblioteca Estense, Modena. Published by P. Arrizoli-Clementel, Paris, 1998. By permission of the Ministero per i Beni e le Attività Culturali.

the architect's design, through a crack above the bed could be seen the whole meadow and everyone who might have wanted to find this mysterious hiding place, while a dark staircase leading to the top of the rock in a thicket could hide from importunate eyes what you wanted to keep secret [Fig. 39]. . . . At the end of the Trianon garden, a whole host of cottages bordered the stream. From the outside, they looked totally rustic, but their interiors were elegant and sometimes even exquisite. In the middle of this hamlet stood a tall tower, known as the Tour de Marlborough, which overlooked the surroundings. Its outside staircase, decorated with wallflowers and geraniums, created the effect of an aerial parterre. One of the cottages contained the dairy, and the cream in porcelain bowls on white marble tables was kept cool by the stream, which changed the nature of the room. Nearby was the real farm, where the queen kept a magnificent herd of Swiss cows, which grazed in the surrounding meadows.

Near the château a large Chinese pavilion, its azure and gold brilliantly reflecting the sun's rays, enclosed a jeu de bagues. Three Chinese figures seemed to activate the machine, though it was actually moved by servants out of sight in an underground passage.[14]

This passage illustrates all the fragility of Marie-Antoinette's world as well as the charm of places which, once seen, are never to be forgotten. That fragility can be explained by some blatant contradictions: the porcelain bowls and marble tables of the dairy strike a discordant note beside the thatched roofs and seem to be the perfect illustration of Rousseau's theories on luxury and the contrast he denounced in the *Contrat social* between cottages and palaces;[15] the innocent way of life, which characterizes the place (or is said to), cannot fit in with the dangerous games played by the queen when she had an opening made in the grotto wall to watch for undesired visitors, a veritable Pandora's box for every kind of gossip; praise for the laborers in the fields and the kitchen gardens is difficult to reconcile with the floral decoration of an "aerial parterre"; and what is one to make of a jeu de bagues operated by servants hidden underground engaged entertaining the so-called shepherdess thankfully escaping the simple country ways of the farm?

Some critics are irritated by the artificial pastoral setting of the Hameau de la Reine, and others make fun of the Chinese jeu de bagues, but garden history is never submitted to the whims of one person, however powerful or wealthy. In her hamlet, Marie-Antoinette was assisted by a group of brilliant designers who developed a French version of the picturesque style. The taste for chinoiserie, by encouraging a break with symmetry and its constraints, helped develop new aesthetic categories, such as the frightening and the eerie. During the 1770s, a plethora of splendid works endorsed the new style. These appeared almost on an annual basis: Duchesne's *Sur la formation des jardins* (1775); Morel's *Théorie des jardins* (1776); Girardin's *De la composition des paysages* (1777); Hirschfeld's *La théorie de l'art des jardins* (1779–85); and Watelet's *Essai sur les jardins* (1774). During the same period, the marquis of Girardin was working on the gardens of Ermenonville, as was the marquis of Laborde at Méréville. Monsieur de Monville was creating the Désert de Retz and Carmontelle was designing the Parc Monceau, while Bélanger, after traveling in England, created the Folie Saint-James in Neuilly (1778) as soon as he returned. In Versailles itself, behind the Potager du Roi, Chalgrin designed a wonderful miniature landscape garden, complete with grotto, belvedere, and Chinese bridges, for Madame de Balbi, the mistress of Louis XVI's brother, the count of Provence.[16]

Roger de Piles, writing about what he called "heroic landscapes," described them as enchanting. Rustic landscapes seemed enchanting at that

Fig. 40. Hubert Robert, *Night Fête Given by the Queen at Trianon*, in honor of the count of Nord's visit, 6 June 1782. Musée des Beaux-Arts, Quimper.

time because the dreams of human perfectibility, encompassing all of humanity, gave them the power to regenerate the people inhabiting them. Enchantment reigned by night as well as by day, as is clear from an account of the nocturnal fête in honor of Marie-Antoinette's brother, Emperor Joseph II: "A new kind of fête was held in the Petit Trianon; the art with which the garden had been lit, rather than illuminated, created a charming effect: earthenware pots, hidden by painted green planks, lit all the banks of shrubs and flowers, bringing out the different shades in the most delightful and varied ways; hundreds of pieces of wood burning in the ditch behind the Temple de l'Amour created a great glow that made it the brightest spot in the garden" (Fig. 40).[17] Before the beneficial effect of these landscapes could be enjoyed, you had to learn to appreciate them visually. As Carmontelle put it,

> We have masters to teach us the art of speaking, singing, and dancing, etc., but it never occurs to us that we should be taught to see. How many pleasures does the ignorance of that knowledge keep from us!

Fig. 41. Claude-Louis Châtelet, *Vue générale du Hameau en amont de l'Etang* (General view of the Hameau seen from above the pond). Plate 29 in *Vues et plans du Petit-Trianon at Versailles*, Biblioteca Estense, Modena. Published by P. Arrizoli-Clementel, Paris, 1998. By permission of the Ministero per i Beni e le Attività Culturali.

> With painters we can travel through nature in their company. They will stop us at every turn so that we can observe its beauties. They bring light to everything we see; they show us the gradations of linear and aerial perspective; they reveal space; they introduce us to the range of different tones and colors and bring out their relationships and harmony.[18]

It was to allow the totality of the landscape to be appreciated that towers were built in various places: a ruined column in the Désert de Retz, the Tour Gabrielle in Ermenonville, the Colonne Trajan in Méréville, and, of course, the Tour de Marlborough, known also as the Tour de la Pêcherie, in the Petit Trianon. This "expansibility" of visual awareness, to borrow Turgot's term, was perhaps just an illusion, but it opened the way to the modern idea of landscape (Fig. 41).

CHAPTER FOURTEEN

From the Ancien Régime to the Present Day

WHEN LOUIS XVI and Marie-Antoinette left the château of Versailles on 6 October 1789, everything pointed to sudden and rapid change. The king had perhaps failed to grasp the political importance of the storming of the Bastille, but he had nonetheless learned a great deal during the summer months, and knowing that his return to Paris would be fatal to the political edifice constructed by Louis XIV, he said to M. de La Tour du Pin as he left, "I leave you in charge here. Try to save my poor Versailles for me." Even so, he was still popular, and the Fête de la Fédération served as a kind of royal investiture, this time of the first constitutional monarch. However, the uneasy compromise that had been established after the flight to Varennes was clearly threatened by impending foreign wars, the flight of the royal family, and the radicalization of the political struggles. The day of 10 August 1792 endangered the very existence of the monarchy, and the reverberations immediately reached Versailles.

In September 1792, a temporary Commission for the Arts was set up by the Legislative Assembly after the king had been removed. This commission decided that the collection of works of art at Versailles should be divided into several lots. The objets d'art, antiques, and gems would go to the museum, that is, the Louvre; the books and medals to the Bibliothèque nationale; the clocks and scientific instruments to the Conservatoire des Arts et Métiers; and the furniture sold. The château thus became a museum where superbly framed paintings hung on the walls of richly decorated but empty apartments. Three inspectors were appointed by the Legislative Assembly to look after the gardens and the château: Loiseleur was responsible for the buildings in the town

and in the Petit Parc; Devienne was in charge of the Grand Parc and the supply and distribution of water; and Le Roy was responsible for the upkeep of
the buildings and the "national garden." For a few months it seemed as
though the situation had stabilized, but events were moving very quickly and
all the compromises designed to preserve the constitutional monarchy broke
down. The monarchy was abolished by the Convention in September 1793.

With the enemy at the frontiers of France, the king executed, and the
country declared a republic, Versailles was in real danger of becoming the very
symbol of the regime that had been abolished. In the turmoil were heard
sharply differing views: whereas Lenoir and the Abbé Grégoire were trying to
safeguard historic monuments by creating the concept of national heritage,
others would cheerfully have seen the seat of power of the ancien régime suffer the same fate as the British monasteries under Henry VIII. There was clear
evidence of this in Versailles: the Convention decreed that the royal châteaux
would not be sold but maintained at public expense by the Republic "for the
entertainment of the people and the foundation of institutions useful to agriculture and the arts,"[1] but at the same time Charles Delacroix, one of its representatives on the spot, talked of "plowing up" the park. On 7 November
1793 he declared that it was time to "break the kind of spell that seems to protect all the embellishments of a tyrant's domain," adding, "All the gates of the
palace are being demolished and the ax is poised to cut down the trees in its
vast avenues."[2]

In fact, this accomplished administrator, who became prefect of the
Gironde under Napoleon and was also the presumed father of the famous
painter, seems to have been more vehement in his words than in his deeds. No
irreparable damage was done, even if the gate to the Cour Royale was actually
demolished, the paving stones removed from the approaches to the château,
and some of the trees in the Grand Parc chopped down to supply the navy and
for use as firewood. The buildings were protected by guards wearing armbands
and with keys to the bosquets where they showed visitors around. But the gardens were not well maintained and the local people were allowed to encroach
on them; fruit trees were planted around the Grand Canal, in the quincunxes
and around the Bassin d'Apollon.

During the Directoire, the gardens began to resemble those in the
Roman palaces that Hubert Robert had painted during his visit to Italy. Ruins
stood alongside ancient splendor. The fountains were turned on in August
1795, but in February of the same year the Grand Canal had been drained and
divided into three lots. On 18 March 1796, Le Roy, who was still in post, sent

a note rebuking the soldiers billeted in the château for showing a lack of respect since they had been "doing their washing in the bassins, known as the Bassins des Buffets on each side of the Terrasse, beating it on the marble tablets, and hanging it out to dry on the arbors."[3] According to one Swiss visitor, Charles de Constant, writing in 1796, there was no longer any furniture in the apartments, but the mirrors, books, and gilt decoration were still intact. He felt, he said, as though he were "surrounded by ghosts,"[4] and this fits completely with the impression of unreality, "this kind of enchantment" that Charles Delacroix described.

The château was awaiting a new mission. During the Directoire, an exhibition of natural history was housed there and a gallery of French painting was established, containing three hundred and fifty paintings, including twenty-three by Poussin, and two hundred and fifty sculptures taken from the gardens. The trend was toward a solution that would make the museum at Versailles a counterpart to the Louvre, the latter showing works from foreign schools of art and the former the great works of the French school. During this period, the gardens survived: Antoine Richard, who had been Marie-Antoinette's gardener, had become close enough to the Republican regime to obtain from the Convention a decree defining the gardens as "agriculturally useful establishments." He was maintained in post during the Directoire and was thus able to work at saving the exotic trees he had planted in the Petit Trianon in the time of Mique and Hubert Robert.

The fall of the Republic marked a predictable change of direction. Napoleon planned to make his position as head of state visible by reoccupying the royal residences, but he was daunted by the expense of doing this at Versailles. Perhaps he was politically astute enough to realize that the château was still linked to the memory of the Bourbons. Perhaps he wanted to build himself an even grander palace in the capital. When he was in exile at St. Helena, he confided to Las Cases details of the grandiose projects he had conceived when he was at the height of his power. He had meant at that point to make Paris the capital of Europe and to transform Versailles, whose "guiding principle" he deplored, into a kind of outpost of the vast metropolis. This meant that the gardens would be completely transformed, and he already envisaged a campaign against their statuary.

> I intended to banish from these beautiful bosquets all those nymphs in
> bad taste and these ornaments of Turcaret-like extravagance,[5] and I was
> going to replace them with stone panoramas of all the capitals from

which we had returned in triumph and all the famous battles for which our armies are renowned. These would have been so many everlasting monuments to our victories and our national glory, built at the gates of Europe's capital, which perforce the rest of the universe would visit.[6]

The relationship between statues by Girardon and Tuby and the financial circles described in Lesage's play may be hard to fathom, but on the other hand it is easy to see the political capital that Napoleon intended to make from this initiative. He had little concern for the gardens, which he had once described as "bankers' follies," adding, "my own garden is the Fontainebleau forest."[7] He wanted to make the gardens into a kind of exhibition space by constructing panoramas, those curious theaters that attracted crowds from big cities at the beginning of the nineteenth century.

The first panoramas had appeared in Britain in the 1780s. They took the form of large rotundas with a spiral staircase around a central column. The staircase led to a balcony halfway up the column, and as you walked around the balcony you could see a painted panorama right across the facing wall. The subjects of these huge paintings were not always the same, but the most popular themes were clearly established: a view across a capital city, different scenes from a big-game hunt in Asia or Africa, and, of course, a great battle with its usual quota of feats of arms, gold-braided generals, heroic regiments, and overworked stretcher bearers. It is easy to see how the emperor planned to use this modern device to capture public imagination by displaying to the whole universe the great scenes from a modern epic, which reduced Louis XIV's campaigns to no more than military parades. But *sic transit*—the only panorama showing Napoleon on the battlefield is to be seen at Waterloo.

Fortunately Napoleon never carried out these grand projects and did no more than visit the Grand Trianon from time to time to ride in the park or hunt. He set the Petit Trianon up as a residence for his mother but she disliked it, and he had the Hameau de la Reine restored for his second wife, Marie-Louise, who, like her aunt Marie-Antoinette, was Austrian. On that occasion, he rebuilt the staircase of the Tour de Marlborough (or Tour de la Pêcherie), and perhaps he remembered that in the despised "bankers' follies" of Méréville, the Désert de Retz, or Ermenonville, similar towers had been constructed to provide a circular view of the landscape, making them the peacetime forerunners of the panoramas he wanted to build.[8]

After the restoration of the Bourbons, Louis XVIII briefly considered returning to Versailles, but he, too, was deterred by the cost of restoring the buildings. However, he did proceed with work on the gardens, and the present Jardin de Roi dates from this period. It was built on the site of the Ile Royale where the bassin and the islands had fallen into disrepair. The Jardin du Roi was typical of the trends of the Romantic period. With its gently undulating lawn, exotic trees, and medallion-shaped corbeils of flowers, it is a good illustration of the emerging compromise between the style of the late eighteenth-century landscape garden and the geometric forms that were coming back into favor.

One talented and knowledgeable champion of geometric forms was Quatremère de Quincy, whom Louis XVIII had appointed intendant des arts et monuments publics. A member of the Institut since 1804, Quatremère de Quincy was a devotee of architectural history and was seen as a firm champion of the classical heritage. From 1788, Charles Joseph Pancoucke had put him in charge of the *Dictionnaire d'architecture* in the *Encyclopédie méthodique*, and in the article "Jardins" he had attacked the fashion for landscape gardens. He thought in fact that art is not simply a copy of nature but an imitation of it, and that a garden that is merely a piece of nature is not a work of art. He used the same argument in his *Essai sur la nature: Le but et les moyens de l'imitation de la nature dans les beaux-arts* (Essay on nature: The purpose and means of imitating nature in the fine arts), published in 1823, shortly after the architect Dufour had created the Jardin du Roi: "What does one enjoy in such a creation? 'Nature' is the reply. But pleasure in nature is one thing; pleasure in imitation another. The pleasure that a landscape painting gives is one thing: the pleasure afforded by a natural landscape is something else. What makes this so-called art of gardening as far from art as it could be is that it contrives to be as realistic as possible."[9]

The Jardin du Roi seems to illustrate quite well the compromise that Quatremère de Quincy was advocating. Its vast lawn has the flexibility of Capability Brown's landscape style; its medallion-shaped corbeils of flowers reintroduce geometry in their large borders, giving gardeners the chance to show their talents in floral designs. The bright colors of exotic flowers became familiar thanks to the steamships that ensured speedy links between France and America, Asia, and Africa. New colors were constantly being produced by more sophisticated chemical dyes.[10] Gardens in the Romantic period thus managed to rival the decor of Restoration salons (Figs. 42 and 43). Sumptuous colors were allied to classically elegant forms. The atmosphere was calm and luxurious. One is reminded of what Hegel says about gardens in his *Cours d'esthétique* (Introductory lectures on aesthetics), which probably dates from

Fig. 42. The Jardin du Roi in the spring. Photograph by Jean-Baptiste Leroux.

the 1820s, when Romanticism was at its height: "A garden, as such, should be a pleasant place and nothing else, not a place that makes its mark by its intrinsic value, not distancing man from what is human or distracting him from his inner life. Here, architecture with its rational lines makes an effective contribution, introducing order, regularity, and symmetry, imposing an architectonic elaboration on objects that are themselves natural." Hegel ended his analysis of the role of gardens by praising formal French gardens in which "the architectonic principle is most fully illustrated" and which has therefore transformed nature into "a vast dwelling open to the sky."[11] This describes perfectly the impression that the Jardin du Roi makes today when you come upon it after admiring the Bassin du Miroir vertugadin, where, thanks to Le Nôtre's art, the forms you see before you are those not of a vast residence but of a veritable open-air palace.

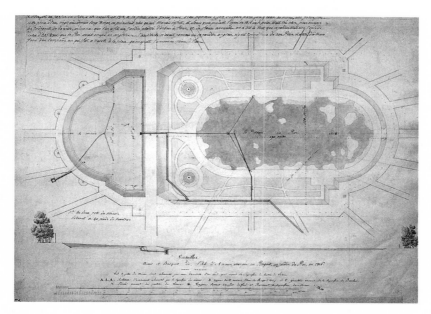

Fig. 43. The Jardin du Roi before Dufour's restoration. *Recueil des plans relatifs aux eaux des jardins et des bâtiments des châteaux de Versailles et des Trianon fait depuis 1809 jusqu'à 1830 par Dufour architecte du roi.* Archives, Service des fontaines, Versailles. In his manuscript annotations Dufour explains that he was asked to remodel Le Nôtre's Bosquet de l'Ile Royale, which had become a "stinking bog," to which he adds, "During the winter of 1816, in which the price of bread ran very high, Louis XVIII ordered that the paupers should be employed by the city to plant a garden of flower trees and natural flowers." He specifically mentions that this garden owes nothing to Harwell, where the king resided when he was exiled from France.

After the creation of this bosquet, the vicissitudes of political life had little impact on the gardens. Following the replanting during Louis XVI's reign, they had survived the serious threat that their future and that of the buildings might no longer be linked. When that danger had been averted, doubtless because of the additional "charm" they lent to the château, they were able to drift along, getting quietly older, while the buildings were being radically changed by Louis-Philippe. Views differ about these alterations: undoubtedly the apartments suffered from the installation of large rooms that were, in effect, exhibition halls displaying the military glories of France. Certain choices had to be made, however, and the king of France, the grandson of a regicide, whose authority was conferred by the barricades, could not establish his court outside

Paris, in a residence to which the Bourbons themselves had not returned. The solution adopted is a curious synthesis of plans outlined during the Revolution and the aspirations of the empire. The royal palace would be used to educate the nation by means of canvases as vast as panoramas. By giving the palace over to the glories of France, it was spared the fate that befell Cluny in the same period. It became a memorial, recognized as such by a national consensus; the Legitimists saw this initiative as public recognition of the achievements of the French kings, the Bonapartists as sanctioning the Napoleonic legend, the Republicans as a gesture by the French people, and the Orleanists as a great achievement for their cause. Victor Hugo summed this up in one of his memorable apothegms: "King Louis-Philippe has done a great thing at Versailles. This accomplishment had the stamp of kingly greatness and philosophic impartiality: a royal monument has been transformed into a national monument."[12]

A few untroubled years followed for Hugo's "national monument." The gardens were flourishing and gave no particular cause for concern. No major event supervened in the Second Republic or the Second Empire. Napoleon III used Versailles to hold fêtes, and on the occasion of Queen Victoria's visit in 1855 the architect Charles Auguste Questel "put up temporary decorations of colored glass all along the parterres."[13] These decorations were so successful that they were subsequently copied on many occasions at fêtes in Paris. Questel (1807–1887) was also responsible for the gardens in the turbulent years of the French military defeat, the Paris Commune, the transfer of the seat of government to Versailles, and the declaration of the German Empire in the Galerie des Glaces. The gardens were also the scene of one of the most painful episodes in this tragedy: the orangerie housed the Council of War that sent scores of Federalist supporters to face the firing squads in the Bois de Satory.

The government remained in the château until the 1875 vote on the constitution and the Wallon amendment, which put the republican regime on a firm footing. While the Senate and Chambre des députés returned to Paris, Questel completed the replanting of the gardens, which had been going on for nearly twenty years from 1863 to 1880. Most of the essential features were preserved in the replanting, but the upkeep of the bosquets was precarious. Few tourists visited the gardens and Pierre de Nolhac, who played a key role in the rediscovery of the authentic Versailles, has left a graphic description of the general atmosphere.

The state's indifference to Versailles was also apparent from the disrepair into which the bosquets had been allowed to fall. The bassins were collapsing and the fountains were gradually being reduced to ruins. The Bassin de Neptune was the only site, albeit one of considerable size, where work was still going on. There were few visitors from elsewhere, and people from the town treated the park, or rather the garden, to use the old term, as if they were its rightful owners. Retired people and youngsters would congregate in the very sheltered allée known as "La Petite Provence." Children would play beneath Girardon's sculpture group "Winter," quite close to the charming Marmousets bronzes. On fine summer days, families would gather on the "Beach," in other words, the *perron* above Latone, where, after sunset, a cooling breeze blew from the woods.[14]

The Bassin du Dragon was restored at the same time as the Bassin de Neptune. In 1889, on the occasion of a fête held to commemorate the centenary of the Serment du Jeu de Paume [Tennis court oath], the people crowding around the president, Sidi Carnot, could see a powerful jet of water spouting from the jaws of the dying monster. They could also see the four cherubim who have slain it scattering across the water, astride their swans. This sculpture group, largely destroyed, had been restored by Tony-Noël and Onésime Croisy; it is still standing today. The two artists created for the bassin a monster straight out of a Romantic painting, a Leviathan, a Gothic gargoyle, spewing water up to the heavens in the throes of death. Every age has its own conception of a monster. The one that the Marsy brothers had sculpted in 1667 probably resembled those that, in 1702, Hardy put into the Bassin du Miroir in Trianon. These are chubby monsters with long necks, endowed by the artists with charming little wings, more like fans than a means of bearing them high into the sky, where only Ariosto's imagination could ever have carried them.

In the 1880s Pierre de Nolhac was the driving force behind the initial restoration of the gardens. He was appointed curator of Versailles in 1887 and remained there until 1920. His memories of those years are full of anecdotes, some of which are entertaining. Carnegie, bored by his visit to the park, heard birds singing and suddenly gave a delighted shout: "Birds! There are birds!" Others are touching, such as Fauré sailing on the Grand Canal with music playing, and others tell a sad story: the demolition of the menagerie by people looking for freestones, for example. Nolhac also recounts how he managed to get rid of the glass panes linking the two wings of the Grand Trianon.

The former peristyle had vanished, leaving only a room that was completely glassed in, conveniently linking the two parts of the building. It is deservedly forgotten except as the courtroom where the Council of War tribunal condemned Maréchal Bazaine to death. I requested the removal of all the glass . . . the peristyle was thus restored to view at little expense, while the former charm of the façades could once again be appreciated, now that the long expanse of shutters had been removed. The moment you arrived, you could now see through the newly visible columns, with the sheen of their marble returning, toward the great bay windows opening onto the gardens and allowing you a glimpse of their beauty.[15]

The "charming" gardens that Delacroix had described were becoming a thing of the past. After the end of World War I when Versailles was the scene of intense diplomatic activity, they took on a more youthful and dynamic appearance in the 1920s, largely as a result of patronage. Thanks to the very generous donations of John D. Rockefeller, the roof of the château, the Petit Trianon, and its Hameau were all restored. Others have followed his example. Large organizations, such as the MATIF (the French exchange market), private donors, and charitable associations such as the Société des amis de Versailles, the Versailles Foundation, and the Friends of Versailles in the United States have raised or given money to supplement French state subsidies. Americans have always shown a warm interest in Versailles, perhaps out of gratitude for the military aid they received from France at the time of Louis XVI, Beaumarchais, and La Fayette, possibly because of nostalgia for a time when Franklin and Jefferson, founding fathers of the nation and sons of the European Enlightenment, were welcomed as heroes in France. Whatever the reason, their support has been unfailing.

Such support was demonstrated once again after the storms in 1990 and 1999, which caused extensive damage to the gardens and château and attracted wide media coverage. The damage, it must be said, would have been less impressive if the replanting, already necessary as far back as the 1970s, had not been so long delayed. In some respects, therefore, the storm damage could be seen as a necessary evil, natural disorder forcing humanity to reimpose its own order. However, before that can be done, you have to reflect carefully. The need to make decisions revealed the full extent of the problems of restoration.

Replanting and restoration presuppose a coherent and responsible approach to the heritage of the past that is transmitted to us through the natural world. In his book *La résurrection de Versailles*, Pierre de Nolhac writes, "Who could claim to reconstitute the magnificence of a long-gone century except through reflection and study? . . . Not only have we lost the right to replace one work of art by another, we may not even replicate those that have disappeared."[16]

Today this seems a very pessimistic view, and it is fortunate that we have moved on from that. Indeed nothing prevents us from using archival research and archaeological digs to recapture "the magnificence of a long-gone century." Garden archaeology helps garden history and both are important guides in re-creating gardens. Surveys to trace canals and stonework; the study of seeds remaining in the soil or on simple shards; purchasing contracts for trees, shrubs, and flowers; contemporary illustrations; accounts and administrative reports—all these are precious sources of information containing the elements needed to establish the state of the gardens at different periods in their history.

That said, which of these periods should we choose? The decisions that have been made are in line with the imperatives of coherence and logic imposed by all good restoration projects: they must "seek to return the gardens to the way they were in Louis XIV's reign with their high arbors and low trees"[17] or, in other words, as they were between 1700 and 1710, just after Le Nôtre's death. The Petit Trianon, the Bosquet des Bains d'Apollon, and the Jardin du Roi are, of course, later than that and must be kept as they were designed, but since they cannot be seen from the Grande Terrasse or the Galerie des Glaces, there is no danger that they will create an awkward hiatus. By choosing to plant low trees, it is possible to remain faithful to the intentions of the team who designed the gardens. Working alongside the king, this team, which included Le Nôtre, Le Brun, and Hardouin-Mansart, sought to create a spacious composition with a clear, readily understood structure: "The present growth of the bosquets, with trees standing almost forty meters high, completely destroys the effect of this composition, makes it impossible to decipher the main axes, and, above all, shortens perspectives by forming a screen close to the spectator that obscures distant views."[18] Thus, the restoration of the Versailles gardens has been carried out in the spirit of Le Nôtre, who, as we have seen, despised "restricted views." To achieve a relatively rapid and efficient restoration of the vegetal architecture after the devastation caused by the storms to some of the bosquets, the range of chosen species had to be diversified. This allowed different growth rates to be harnessed, some ensuring that the bosquets thickened up quickly, others providing the longer-term structure. This diversification has had many other benefits. It gives better resistance to disease and a "wider range and variety of greenery throughout the

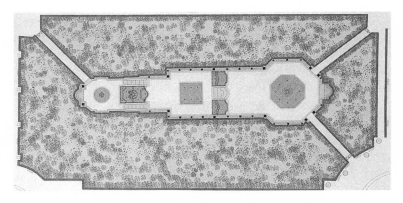

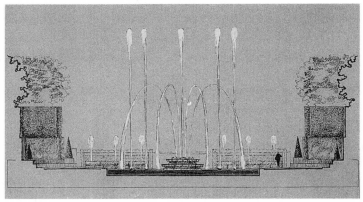

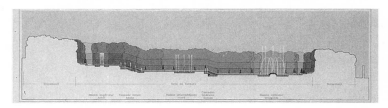

Fig. 44. Three drawings for the *Projet de restauration du Bosquet des Trois Fontaines*, Pierre-André Lablaude. Musée du Château de Versailles.

seasons." It will also obviate "the trauma of clear-cutting," which is inevitable every hundred years if, as has been the case until now, plantings have simply been confined to species more appropriate for forests than gardens. In addition, it will at last reveal "in the corner of the bosquets, these silhouetted outlines of trees, beloved of seventeenth-century landscape artists,"[19] and bring out the colors in the different species of the palisades so as to create a marbled effect on the great flat surfaces of the vegetal architecture. Technical progress is extremely helpful in this respect. Pruning machines now have blades mounted on telescopic arms and the use of lasers allows an unprecedented degree of precision in the alignments.

The restoration program for the bosquets has thus been clearly established and it is proceeding alongside the program for the open spaces, where large-scale topiary is restoring the curved surfaces visible in the paintings of Etienne Allegrain and Jean-Baptiste Martin. These ambitious but realistic goals are not confined to the vegetal architecture. In the Bosquet des Trois Fontaines, the hydraulic system is reemerging, which will eventually allow visitors to see the fountains playing in the garden setting designed by Le Nôtre. They will rediscover not only the interplay of water jets but also the effect of perspective, decelerated in one direction, accelerated in the other, increasing the length of the bosquet when seen from below, decreasing it when seen from above (Fig. 44).

The difficult problem posed by the restoration of the Versailles gardens demonstrates clearly that the approach of the landscape designer must be, as Pierre-André Lablaude puts it, "as rigorous as that required for the restoration of a painting, archaeological object, or cathedral."[20] When directed by such firmly established principles, we can anticipate that, in the not too distant future, Versailles will illustrate, even more clearly than it does today, the heritage of buildings and the heritage of landscape perfectly combined together.

CHAPTER FIFTEEN

History, Gardens, and Landscape

As we leave the Grande Terrasse, passing through the château on our way back to modern civilization, one last look at the Grand Canal will inevitably call to mind some reflections on the part played by history at Versailles. Gardens have a different relationship to history from that of buildings alone. Stone speaks for itself; it is fashioned and put in place by men of another age, drawing visitors imaginatively into the past. Gardens, on the other hand, relate less directly to history. Their foliage and the water in their bassins, constantly moving in the unseen wind, remind us of what they really are: a living fabric reacting to the constant changes of their environment. Some of these changes, like the trembling of a leaf, last only moments, some much longer, as hours slip by. Others follow the passage of the seasons, the evolution of species, and even, in the long term, changes to the climate itself. To these must be added political decisions—or rather lack of them—and technical developments that radically change the ways in which gardens are maintained.[1] But if gardens are constantly changing, bending but not breaking under all the different kinds of pressure exerted by time, and if that flexibility is the source of their strength, why then should one continually work to take them back to a specific point in their history by a process of constant pruning, cutting them back like vines?

There are two answers to this question. The first relates to conservation, the second concerns the surrounding landscape. The gardens were made to be seen as they were at the end of Louis XIV's reign, when the trees had reached maturity and were best suited to the architecture of the façade that was built as they were growing into shape. Unlike the apartments, which were redesigned, then restored, so that several styles blend together, the unity of that façade is absolute and it was designed for the gardens it overlooks. Since the Petit Trianon and the eighteenth- and nineteenth-century bosquets cannot be seen from the Grande Terrasse, this should be turned to advantage and the unity of the whole preserved. When you arrive in Versailles it is this whole group of buildings and gardens that you want to see. Visitors generally know enough history to see Versailles as an ideal image of France at a time when her intellectual life was of exceptional brilliance. Some may even realize that it is also a triumphant assertion of the power of the modern state. Spoiling the unity of the façade and the gardens would be a distortion of the whole: this would be as irresponsible as severing the links at Stowe between Capability Brown's style and the Palladianism of the temples, or the links in Berlin between Schinkel's gardens and his architectural creations.

On the contrary, the landscape that you see stretching beyond the gardens from the top of the Grande Terrasse is not, and cannot be, related to the seventeenth century; it is not, and cannot be, designed in any given style. The question, therefore, arises whether there is a hiatus between the ever-present geometrical rigor of the gardens and the open backdrop of the horizons of the Ile-de-France against which they are set. The difficult problem of that gradual transition was solved by Le Nôtre with an ease that makes him the first of our great landscape gardeners.

When we look out from the château of Versailles across the whole vista, we see below us first a historic garden, then a vast section of the Ile-de-France. This is what we mean when we talk of the landscape heritage of Versailles. To be sure, the château has its gardens that undoubtedly bear the unsullied imprint of the century in which they were created. But these gardens, thanks to the Grand Canal, blend into the eternal landscape of the Ile-de-France. It was this effect that the great artists who inspired Le Nôtre's creative imagination, such as Nicolas Poussin, Francesco Albani, Annibale Carracci, and Claude Lorrain, had expressed from the beginning of the seventeenth century when they painted the Roman campagna; from then on, landscape and history were linked. By placing the earliest traces of our cultural universe against a background of eternal hills, beneath a sky bathed in a tranquil light, they were already expressing the ephemeral character of all human creation confronted with the eternity of nature. These links between landscape and history are stronger than ever today.

When we travel along the motorways of France and read signs that say "Paysages de Cézanne" or "Paysage de Picardie," we mentally connect what we see, what we know, and the forms of the living landscape that is gliding by.

Fig. 45. The Great Perspective seen from the Bassin de Latone. Photograph by Jean-Baptiste Leroux.

These signposts would be meaningless if the vision we have of the countryside they mark were not also the vision of a particular sky, of trees in the wind, roofs in the sun, and people glimpsed working in the fields. These people will go home, once their work is done, to houses that have taken the place of other houses, as they themselves have taken the place of those who lived there before. The landscape accommodates different time schemes, giving us a spontaneous, almost instinctive, sense of history.

When gardens appear in a landscape a new and deeper meaning is given to this historical exchange. Because they are man-made, they can be dated, but they live the life of the landscape because they, too, accommodate different time schemes. Nature and history come together in a garden, and if there is one place where the intellectual fertility of that union can be seen, it is at Versailles.

Any tourist visiting the apartments will feel history come alive. But when you go out on the Grande Terrasse, you feel something quite different. There is still a sense of history in the arrangement of surfaces and volumes, in the statues and the bassins: hydraulic engineers have come and gone, generations of gardeners have tended the parterres, and the gardens have lived on, their appearance unchanged. But these living gardens draw your gaze toward the immutable vastness of the horizon. There you can see the Ile-de-France as it appears in French painting from miniatures in a medieval book of hours to the Impressionists, to Delaunay, or to Marquet. The brilliant whites of the clouds, the deep, luminous blues of the skies, and the greens that the fields and the woods spread over the landscape have remained the same over the centuries.

You then realize that the trees in the countryside are no different from those in the bosquets before you; together with the shimmering waters of the Grand Canal, they fuse their colors with those of the gardens. The imperceptible transitions orchestrated by Le Nôtre from the château to the end of the Grand Canal take history toward the horizon, where it is caught up in the immense theater of nature (Fig. 45).

MAPS

Map 1. Versailles between 1688 and 1704. Musée du Château de Versailles.

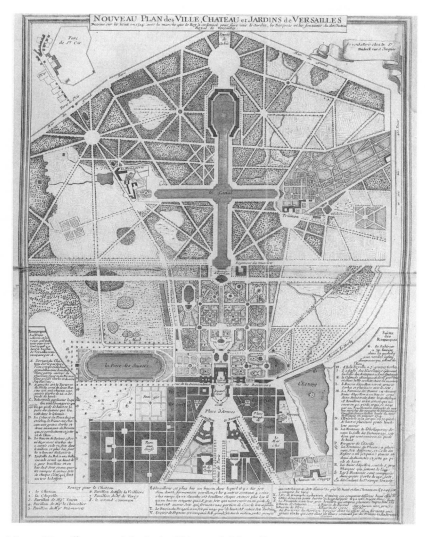

Map 2. Versailles, 1714. Musée du Château de Versailles.

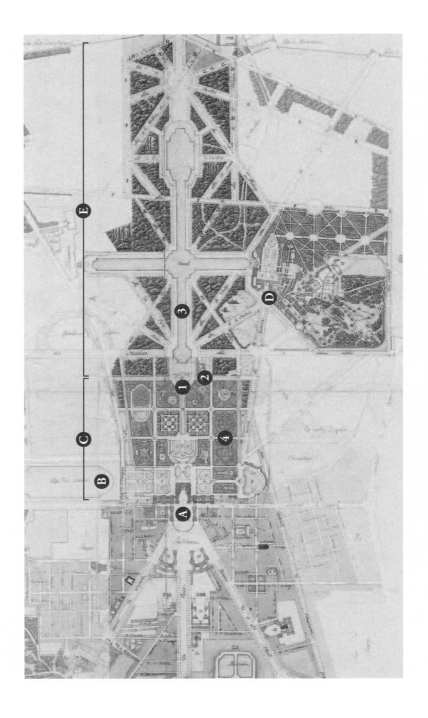

Map 3. Plan of the château, gardens, Petit Parc, Trianon, and the town of Versailles during the First Empire. A. Château. B. Pièce d'Eau des Suisses. C. Petit Parc. D. Trianon. E. Grand Parc. 1. Bassin d'Apollon. 2. Allée d'Apollon. 3. Grand Canal. 4. Etoile Royale.

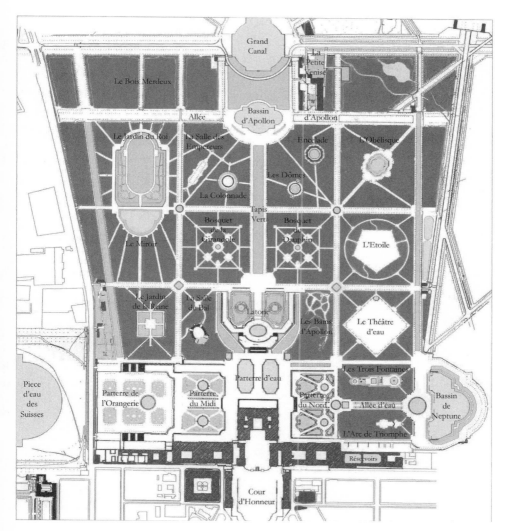

Map 4. Petit Parc.

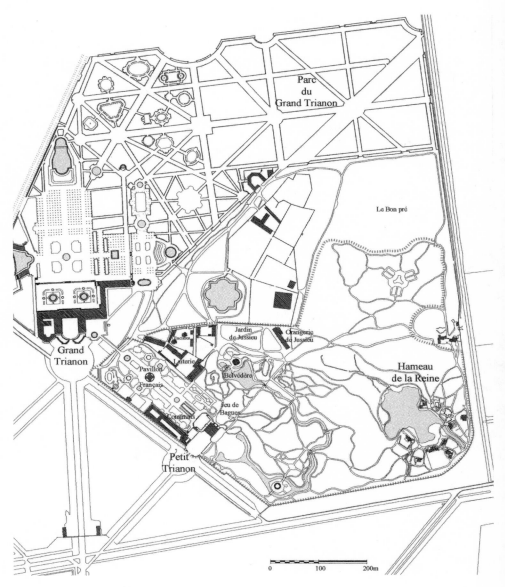

Map 5. The Trianon.

CHRONOLOGY

1623	Louis XIII has a hunting lodge built in Versailles, turning it into a small château ten years later
1633–39	Construction of the château, town, and Richelieu's garden
1650	Mansart finishes the Château de Maisons
1656	Le Nôtre at Vaux-le-Vicomte
1661	Start of Louis XIV's reign
1662	Menagerie and the first orangerie built
1664	Creation of the north bosquet, which becomes the Bosquet du Dauphin in 1669
	Creation of the south bosquet, which becomes the Bosquet de la Girandole in 1669
1665–70	Construction of the Grotte de Thétys and the Trianon de Porcelaine
	Creation of the Fer à Cheval, the Bassin de Latone, the Lézards, the Bassin d'Apollon, and the Grand Canal
	Widening of the Allée Royale (Tapis Vert)
	Creation of Le Labyrinthe and the Bosquet du Marais, to which will be added the Bains d'Apollon in 1704
	La Quintinie appointed director of the fruit and vegetable gardens of the royal houses (1670)
	The shape of the gardens emerges in the course of these five years; construction of an "envelope" around Louis XIII's château begins
1671	Creation of the Berceau d'Eau, which becomes the Trois Fontaines in 1677–78
	Creation of the Pavillon d'Eau, which becomes the Arc de Triomphe in 1677–78
1671–72	Creation of the Etoile, which becomes the Montagne d'Eau

1671–74   Creation of the Ile Royale and the Miroir
           Creation of the Théâtre d'Eau
           Creation of the Salle des Festins, which becomes the Salle du
               Conseil and then the Salle de l'Obélisque in 1706
1672   Creation of the Bassin de Cérès
           Creation of the Bassin de Flore
1673   Creation of the Bassin de Bacchus
1674   Creation of the Bassin de Saturne
           Celebrations to mark the conquest of Franche-Comté
           Colbert's Grande Commande
1675   Creation of the Bosquet de l'Encelade
           Creation of the Bosquet de la Renommée, which becomes the
               Bosquet des Dômes in 1681; the three Grotte de Thétys sculp-
               ture groups will be sited here until 1705
           Creation of the Galerie d'Eau, which becomes the Galerie des
               Antiques around 1683, then the Salle des Marronniers in 1704
           The Bassin de Neptune is excavated
1678   Creation of the Bosquet des Sources, which becomes the Colon-
               nade in 1685
1678–82   The Pièce d'Eau des Suisses is excavated
1681–83   Creation of the Salle de Bal or Bosquet des Rocailles
1682   The Parterre d'Eau is replaced by the two water mirrors on the
               Grande Terrasse
           The Machine de Marly is built
1683   Demolition of the Grotte de Thétys
           Construction of the new orangerie, completed in 1688
1683–89   Twelve statues and twelve white marble vases placed in the Allée
               Royale (or Tapis Vert)
1684   Work begins on the Canal de l'Eure
1684–89   The Colonnade is built on the site of the Bosquet des Sources
1686   The height of the statue of Latone is increased and it is turned to
               face the Bassin d'Apollon and no longer the château
1687–88   The Trianon de Porcelaine is replaced by the Trianon de Marbre
1699   Girardon's *Enlèvement de Proserpine* is placed in the center of the
               Colonnade
1700   Death of Le Nôtre
           Cast-iron pipes replace lead piping
1715   Death of Louis XIV

1741	Redecoration of the Bassin de Neptune
1743	Demolition of the Théâtre d'Eau, which will become the Rond Vert in 1774
1749–50	Jacques Ange Gabriel builds the Pavillon Français and the Jardin Français in the Petit Trianon
1760–64	The château of the Petit Trianon is built
	The Bosquet de la Girandole and the Bosquet du Dauphin are demolished; they will become the north and south Quinconces
1774	Death of Louis XV; accession of Louis XVI
1774–76	Louis XVI orders the replanting of Versailles
	The Bosquet de la Girandole and the Bosquet du Dauphin become the Quinconce du Nord and the Quinconce du Midi
	The Labyrinthe is demolished and becomes the Bosquet de la Reine
	Hubert Robert creates the Bosquet des Bains d'Apollon, completed in 1778
1777	Work begun on the Petit Trianon in Marie-Antoinette's English garden
	The Temple de l'Amour and the Belvédère are completed in 1778 and the Hameau in 1787
1789	The royal family leaves Versailles
1793	On the advice of Antoine Richard, the Convention decides to make the Versailles gardens "a place serving agriculture and the arts"
1815	Accession of Louis XVIII
1817–18	Dufour creates the Jardin du Roi on the site of the Ile Royale
1820	Demolition of the pavilions in the Bosquet des Dômes
1837	Louis-Philippe makes Versailles a museum dedicated to "all the splendors of France"
1860	Napoleon III begins the second replanting of the gardens
1889	Popular festival celebrating the centenary of the Serment du Jeu de Paume (Tennis court oath) and the redecoration of the Bassin du Dragon
1991	The third replanting begins
1992	Restoration of the Jardin Français in the Petit Trianon
1997	Restoration of the Bosquet de l'Encelade
1999	Storm damage speeds up the progress of the third replanting
2001	Restoration of the Parterre de l'Orangerie
	Quinconce du Nord and Quinconce du Midi are transformed back into the Bosquet du Dauphin and the Bosquet de la Girandole

NOTES

PART I. THE STATE, THE KING, AND THE GARDENS

Note to epigraph: Mandrou, *La France aux XVIIe et XVIIIIe siècles,* 228.

CHAPTER ONE. THE MONARCHY AND THE GARDENS BEFORE THE REIGN OF LOUIS XIV

1. Machiavelli, *Oeuvres complètes* (Paris, 1952), 136.

2. Cottret, *La vie politique en France au XVIe, XVIIe et XVIIIe siècles,* 11.

3. C. Acidini Luchinat, "Les jardins des Médicis: Origines, développements, transformations," in *Les jardins des Médicis,* 50.

4. M.-A. Giusti, "Les Demeures laurentiennes à Pise et aux alentours," in *Les jardins des Médicis,* 207.

5. Cloulas, *Cathérine de Médicis,* 340.

6. *Les triomphes faits à l'entrée de François II et de Marie Stuart au château de Chenonceau,* reedited by prince A. Golitsyn (Paris, 1857).

7. Quoted by Solnon, *La cour de France,* 129.

8. Marie, *Naissance de Versailles,* 1, 7.

9. A.-M. Lecoq, "Le jardin de la sagesse de Bernard Palissy," in Mosser and Teyssot, *Histoire des jardins de la Renaissance à nos jours,* 73.

10. *Relations des ambassadeurs vénitiens sur les affaires de France,* 2, 593.

11. Woodbridge, *Princely Gardens,* 81.

12. A. Babeau, *Le Louvre et son histoire,* 1895, quoted by Daufresne, *Le Louvre et les Tuileries,* 26.

13. *Les fêtes de la Renaissance.*

14. Ganay says that he was the true creator of the park. See *André le Nostre,* 69.

15. The Ligue was founded by the duke of Guise in 1576 to defend Catholicism against Calvinism and remove Henri III from the throne.

16. Lecoq, *François I imaginaire,* 362.

17. Mollet, *Théâtre des plans et jardinages.*

18. Barbiche and Dainville-Barbiche, *Sully*, 314.

19. A. de Montchrestien, *Traité d'économie politique*, 241 (Paris, 1615).

20. Olivier de Serres, "Adresse au Roi," in *Théâtre d'agriculture et ménage des champs*, 8.

21. Baridon, *Les jardins*, 610–11.

22. Batiffol, *Autour de Richelieu*, 155.

23. Ibid., 187.

24. Ibid., 189.

25. Quoted in ibid., 144.

26. Boudon, *Richelieu, ville nouvelle*, 160.

27. Quoted by Paul Guth in *Mazarin*, 579.

CHAPTER TWO. THE NATURE AND SPLENDOR OF THE MONARCH

1. Quoted by Petitfils, *Louis XIV*, 253.

2. For the role played by the king's ministers and secretaries in the composition of the *Mémoires*, see the preface by B. Champigneulles in Louis XIV, *Mémoires*.

3. Ibid., 4.

4. Murat, *Colbert*, III.

5. Ibid.

6. R. Mousnier, *Les institutions de la France sous la monarchie absolue* (Paris, 1992), 193–94.

7. Petitfils, *Louis XIV*, 10.

8. People who negotiated with the minister to agree to the sums due from the farms either in whole or in part.

9. Louis XIV, *Mémoires*, 253.

10. Voltaire, *Le siècle*, 705.

11. *Le triomphe royal*, 1649, 73.

12. Bossuet, *Politique*, V, iv, 1, 178.

13. H. du Boys in his treaty, *De l'origine et auctorité des roys*, 1604, quoted by Jacques Ellul, *Histoire des institutions*, vol. 1, *L'Antiquité*, 334.

14. "I asked the Cardinal if Louis XIV was well versed in the teaching of the Church he had always supported so ardently. He replied to me in these very words: 'He had a naive and simple faith.'" *Supplément du siècle de Louis XIV* (Paris, 1957), 1242.

15. Bossuet, *Politique*. In his introduction to the book, E. Le Brun stresses that Bossuet came from a legal family of *parlementaires* who had remained loyal to the crown during the Fronde. The king and the churchman thus had a similar outlook.

16. On kingship and the theoretical foundations of monarchical power, see Kantorowicz, *The King's Two Bodies*.

17. Sermon for Palm Sunday, preached before the king on 2 April 1662.

18. Bossuet, *Politique*, V, iv, 63.

19. Louis XIV, *Mémoires*, 193.

20. Bossuet, *Politique*, V, iv, 96.

21. Louis XIV, *Mémoires*, 177.

22. Ibid., 42–43.

23. "He is shrewdly observant, knows the heart of each of his subjects, and once he has seen or heard of someone, he never forgets him." J.-B. Visconti, *Mémoires sur la cour de Louis XIV, 1673–1681* (Paris, 1988), 27.

24. Bossuet, *Politique*, V, iv, 1, 177.

25. Cardin Le Bret, *De la souveraineté du roi* (Paris, 1632).

26. Quoted by Sabatier, *Versailles ou la figure du roi*, 428.

27. Hobbes, *Leviathan*, 89.

28. Ibid., 111.

29. Letter dated 15 April 1630, quoted in J. Cormette, "L'alchimiste, le prince, et le géomètre," *Revue de synthèse* (July–Dec. 1991): 1, 492–93.

30. Louis XIV, *Mémoires*, 177.

31. Dangeau, *Journal*, XVI, 128.

32. Quoted in M. M. McGowan, "Les images du pouvoir royal au temps de Henri III," in *Théories et pratiques politiques à la Renaissance*, 305.

33. Laurent de Morellet (le sieur Combes), *Explication historique de ce qu'il y a de plus remarquable dans la maison royale de Versailles et en celle de Monsieur à Saint-Cloud* (Paris, 1681), 1.

34. Saint-Simon, *Mémoires*, V, 533.

35. Voltaire, *Le siècle*, 951.

36. Ibid., 969.

37. Ibid., 912.

38. Ibid., 1020.

39. Saint-Simon, *Mémoires*, V, 531.

40. Ibid., 533.

41. Spanheim, *Relation de la cour de France*, 67.

42. D. Cronström, account published in *La gazette des Beaux-Arts* 66 (July–August 1965): 103–4, by S. de l'Epinois.

43. Ibid., 104.

44. Sourches, *Mémoires*, X, 158.

45. Ibid., XIII, 523.

46. Saint-Simon, *Mémoires*, V, 609–10.

47. Louis XIV, *Mémoires*, 90.

CHAPTER THREE. A NEW IMAGE OF GOOD GOVERNMENT

1. Colbert, *Lettres*, 5:266–67.

2. Ibid., 5:269.

3. Ibid., 5:269–70.

4. See Saule, "Le château de Versailles," 307–24.

5. Expenditure in Versailles rose to 526,954 livres in 1666 and fell to 214,300 livres the following year. It then more than doubled in 1668 and doubled again the following year.

6. Colbert, *Lettres*, 5:330.

7. Ibid., 5:297. Le Nôtre had just finished the Parterre du Nord, the Allée d'Eau, and the Bassin du Dragon.

8. Louis XIV, *Mémoires*, 165.

9. Ibid., 51.

10. Ibid., 76.

11. Ibid., 151.

12. Ibid., 284.

13. Petitfils, *Louis XIV*, 252. Despite its cumbersome procedures, "this great search" for aristocratic parvenus removed between 25 and 40 percent (possibly more) of the aristocracy in some regions of France.

14. Louis XIV, *Mémoires*, 134.

15. Ibid., 90.

16. Bluche, *Louis XIV*, 434–36.

17. Sourches, *Mémoires*, I, 202.

18. Mariage, *L'univers de Le Nostre*, 119.

19. Murat, *Colbert*, 143.

20. Bottineau, "Essais sur le Versailles de Louis XIV," 125.

21. Tr. note: In Greek mythology, Enceladus was a Titan, defeated in battle and buried under Mount Etna by Athena.

22. Sabatier, *Versailles ou la figure du roi*, 556.

23. Louis XIV, *Mémoires*, 58.

24. Lacour-Gayet, *L'education politique de Louis XIV*, 83.

25. Quoted by Nolhac, *La création de Versailles*, 218.

26. Tr. note: a toise was a measure of approximately two meters.

27. Scudéry, *La promenade de Versailles*, 27.

28. Ibid., 50.

29. Saint-Simon, *Mémoires*, V, 532.

30. H. Repton defined the English landscape garden as "the happy medium betwixt the wildness of nature and the stiffness of art; in the same manner as the English constitution is the happy medium betwixt the liberty of savages and the restraints of despotic government." In *Sketches and Hints on Landscape Gardening* in *The Landscape Gardening and Landscape Architecture of the Late Humphrey Repton Esq.* (London, 1840), 106.

31. Quoted by Petitfils, *Louis XIV*, 257.

32. Ibid., 261.

33. Quoted by Murat, *Colbert*, 265.

34. Ibid., 272.

35. Verlet, *Le château de Versailles*, 115.

36. Ibid., 193. Tr. note: A hoy is a small flat-bottomed coaster. A *peotta* is a large seagoing gondola.

37. For an account of the Versailles menagerie, see G. Mabille, "La ménagerie de Versailles," in Mosser and Teyssot, *Histoire des jardins de la Renaissance à nos jours*, 168–70.

38. Verlet, *Le château de Versailles*, 204. Tr. note: An arpent was approximately 0.85 acre.

39. Ibid., 215.

40. Translated by John Evelyn (1620–1706) as *The Compleat Gard'ner* (London: Matthew Gillyflower and James Partridge, 1693).

41. La Quintinie, *Instruction*, 8.

42. Ibid., 988.

43. Ibid., 1038.

44. Ibid., 1040.

45. Ibid., 682.

46. See B. Saule's contribution to the catalogue of the exhibition *Versailles et les tables royales en Europe, XVII–XIX siècles* (Versailles, 1993).

47. Quoted in La Quintinie, *Instruction*, 1154.

PART II. THE EMPIRE OF GEOMETRY

Note to epigraph: Huygens, *Correspondance*, 5:282.

CHAPTER FOUR. VERSAILLES AND THE ACADEMIES

1. Colbert, *Lettres*, 5:363.

2. Perrault, *Mémoires*, 125–126.

3. Ibid., 134.

4. Picon, *Claude Perrault*, 20.

5. Cassini, *Mémoires pour servir à l'histoire des sciences*, 291.

6. Claude Perrault, *Pourquoy et comment l'observatoire a esté baty*, in Colbert, *Lettres*, 5:515.

7. Guiffrey, *Comptes*, vol. 1, year 1665, col. 113.

CHAPTER FIVE. THE ASTRONOMERS IN THE GARDEN

1. "La Révolution scientifique au XVIIe siècle," in René Taton, *Histoire générale des sciences*, vol.2 (PUF, Paris: 1958), p. 196

2. De Caus, *La perspective avec la raison des ombres et des miroirs*.

3. *Pensées*, ed. Louis Lafuma (Paris: Seuil, 1962), 310.

4. On Kepler and the human eye, see G. Simon, *Kepler astronome, astrologue* (Paris, 1979).

5. On the size of shadows and the relationship with Caravaggism, see Kemp, *The Science of Art*.

6. Descartes, *Principes de la philosophie*, in *Oeuvres et lettres*, 612–13.

7. Picard, *Traité,* 180.

8. Colbert, *Lettres,* 4:185.

9. Guiffrey, *Comptes,* vol. 1, year 1680, col. 1309.

10. Charageat, "André Le Nôtre et ses dessins," 26.

11. This extract taken from Perrault's *Mémoires* is quoted by Ganay, *André Le Nostre,* 28.

12. Picard, *Traité,* 142.

13. Boyceau de la Barauderie, *Traité,* II, 4, 72.

14. Quoted by Mariage, *L'univers de Le Nôstre,* 100.

15. La Quintinie, *Instruction,* 27–28.

CHAPTER SIX. ENGINEERS AND GARDENERS

1. Pierre Clément, *Lettres, instructions et mémoires de Colbert, Paris 1861–1882,* 5, 267.

2. Guiffrey, *Comptes,* vol. 1, year 1671, col. 518.

3. "To René Hermel, laborer, payment for 88 toises of rigolles" in Guiffrey, *Comptes,* vol. 1, 1664, col. 25.

4. Tr. note: a "rayon" was a smaller gully than a "rigole," and a "repaire" served to mark the level on the pole.

5. Dézallier d'Argenville, *La théorie* (1709), 112.

6. Tr. note: a convex talus named after the hooped shape of the farthingale.

7. Colbert, *Lettres,* April 1677.

8. Dézallier d'Argenville, *La théorie* (1709), 100.

9. Du Breuil, *L'art universel des fortifications,* 6.

10. Ibid., 105.

11. Blanchard, *Les ingénieurs du "Roy" de Louis XIV à Louis XVI,* 111.

12. Rorive, *La guerre de siège sous Louis XIV,* 57.

13. Quoted in ibid., 180.

14. Dézallier d'Argenville, *La théorie,* 143.

CHAPTER SEVEN. HYDRAULICS AND PHYSICS

1. Dézallier d'Argenville, *La théorie* (1709).

2. Desgots, "Abrégé de la vie d'André Le Nôtre," 122.

3. Quoted by Verlet, *Le château,* 121–29.

4. The document is reproduced in Barbet, *Les grandes eaux de Versailles,* 28.

5. The text appears in Barbet, *Les grandes eaux de Versailles,* 382.

6. By "adjutage" the author of the report means a piece at the end of the conduit through which the water is brought. This modified the flow of the water and gave the jet its shape.

7. F. Boudon has drawn attention to the interesting plans provided by L.-A. Barbet of the canalizations in the gardens in his study "Histoire des jardins et cartographie en France," in Mosser and Teyssot, *Histoire des jardins de la Renaissance à nos jours,* 121–29.

8. Quoted by Barbet, *Les grandes eaux de Versailles*, 39. See also Colbert, *Lettres*, 5:354–55.

9. Picard, *Traité*, 175.

10. Dézallier d'Argenville, *La théorie* (1709) 315.

11. See Christiany, *Le Canal de l'Eure*.

12. Ibid.

13. Barbet, *Les grandes eaux de Versailles*, 80.

14. Dézallier d'Argenville, *La théorie* (1709), 382.

15. *Mémoires de l'Académie des sciences*, 1733, I, 360.

16. Mariotte, *Traité du mouvement d'eau*, 325.

17. Ibid., 278.

CHAPTER EIGHT. THE WORLD OF PLANTS AND THE SILENT PROGRESS OF
THE LIFE SCIENCES

1. Colbert, *Lettres*, 5:354.

2. Ibid., 5:368.

3. Ibid., 5:362.

4. Ibid., 5:413.

5. Guiffrey, *Comptes*, vol. 1, year 1668, col. 305, and year 1671, col. 586.

6. Tessin le Jeune, "Relation de la visite de Nicodème Tessin," 12.

7. Guiffrey, *Comptes*, vol. 2, year 1686, col. 1019.

8. Colbert, *Lettres*, 5:371.

9. Francastel, "La replantation du parc de Versailles au XVIIIe siècle," *Bulletin de la Société de l'histoire de l'art français*, 1950, 53–57.

10. La Quintinie, *Instruction*, 517, 530.

11. Guiffrey, *Comptes*.

12. See Bouchenot-Déchin, *Henry Dupuis, jardinier de Louis XIV*.

13. Tr. note: *Fagus sylvatica*.

14. Dézallier d'Argenville, *Théorie et pratique*, 197–201.

15. Thierry Mariage, "L'univers de Le Nôtre et les origines de l'aménagement du territoire," *Revue des monuments historiques* 143 (1986): 12.

16. Ganay, *André Le Nostre*, 51.

17. La Quintinie, *Instruction*, 237.

18. Descartes, *Traité de l'homme*, in *Œuvres et lettres*, 873.

19. Tauvry, *Nouvelle anatomie raisonnée*, 1690, preface.

20. La Quintinie, *Instruction*, 1048.

21. In this context we should remember that Louis XIV was interested in the work of the botanist Tournefort and personally sponsored his long journey in the East (see the preface to Tournefort's *Relation d'un voyage du Levant*). Moreover, Tournefort was the protégé of Fagon and knew Dodart, two of the king's doctors: Fagon gave up in his favor his post as director of the Jardin du Roi, now the Jardin des plantes in Paris. Once Tournefort was in place, Louis XIV asked him to build hothouses.

22. La Quintinie, *Instruction,* 1066.

23. For Charles Perrault, see Picon, *Claude Perrault.*

24. Ibid., 74.

25. On the rise of chemistry and the empirical methodology, see Koyré, *Etudes newtoniennes,* 33–34.

PART III. AN OPEN-AIR PALACE

Note to epigraph: Mme. de Sévigné, letter dated 7 August 1675 in *Lettres,* 1974, II, 38.

CHAPTER NINE. GARDENS AND CULTURE AT COURT

1. Scudéry, *La promenade,* 27.

2. Voltaire, *Le siècle,* 93.

3. La Fontaine, *Les amours de Psyché et de Cupidon,* in *Œuvres complètes,* 427.

4. Félibien, *Recueil de descriptions,* 107.

5. Tr. note: *Artamène ou le Grand Cyrus,* a novel originally attributed to Georges de Scudéry and subsequently to Madeleine de Scudéry.

6. A survey of these has been carried out. See Rostaing, "André Le Nôtre et les jardins français du XVIIe siècle."

7. Mme. de Sévigné, letter dated 7 August 1675 in *Lettres,* 1974, II, 38.

CHAPTER TEN. LE NÔTRE

1. Boyceau de la Baraudière, *Traité.*

2. Thuillier, *Simon Vouet,* 13–14.

3. Quoted by Ganay, *André Le Nostre,* 123.

4. The plan is held in the Institut de France library.

5. Colbert, *Lettres,* 5:400.

6. This letter is held in the Château de Chantilly.

7. Lister, *Voyage à Paris en 1698,* 48.

8. Du Breuil, *La perspective pratique,* 2.

9. Mariage, *L'univers de Le Nostre,* 100.

10. Boyceau de la Baraudière, *Traité,* III, 3, 71.

11. Ibid., II, 1, 69.

12. Mollet, *Le jardin de plaisir,* 31.

13. Dangeau, *Journal,* XVI, 128.

14. Dézallier d'Argenville, *La théorie* (1709).

15. Dézallier d'Argenville, *La théorie* (1709), 13.

CHAPTER ELEVEN. LE NÔTRE'S AESTHETIC

1. Piles, *Cours de peinture*, 42.

2. Wren, *Parentalia*, 351.

3. Descartes, *Discours de la méthode*, in *Œuvres et lettres*, 132–33.

4. Alberti, *L'architecture*, 187.

5. For details of the polemics provoked by aesthetic problems in Florence, see Antal, *Florentine Painting and Its Social Background*, II, 4, and III, 4.

6. Vitruvius, *De l'architecture*, III, 7.

7. Rykwert, *Les premiers modernes*, iii, ix, x.

8. Mollet, *Le jardin de plaisir*, 31.

9. Poussin, *Mesures de la célèbre statue de l'Antinoüs*, 2.

10. Pascal, *Pensées*, in *Moralistes du XVIIe siècle* (Paris, 1992), p. 330, no. 55.

11. Louis XIV, *Manière de montrer les jardins de Versailles*.

12. Boyceau de la Baraudière, *Traité*, III, 4, 72.

13. Kemp, *The Science of Art*, 93–96.

14. Caus, *La perspective avec la raison des ombres et des miroirs*, II.

15. Du Breuil, *La perspective pratique*, 115.

16. Piles, *Cours de peinture*, 200.

17. Racine, "La promenade de Port-Royal," 30–31.

18. Tr. note: A legendary monster from the Nerluc area in Provence.

19. La Fontaine, *Les amours de Psyché et de Cupidon*, in *Œuvres complètes*, 427.

20. Descartes, *Traité de l'homme*, in *Œuvres et lettres*, 814.

21. Lablaude, *Les jardins de Versailles*, 50.

22. Piganiol de la Force, *Nouvelle description des châteaux de Versailles et de Marly*, 103.

23. Rostaing has drawn up a valuable chronology of the early canals in "André Le Nôtre et les jardins français du XVIIe siècle."

24. Farhat, "Pratiques perspectives et histoire de l'art des jardins."

25. Boyceau de la Baraudière, *Traité*, III, 4, 72.

26. See Chapter 7, note 13.

27. Piles, *Cours de peinture*, 201–2.

28. A.-J. Dézallier d'Argenville, *Abrégé de la vie des plus fameux peintres* (Paris, 1972), 68.

29. Félibien, *Description de la grotte de Versailles*, 70.

30. Mme. de Sévigné, letter to Mme. de Grignan, in *Lettres*, 1956, I, 265.

31. Montesquieu, *De l'esprit des lois*, 2 vols. (Paris, 1956), book IV, chapter 2, 35–36.

32. Piles, *Cours de peinture*, 201–2.

33. Piganiol de la Force, *Nouvelle description des châteaux et parcs de Versailles et de Marly*, 9th ed. (Paris, 1764), II, 107.

34. Francastel, *La sculpture de Versailles* (Paris, 1930), ch. 3, "Le triomphe de Le Brun et de l'antique," 103–41.

35. Quoted by Mirka Beneš in "Inventing a Modern Sculpture Garden at the Museum of Modern Art New York," *Landscape Journal* 13, no. 1 (1994): 13.

36. Poussin, *Lettres et propos sur l'art*, 192.

37. La Fontaine, *Les amours de Psyché et de Cupidon*, in *Œuvres complètes*, 427.

38. Félibien, *Description de la grotte de Versailles*, 74.

39. La Fontaine, *Les amours de Psyché et de Cupidon*, in *Œuvres complètes*, 407.

40. According to Furetière's *Dictionnaire universel*, this term was used for a small ornament placed at the top of a cornice and ending in a kind of volute.

41. Piganiol de la Force, *Nouvelle description des châteaux de Versailles et de Marly*, 164.

42. F. Colonna, *Le songe de Poliphile* (Paris, 1994), 290.

43. Christout, *Le ballet de cour de Louis XIV*, 29.

44. Woodbridge, *Princely Gardens*, 220.

45. Piganiol de la Force, *Nouvelle description des châteaux de Versailles et de Marly*, 107.

46. Ibid., 110. The lines are by Benserade.

47. Fumaroli, *Le poète et le roi*, particularly the chapter entitled "Olympe et le Parnasse."

48. See Jean-Pierre Colinet's edition of Perrault's *Contes* (Paris, 1981), and M. Baridon, "Le labyrinthe de Versailles," in *Labyrinthes: Du mythe au virtuel* (Paris, 2003), 83–91. Whether the king approved of this profane version has remained a mystery.

49. Quoted by Néraudau, *L'Olympe du Roi-Soleil*, 65.

50. Pascal, *Pensées*, 115, in the Brunschvicg edition; 65 in the Lafuma edition (Paris, 1978).

51. Molière, *Amphytrion*, Act II, Scene 2.

52. Félibien, *Les divertissements de Versailles*.

53. For translation, see above.

54. Voltaire, *Le siècle*, 1012.

55. A chronology of court fêtes is given by Moine in *Les fêtes à la cour du Roi Soleil*, 221–23. On the fête known as the Plaisirs de l'Ile Enchantée, see Marie, "Les Plaisirs de l'Ile Enchantée."

56. Molière, *Œuvres complètes*, I, 603–4.

57. Ibid.

58. Félibien, *Receuil de descriptions de peintures et d'ouvrages faits pour le roi*, 208–30.

59. A. Félibien, *Relation de la fête de Versailles du 18 juillet 1668* (Paris, 1999), 56–57.

60. Sourches, *Mémoires*, 273.

61. For further information on this text, see Rostaing, "André Le Nôtre et les jardins français du XVIIe siècle," 26. This description of the Jardin des Sources is corroborated by the testimonies of Tessin and Madame Palatine, who was an authority on gardens.

62. Mariage, *The World of André Le Nôtre*, 89.

63. Walpole said of the trellises in the gardens of Paris, "They form light corridors, and transpicuous arbors through which sunbeams play and checker the shade, set off the statues, vases, and flowers, that marry with their gaudy hotels, and suit the gallant and idle society, who paint the walks between their parterres, and realize the fantastic scenes of Watteau and Durfé." *Essay on Modern Gardening by M. Horace Walpole*, trans. M. le duc de Nivernois, 17–18 (parallel text).

64. D'Urfé, *L'Astrée*, 25.

CHAPTER TWELVE. LOUIS XV

1. Saint-Simon, *Mémoires*, 6:167.

2. Lablaude, *Les jardins de Versailles*, 117.

3. Barbier, *Journal historique et anecdotique du règne de Louis XV*, 4 vols., I, 155.

4. Ibid., II, 258.

5. Croÿ, *Mémoires*.

6. Ibid., 225.

7. Nolhac, *La création de Versailles*, 7.

8. On the life sciences and empirical methods of observation, see Baridon, "Les deux grands tournants du siècle des lumières."

9. See Part II.

10. Antoine, *Louis XV*, 513.

11. Usually small drawings of burlesque rustic or city scenes depicting the daily life of the common people.

12. Himelfarb, "Versailles, fonctions et légendes," in *Les lieux de mémoire*, 2. *La Nation* (Paris, 1986), 267.

13. J.-M. Drouin, *L'écologie et son histoire* (Paris, 1993), 35.

CHAPTER THIRTEEN. LOUIS XVI AND MARIE-ANTOINETTE

1. Taylor-Leduc, "Louis XVI's Public Gardens."

2. Baridon, "The Conservation and Rehabilitation of Le Nôtre's gardens at Versailles."

3. Cayeux, *Hubert Robert*, 77.

4. Letter from d'Angiviller to Soufflot, cited by Cayeux, *Hubert Robert*, 77.

5. Francastel, *La sculpture de Versailles*, 46.

6. Quoted by Cayeux, *Hubert Robert*, 78.

7. Quoted by Arrizoli-Clémentel, *Vues et plans du Petit Trianon*, 10.

8. Mique was born in Nancy in 1728 and became director-general of the Bâtiments du Roi of Poland after the death of Héré.

9. Cayeux, "Des amateurs compromettants," 13.

10. On 25 July 1774, the queen commissioned the count of Caraman to follow the example of M. Botin and the duke of Chartres and create an English garden at the Petit Trianon, which she had dubbed Le Petit-Vienne (Bandeau, *Revue rétrospective*, III). Cited by Morey, *Richard Mique*, 17.

11. Morey, *Richard Mique*, 17. This text appears in Campan's *Mémoires* (1988), 150.

12. Croÿ, *Mémoires*, 8.

13. Ibid., 8.

14. Hezecques, *Page à la cour de Louis XVI*, 100.

15. As early as 1750, Rousseau contrasts "the simplicity of primitive times" and the "vices that were never so marked as when they could be at the gates of a great man's palace, upheld, so to speak, by marble columns." *Discours sur les sciences et les arts*, in *Œuvres complètes*, I, 22.

16. Scott, "Madame's Pavillon de musique."

17. Campan, *Mémoires* (1822), 123.

18. Carmontelle, *Le jardin de Monceau,* 1.

CHAPTER FOURTEEN. FROM THE ANCIEN RÉGIME TO THE PRESENT DAY

1. Caffin-Carcy and Villard, *Versailles et la Révolution,* 44.

2. Ibid. Charles Delacroix later successfully organized support for the empire and ended his career as prefect of the Gironde.

3. L. A. Gatin, "Versailles pendant la Révolution," *Revue de l'Histoire de Versailles et de la Seine et Oise* (1908): 334.

4. Quoted by Nolhac, *La création de Versailles,* 49.

5. Tr. note: Turcaret, the eponymous hero of a play by Lesage, was a rich financier who gave extravagant presents to the woman he loved.

6. Las Cases, *Le Mémorial de Sainte-Hélène,* 2 vols. (Paris, 1956), I, 970.

7. Quoted by G. Teyssot, "Un art si bien dissimulé, le jardin éclectique et l'imitation de la nature," in Mosser and Teyssot, *Histoire des jardins de la Renaissance à nos jours,* 360.

8. Baridon, *Les jardins,* 835.

9. Quatremère de Quincy, "Jardin," in *Encyclopédie méthodique,* 2nd ed.

10. On this evolution of taste and the essential part played by Chevreul, see Baridon, *Les jardins,* 969–74, 1025–30.

11. Hegel, *Cours d'esthétique,* III, 99.

12. V. Hugo, *Choses vues,* 1830–1846 (Paris, 1972), I, 133. This appears as an epigraph to Gaehtgens, *Versailles, de la résidence royale au musée historique.*

13. H. Delaborde, *Notice sur la vie et les ouvrages de Monsieur Questel,* 17.

14. Nolhac, *La résurrection de Versailles,* 8.

15. Ibid., 130.

16. Nolhac, *La creation de Versailles,* 14.

17. Lablaude, "Restauration et régénération de l'architecture végétale des jardins de Versailles," 80.

18. Ibid., 79.

19. Ibid., 83.

20. Ibid.

CHAPTER FIFTEEN. HISTORY, GARDENS, AND LANDSCAPE

1. For an account of the changes in the Versailles estate from its origins to the present day, see Maroteaux, *Versailles, le roi et son domaine* (Paris, 2000).

GLOSSARY

ajutage. A nozzle or a head fixed on the extremity of a pipe in order to give a distinct shape to a water jet.

allée. A broad walk bordered by trees or palisades (see *palissades*).

bambochade. A picture depicting, usually in a burlesque way, everyday urban or rural scenes.

bassin. An ornamental pond of stone construction, generally geometric, in which fountains might feature.

bosquet. An ornamental grove (the term is derived from the Italian *boschetto*, a small wood), generally square or rectangular and enclosing a large open space displaying fountains, statues, or a theater.

boulingrin. A sunken turf parterre surrounded by a sloping bank. A corruption of the English "bowling green."

buffet d'eau. An architectural garden feature placed against a wall, a palisade, or an embankment, or in a niche with water flowing over it into bowls, basins, or troughs (*Oxford Companion to Gardens*).

cabinet. A garden enclosure forming a small room with green walls cut to shape.

corbeille de fleurs. A round or oval flower bed.

enroulement. A scroll-like border decorating a parterre (see *parterre*).

girandole. A group of powerful jets designed to play together and project a massive column of water in the air.

glacis. A long incline sloping gently down to ground level, usually planted with grass.

guéridon. A small table with a central pedestal.

jeu de bagues. A Chinese game in which players use a stick to remove rings hanging from a revolving wheel.

miroir d'eau. A formal bassin reflecting the light like a mirror.

palissade (from *palis*, a fence of pales). Palisade—a row of trees or shrubs forming a hedge clipped into a green wall (*Oxford Companion to Gardens*).

parterre. A level section in a formal garden, usually containing flowers, lawns, and sometimes water.

parterre de broderie. A parterre decorated with flowing lines of boxwood and flowers imitating embroidery.

parterre de pièces coupées. A parterre made of individual pieces, sometimes lined with box, between which one could walk. (The Parterre de l'Orangerie at Versailles is a fine example.)

patte d'oie. A "goosefoot" intersection with three paths radiating from a central point.

pièce d'eau. A general term for an ornamental water feature; a water parterre and a bassin are pièces d'eau.

plate-bande. In the modern sense, simply a small plot of ground where one can grow flowers or vegetables. In the seventeenth century it was a border extending along the sides of a parterre like a frame.

rocaille. Rock and shellwork.

salle de verdure. A space enclosed by palisades and resembling a room.

saut-de-loup. A ha-ha; a wide ditch.

talus. An embankment generally planted with grass.

vertugadin. Originally a pad women fastened around their hips to puff out their skirt. It was said to protect their virtue (*vertu gardien*). In formal gardens it was a crescent-shaped embankment gently rising from the ground at both ends and reaching its maximum height in the middle. Le Nôtre's most famous vertugadins can be seen at Chantilly and at Versailles in the Bassin du Miroir, opposite the Jardin du Roi.

BIBLIOGRAPHY

SOURCES

Académie royale des sciences. *Histoire de l'académie royale des sciences depuis son établisse-ment en 1666 jusqu'à 1699.* Paris, 1729–33.

———. *Mémoires . . . depuis 1666 jusqu'à 1699.* Paris, 1729–33.

Alberti, Leon Battista. *L'architecture et art de bien bastir.* Trans. Jean Martin. 1568.

Barbier, Edmond Jean-François. *Journal historique et anecdotique du règne de Louis XV.* 4 vols. Paris, 1847–56.

Belidor, Bernard Forest de. *Architecture hydraulique.* 1737.

———. *Le bombardier français ou nouvelle méthode pour jeter les bombes avec précision, avec un traité des feux d'artifice.* 1734.

Blondel, Jacques François. *Cours d'architecture civile.* 1771–77.

Bosse, Abraham. *Moyen universel de pratiquer la perspective sur les tableaux ou surfaces ir-régulieres, ensemble quelques particularités concernant cet art et celui de la gravure en taille douce.* 1653.

Bossuet. *Politique tirée des propres paroles de l'écriture sainte.* Critical edition by Jacques Le Brun. Geneva, 1967.

Boyceau de la Baraudière, Jacques. *Traité du jardinage selon les raisons de la nature et de l'art.* Paris, 1638.

Campan, Jeanne Louise. *Mémoires sur la vie privée de Marie Antoinette.* Paris, 1822. Reprint, Paris: Hachette, 1988.

Cardin Le Bret, *De la souveraineté du roi.* Paris, 1632.

Carmontelle, Louis Carrogis dit. *Le jardin de Monceau.* Paris, 1779.

Cassini, Jean-Dominique. *Mémoires pour servir à l'histoire des sciences et à celle de l'Observa-toire royal de Paris avec une vie de J.-D. Cassini écrite par lui-même.* 1810.

Caus, Salomon de. *La perspective avec la raison des ombres et des miroirs.* 1612.

Chaufourier, Jean. *Recueil des plans des château et jardins de Versailles en 1720 accompagné de gravures de Jacques Rigaud, Présentation et commentaire de Piere Arizzoli-Clémentel.* Paris, 2000.

Choisy, François-Timoléon, abbé de. *Mémoires.* 1727.

Colbert, Jean-Baptiste. *Lettres, instructions, et mémoires de Colbert.* Ed. Pierre Clément. 10 vols. Paris, 1861–82.

Colonna, Francesco. *Le Songe de Poliphile.* Paris: Imprimerie nationale, 1994.

Croÿ, duc de. *Mémoires sur les cours de Louis XV et Louis XVI.* Published by the viscount of Grouchy. Paris: La Nouvelle Revue Rétrospective, 1897.

Dangeau, Philippe de Courcillon, marquis de. *Journal du marquis de Dangeau.* Ed. and annot. duke of St. Simon by J. Feuillet de Conches, 19 vols. Paris: Firmin-Didot frères, 1854–60.

Descartes. *Œuvres et letters.* Paris: La Pléiade, 1953.

Dézallier d'Argenville, Antoine Joseph. *La théorie et la pratique du jardinage où l'on traite à fond des beaux jardins appelés communément les jardins de plaisance et de propriété.* 1747. Reprint, Paris: Connaissance et mémoires, 2002.

Du Breuil, le Père Jean. *L'art universel des fortifications.* Paris, 1665.

———. *La perspective pratique.* 1642–49.

Félibien, André. *Description de la grotte de Versailles.* Paris, 1672.

———. *Description sommaire du chateau de Versailles.* 1674.

———. *Les divertissements de Versailles . . . au retour de la conquête de la Franche-Comté de 1674.* Reprint, Paris, 1994.

———. *Recueil de descriptions de peintures et d'ouvrages faits pour le roi.* Paris, 1689.

Guiffrey, Jules. *Comptes des Bâtiments du Roi sous le règne de Louis XIV.* 5 vols. Paris, 1881–1901.

Hegel, Georg Wilhelm Friedrich. *Cours d'esthétique.* Trans. Jankélévitch. Paris, 1944.

Hezecques, comte de. *Page à la cour de Louis XVI.* Paris: Tallandier, 1987.

Hobbes, Thomas. *Leviathan.* 1651. Reprint, London: Dent, 1940.

Huygens, Christiaan. *Correspondance.* In *Œuvres completes.* Vols. 1–10. La Haye, 1888–1910.

La Fontaine. *Œuvres complètes.* Paris: Seuil, 1965.

La Hire, Philippe de. *L'Ecole des arpenteurs.* 1689.

La Quintinie, Jean-Baptiste de. *Instruction pour les jardins fruitiers et potagers.* 1690. Reprint, Versailles-Arles: Actes Sud, 1999.

Le Bret, Cardin, *De la souveraineté du roi.* Paris: J. Quesnel, 1632.

Le triomphe royale. [Conventional title: La Mazarinade]. 1649.

Lister, Martin. *Voyage à Paris en 1698.* Paris, 1873.

Louis XIV. *Mémoires et divers écrits.* Longnon edition. Paris, 1960.

Luynes, duc de. *Mémoires sur la cour de Louis XV.* Dussieux edition. Paris, 1865–65.

Manesson-Mallet, Allain [*sic*]. *Les travaux de Mars.* 1685.

Mariotte, Edme, abbé. *Traité du mouvement des eaux.* 1686. Reprint, Paris, 1700.

Molière. *Œuvres completes.* M. Rat edition. Paris: La Pléiade, 1959.

Mollet, André. *Le jardin de plaisir.* 1652. Reprint, Michel Conan. Paris, 1981.

Montchrestien, Antoine de. *Traicté de l'œconomie politique.* 1615. Reprint, Geneva: Slatkine, 1970.

Orléans, Charlotte Elisabeth de Bavière, duchesse d'. *Lettres de Madame, duchesse d'Orléans, née Princesse Palatine.* New ed. by M. Goudeket. Paris, 1943–47.

Pascal, Blaise, *Pensées,* ed. Louis Lafuma. Paris: Seuil, 1962.

Perrault, Claude. *Memoires de ma vie*. Reprint, Paris: Macula, 1993.

Picard, Jean. *Traité du nivellement mis en lumière par les soins de M. de la Hire*. 1684.

Piganiol de la Force, Jean Aymar. *Description de Paris, de Versailles . . . des environs de Paris*. 1742.

———. *Nouvelle description des châteaux et parcs de Versailles et de Marly*. Paris, 1713.

Piles, Roger de. *Cours de peinture par principes*. Paris, 1708.

Poussin, Nicolas. *Mesures de la célèbre statue de l'Antinoüs suivies de quelques observations sur la peinture*. Bellory, 1672. Italian trans. P. M. Gault de St. Germain. Paris, 1803.

Primi Visconti, G.-B. *Mémoires sur la cour de Louis XIV*, 1673–81. Reprint with introduction and notes by Jean-François Solon. Paris: Perrin, 1988.

———. *Lettres et propos sur l'art*. Paris: Hermann, 1989.

Quatremère de Quincy, Antoine Chrysostome. *Encyclopédie méthodique*. Paris: Panckoucke, 1788.

———. *Essai sur la nature et l'imitation dans les beaux-arts*. Paris, 1822.

Racine, Jean. "La promenade de Port-Royal." In Odes IV, *Œuvres*. Mesnard edition. 1865–73.

Repton, Humphrey. *Sketches and Hints on Landscape Gardening* in *The Landscape Gardening and Landscape Architecture of the Late Humphrey Repton Esq*. Reprint, London, 1840.

Rousseau, Jean-Jacques. *Discours sur les sciences et les arts*. In *Œuvres complètes*. Paris: Gallimard, La Pléiade, 1966.

Saint-Simon, L. de Rouvroy, duc de. *Mémoires*. Yves Coirault edition. Paris: La Pléiade, 1983–86.

Scudéry, Madeleine. *La promenade de Versailles*. 1669. Reprint, Paris: Mercure de France, 1999.

Serres, Olivier de. *Théâtre d'agriculture et ménage des champs*. Reprint, Arles: Actes Sud, 1996.

Sévigné, Marie de Rabutin Chantal, marquise de. *Lettres*. 3 vols. Paris: La Pléiade, 1953–57.

Sourches, Marquis de. *Mémoires*. Published by the count of Cosnac and Arthur Bertrand. Paris: Hachette, 1882–93.

Spanheim, Ezechiel. *Relation de la cour de France en 1690*. Published by Emile Bourgeois Annales de l'Université de Lyon, facsimile 5. Lyon: Picard, 1900.

Tauvry, Daniel. *Nouvelle anatomie raisonnée*. 1690.

Tessin le Jeune, Nicodème. "Relation de la visite de Nicodème Tessin à Marly, Versailles, Clagny, Rueil et Saint Cloud en 1687." *Revue de l'histoire de Versailles et de Seine et Oise* 28 (1926): 274–300.

Thomassin, Simon. *Recueil des figures, groupes, termes, fontaines et vases et autres ornements tels qu'ils se voient à présent dans le château et le parc de Versailles*. 1694.

Tournefort, Joseph Pitton de. *Relation d'un voyage du Levant fait par ordre du roi*. 1727.

Urfé, Honoré d'. *L'Astrée*. 1607–27. Reprint, Lyon, 1911.

Vauban, Sébastien Le Prestre, marquis de. *Traité des sièges et de l'attaque des places*. Paris: Découvertes, 1992.

Vitruve. *De l'architecture*. Paris: Les Belles-Lettres, vol. 3, 1990.

Voltaire. *Le siècle de Louis XIV*. Paris: La Pléiade, 1957.

Wren, Christopher. *Parentalia, or Memoirs of the Family of the Wrens*. London, 1750.

STUDIES

Versailles in the Time of Louis XIV

HISTORICAL CONTEXT, IDEAS, AND ART

Actes du colloque international sur les plans reliefs. Paris: SEDES, 1993.

Antal, Frederick. *Florentine Painting and Its Social Background*. London, 1948. French translation, *Florence et ses peintres: La peinture florentine et son environnement social (1300–1450)*. Paris: Gérard Monfort, 1991.

Apostolidès, Jean-Marie. *Le Roi-machine: Spectacle et politique au temps de Louis XIV*. Paris: Minuit, 1981.

Barbiche, Bernard, and S. de Dainville-Barbiche. *Sully*. Paris: Fayard, 1997.

Batiffol, Louis. *Autour de Richelieu*. Paris, 1937.

Bellaigue, Raymonde de. *Le Potager du Roi*. Versailles: ENSH, 1982.

Bluche, François (sous la direction de). *Dictionnaire du grand siècle*. Paris: Fayard, 1990.

———. *Louis XIV*. Paris: Fayard, 1986.

Bottineau, Yves. "Essais sur le Versailles de Louis XIV." *Gazette des Beaux-Arts* 92, nos. 1436 and 1437 (September–October 1988).

Boudon, Philippe. *Richelieu, ville nouvelle*. Paris: Dunod, 1978.

Chaunu, Pierre. *La civilisation de l'Europe classique*. Paris: Arthaud, 1966.

Christout, Marie Françoise. *Le ballet de cour de Louis XIV, 1643–1672: Mises en scène*. Paris: Picard, 1967.

Cloulas, Ivan. *Catherine de Médicis*. Paris: Fayard, 1979.

Cormette, J. "L'alchimiste, le prince, et le géomètre." *Revue de synthèse* July–Dec. 1991: 492–93.

Cottret, Monique. *La vie politique en France aux XVIe, XVIIe et XVIIIe siècles*. Paris: Ophrys, 1991.

Les fêtes de la Renaissance. Studies collected by J. Jacquot. Paris: Editions du CNRS, 1956.

Ellul, Jacques. *Histoire des institutions, vol. 1, L'Antiquité*. Paris: Presses universitaires de France, 1970.

Fumaroli, Marc. *Le poète et le roi*. Paris: Fallois, 1997.

Guiffrey, Jules. *Comptes des Bâtiments du Roi sous le règne de Louis XIV*. 5 vols. Paris, Imprimerie nationale, 1881–1901.

Guth Paul. *Mazarin*. Paris: Flammarion, 1999.

Kantorowicz, Ernst H. *The King's Two Bodies: A Study in Mediaeval Political Theology*. Princeton, N.J., Princeton University Press, 1957.

Kemp, Martin. *The Science of Art*. New Haven: Yale University Press, 1992.

Lacour-Gayet, Georges. *L'éducation politique de Louis XIV*. Paris, 1898.

Lecoq, Anne Marie. *François I imaginaire*. Paris: Macula, 1987.

Maindron, Ernest. *L'ancienne académie des sciences*. Paris, 1895.

Mandrou, Robert. *La France aux XVIIe et XVIIIe siècles*. Paris: Presses universitaires de France, 1987.

Murat, Ines. *Colbert*. Paris: Fayard, 1980.

Néraudau, Jean-Pierre. *L'Olympe du Roi-Soleil*. Paris: Les Belles Lettres, 1986.

Newton, William R. *L'espace du roi: La cour de France au château de Versailles*. Paris: Fayard, 2000.

Niderst, Alain. *Madeleine de Scudéry, Paul Pélisson et leur monde*. Paris, 1976.

Petitfils, Jean-Christian. *Louis XIV*. Paris: Perrin, 1995.

Picon, Antoine. *Claude Perrault ou la curiosité d'un classique*. Paris: Picard, 1988.

Plans en relief de villes belges. Intro. Grodecki. 1965.

Poudra, Noël Germinal. *Histoire de la perspective ancienne et moderne*. Paris, 1864.

Relation des ambassadeurs vénitiens sur les affaires de France. Trans. M. N. Tommaseo. Paris, 1838 (Collection des documents inédits pour servir à l'histoire de France).

Rorive, Jean-Pierre. *La guerre de siège sous Louis XIV*. Brussels: Editions Racine, 1998.

Rykwert, Joseph, trans. *Les premiers modernes*. Paris: Hazan, 1991.

Sabatier, Gérard. *Versailles ou la figure du roi*. Paris: Albin Michel, 1999.

Salomon-Bayet, Claire. *L'institution de la science et l'expérience du vivant: Méthode et expérience à l'académie royale de sciences, 1666–1793*. Paris: Flammarion, 1978.

Saule, Béatrix. "Le château de Versailles." In *Colbert 1619–1683, Catalogue, Exposition, Hôtel de la Monnaie*. Paris, 1983. 307–11.

———. *Versailles triomphant: Une journée de Louis XIV*. Paris: Flammarion, 1996.

Serres, Michel (sous la direction de). *Eléments d'histoire des sciences*. Paris: Bordas, 1989.

Simon, Gérard, *Kepler, astronome, astrologue*, Paris: Gallimard, 1979.

Solnon, Jean-François. *La cour de France*. Paris: Fayard, 1987.

Taton, René (general editor). *Histoire générale des sciences*. Vol. 2, *La science moderne de 1450–1800*. Paris: Presses universitaires de France, 1958.

———. *Les origines de l'académie royale des sciences*. Paris: Palais de la Découverte, 1965.

Théories et pratiques politiques à la Renaissance. Paris: Vrin, 1977.

Thuillier, Jacques. *Simon Vouet*. Paris: Réunion des Musées Nationaux, 1990.

THE GARDENS

Adams, William Howard. *Les jardins de France*. Paris: Editions de l'Equerre, 1980.

Barbet, Louis Albert. *Les grandes eaux de Versailles*. Paris: Dunod and Pinat, 1907.

Barchilon, Jacques. "Les frères Perrault à travers la correspondance et les oeuvres de C. Huygens." *XVIIe siècle* 56 (1962): 19–36.

Baridon, Michel. *Les jardins: Paysagistes, jardiniers, poètes*. Paris: Laffont-Bouquins, 1998.

———. "The Scientific Imagination and the Baroque Garden." *Studies in the History of Gardens and Designed Landscapes* 18, no. 1 (1998): 5–19.

Beaussant, Philippe, and P. Bouchenot-Déchin. *Les plaisirs de Versailles*. Paris: Fayard, 1996.

Berger, Robert W. *In the Garden of the Sun King: Studies on the Park of Versailles Under Louis XIV*. Washington, D.C.: Dumbarton Oaks, 1985.

Bouchenot-Déchin, Patricia. *Henry Dupuis, jardinier de Louis XIV*. Paris: Perrin, 2001.

Castelluccio, Stéphane. "Les collections d'André Le Nôtre." *L'Estampille—L'objet d'art* (July–August 2000): 42–58.

Charageat, Marguerite. "André Le Nôtre et ses dessins." *Gazette illustrée des amateurs de jardins* (1953–54): 21–27.

Christiany, Janine. "Le Canal de l'Eure, un ouvrage inachevé: Inscriptions et traces dans le paysage." Ph.D. thesis, University of Paris I, 1995.

Conan, Michel. "The Conundrum of Le Nôtre's Labyrinth." In *Garden History: Issues, Approaches, Methods*. Washington, D.C.: Dumbarton Oaks Foundation, 1992. 119–50.

———. *Dictionnaire historique de l'art des jardins*. Paris: Hazan, 1999.

———. "Les jardins chez La Fontaine." *Studies in the History of Gardens and Designed Landscapes* 18, no. 1 (1998).

Constans, Claire. *Versailles: Château de la France et orgueil des rois*. Reprint, Paris: Gallimard, 2000.

Dauchez, Chantal. "L'administration des jardins au Grand siècle." Ph.D. thesis, University of Paris II, 1993.

———. *Les jardins de Le Nôtre*. Paris: La Compagnie du Livre, 1994.

Daufresne, Jean-Claude. *Le Louvre et les Tuileries*. Paris: Mengès, 1994.

Davy de Wirville, Adrien. *Histoire de la botanique en France*. Paris, 1954.

Demoris, René. "Le corps royal et l'imaginaire au XVIIe siècle: Le portrait du roi par Félibien." *Revue des sciences humaines* 44 (1972): 10–30.

Desgots, Claude. "Abrégé de la vie d'André Le Nôtre." *Continuation des mémoires de littérature et d'histoire*, vol. 9. Paris, 1730.

Farhat, Georges. "Pratiques perspectives et histoire de l'art des jardins." *La revue de l'art* 129 (2000): 28–40.

Francastel, Pierre. *La sculpture de Versailles*. Paris: Mouton, 1970.

Friedman, Ann. "The Evolution of the Parterre d'Eau." *Journal of Garden History* 8, no. 1 (1988): 1–30.

Ganay, Ernest de. *André Le Nostre*. Paris: Vincent, Fréal, 1962.

———. *Bibliographie de l'art des jardins*. Reprint, Paris: Bibliothèque aes Arts Décoratifs, 1989.

Garnier-Pelle, Nicole. *André Le Nôtre et les jardins de Chantilly*. Somogy: Editions d'art, 2000.

Garrigues, Dominique. *Jardins et jardiniers de Versailles au Grand Siècle*. Seyssel: Champ Vallon, 2001.

Guiffrey, J. *André Le Nôtre*. Paris: Institut de France, 1908.

Guillou, Edouard. *Versailles, palais du soleil*. Editions d'histoire et d'art. Paris: Plon, 1963.

Hautecoeur, Louis. *Les jardins des dieux et des hommes*. Paris, 1959.

Hazlehurst, Francis Hamilton. *Gardens of Illusion: The Genius of André Le Nôtre*. Nashville: Vanderbilt University Press, 1980.

Hedin, Thomas F. "Le Nostre to Mansart: Transition in the Gardens of Versailles." *Gazette des Beaux-Arts* 130 (1997): 191–343.

Hoog, Simone. *Manière de montrer les jardins de Versailles par Louis XIV*. Paris: RMN, 1992.

Les jardins des Médicis. Milan: Motta, 1996. French translation, Arles: Actes Sud, 1997.

Jeannel, Bernard. *Le Nôtre*. Paris: Hazan, 1985.

Josephson, Ragnar. "Description de Trianon en 1694." *Revue de l'Histoire de Versailles et de Seine et Oise*, 1927, 149–67.

———. "Relation de la visite de Nicodème Tessin en 1687." *Revue de l'Histoire de Versailles et de Seine et Oise*, 1926, 274–300.

Lablaude, Pierre-André. *Les jardins de Versailles*. Paris: Scala, 1995.

Le Nôtre, un inconnu illustre. Actes du colloque international organisé à Paris et Chantilly en l'honneur du tricentenaire de la mort de Le Nôtre. Paris: Monum. ed. du patrimoine, 2003).

Lodari, Renata. *I Giardini di Le Nôtre*. Turin: Umberto Allamandi, 2000.

Mabille, Gérard. *Vues du jardin de Marly*. Paris: A. de Gourcuff, 1998.

Mariage, Thierry. *L'univers de Le Nostre*. Brussels: Mardaga, 1990. English translation by Graham Larkin, *The World of André Le Nôtre*. Philadelphia: University of Pennsylvania Press, 1999.

Marie, Alfred. *Naissance de Versailles*. Paris: Fréal, 1968.

———. "Les plaisirs de l'Ile Enchantée." *Bulletin de la société de l'histoire de l'art français* (1941–44): 118–25.

Maroteaux, Vincent. *Versailles, le roi et son domaine*. Paris: Picard, 2000.

"La ménagerie de Versailles." In Monique Mosser and G. Teyssot, *Histoire des jardins de la Renaissance à nos jours*. Paris: Flammarion, 1992. 168–71.

Moine, Marie Christine. *Les fêtes à la cour du Roi Soleil*. Paris: François Sorlot, 1984.

Mollet, Claude. *Théâtre des plans et jardinages, contenant des secrets et des inventions incognues à tous ceux qui jusqu'à présent se sont meslez d'escrire sur cette matière, avec un traicté d'astrologie, propre pour toutes sortes de personnes, et particulièrement pour ceux qui s'occupent de la culture des jardins*. Paris: C. de Sercy, 1652.

Mosser, Monique, and G. Teyssot. *Histoire des jardins de la Renaissance à nos jours*. Paris: Flammarion, 1992.

Moulin, Jacques. *Vaux-le-Vicomte: Etude préalable à la restauration des parcs et des jardins: Bilan historique*. Paris, 1995.

Nolhac, Pierre de. *La création de Versailles*. Versailles: Librairie Bernard, 1901.

———. *Versailles, les extérieurs et les jardins*. Paris, 1930.

Orsenna, Eric. *Portrait d'un homme heureux, André Le Nôtre, 1613–1700*. Paris: Fayard, 2000.

Pérouse de Montclos, Jean-Marie. *Vaux-le-Vicomte*. Paris: Mengès, 1997.

———. *Versailles*. Paris: Scala, 1996.

Pincas, Stéphane. *Versailles, un jardin à la française*. Paris: Editions La Martinière, 1995.

Pommier Edouard. "Versailles: L'image du souverain." In *Les lieux de mémoire*. Vol. 2, 2. Paris: Gallimard, 1986.

Le Potager du Roi. Versailles: Ecole Nationale Supérieure du Paysage, 1998.

Projets pour Versailles: Dessins des Archives nationales. Exhibition catalogue, national archives. Paris, 1985.

Rommel, Alfred. *Die Entstehung des Klassischen französischen Gartens im Spiegel der Sprache*. Berlin: Deutsche Akademie der Wissenschaften zu Berlin, 1954.

Rostaing, Aurélia. "André Le Nôtre et les jardins français du XVIIe siècle: Perspectives de recherche et 'vues bornées.'" *La Revue de l'Art* 129 (December 2000): 15–27.

Senna, Erik. *Andre Le Nôtre: Gardener to the Sun King*. London: Braziller, 2001.

Tenenti A. "Claude Perrault et la pensée scientifique française dans la seconde moitié du XVIIe siècle." In *Hommage à Lucien Febvre*. Paris, 1953.

Verlet, Pierre. *Le château de Versailles*. Paris: Albin Michel, 1999.

The Versailles colloquium, Gazette des Beaux-Arts. April 1992.

Weber, Gerold. *Brunnen und Wasserkünste in Frankreich im Zeitalter von Louis XIV*. Worms am Rhein: Wernersche Verlaggesellschaft, 1985.

Woodbridge, Kenneth. *Princely Gardens*. London: Thames and Hudson, 1986.

Versailles After Louis XIV

HISTORICAL CONTEXT, IDEAS, AND ART

Vincent Maroteaux, *Le Roi et son domaine*, cited above, and Theodor W. Gaehtgens, *Versailles, de la résidence royale au musée historique*, cited below, give very complete bibliographies. Learned societies have contributed a great deal to our knowledge of Versailles. See in particular, *Versalia* (Société des Amis de Versailles), *Revue de l'histoire de Versailles et de Seine et Oise*, which became *Revue de l'histoire de Versailles et des Yvelines*.

Antoine, Michel. *Louis XV*. Paris: Fayard, 1989.

Baridon, Michel. "Les deux grands tournants du siècle des lumières." *Dix-huitième siècle* 31 (1999): 15–31.

Bertier de Sauvigny, G. de. *La restauration*. New ed. Paris, 1990.

Blanchard, Anne. *Les ingénieurs du "Roy" de Louis XIV à Louis XVI*. Montpellier: Anne Blanchard, 1979.

Bourde, André-Jean. *Agronomie et agronomes en France au XVIIIe siècle*. Paris, 1967.

Caffin-Carcy, Odile, and J. Villard. *Versailles et la Révolution*. Versailles: Editions d'art Lys, 1988.

Gaehtgens, Theodore W. *Versailles, de la résidence royale au musée historique*. Antwerp: Fonds Mercator, 1984.

Himelfarb, Hélène. "Versailles en notre temps." In Y. M. Bercé et al., *Destins et enjeux du XVIIe siècle*. Paris: Presses universitaires de France, 1985. 140–52.

———. "Versailles, fonctions et légendes." In *Les lieux de mémoire*, vol. 2: *La Nation*. Under the direction of P. Nora. Paris: Gallimard, 1986.

Koyré, Alexandre. *Etudes newtoniennes*. Paris, 1968.

La Rue, Adolphe de. *Les chasses du Second Empire*. Reprint, Paris, 1984.

Las Cases, Emmanuel Auguste, marquis de. *Le Mémorial de Sainte-Hélène*. 2 vols. Paris: Gallimard, La Pléiade, 1956.

Marie, Alfred. "Napoléon et le domaine de Versailles." *Archives de l'Art français* 24 (1969): 119–31.

Montalivet, Comte de. *Le roi Louis-Philippe et sa liste civile*. Paris, 1850.

Sylvestre de Sacy, Jacques. *Le Comte d'Angiviller, dernier directeur des Bâtiments du Roi.* Paris, 1953.

Waresquiel, E. de, and B. Yvert. *Histoire de la Restauration, 1814–1830.* Paris: Perrin, 1996.

Weulersse, Georges. *Le mouvement physiocratique en France de 1756 à 1770.* 2 vols. Paris, 1910.

Zweig, Stefan. *Marie-Antoinette.* Translated from the German. Paris: Grasset, 1934.

THE GARDENS

Arrizoli-Clémentel, Pierre. *Vues et plans du Petit-Trianon.* Paris: A. de Gourcuff, 1998.

Babelon, Jean-Pierre. "La restauration des jardins de Versailles." *Monumental* 4 (September 1993).

Baridon, Michel. "The Garden of the Perfectibilists: Méréville and the Désert de Retz." In J. D. Hunt and M. Conan, eds., *Tradition and Innovation in French Garden Art.* Philadelphia: University of Pennsylvania Press, 2002. 121–34.

———. *Le jardin paysager anglais au XVIIIe siècle.* Presses de l'Université de Bourgogne, 2001.

Cayeux, Jean de. "Des amateurs compromettants." In *Hubert Robert et la Révolution.* Valence: Musée de Valence, 1989.

———. *Hubert Robert et les jardins.* Paris: Herscher, 1987.

Delaborde, Henri. *Notice sur la vie et les ouvrages de Monsieur Questel.* Paris: Institut de France, Académie des Beaux-Arts, 1890.

Desjardins, Gustave. *Le Petit Trianon.* Versailles: Editions Bernard, 1885.

Francastel, Pierre. *La création du musée historique de Versailles.* Versailles: Editions Léon Bernard, 1930.

———. "La replantation du parc de Versailles au XVIIIe siècle." *Bulletin de la Société de l'Histoire de l'Art français* (1950): 53–57.

Ganay, Ernest de. *Les jardins à la française en France au XVIIIe siècle.* Paris, 1943.

Garrigues, Dominique. *Jardins et jardiniers de Versailles au Grand Siècle.* Seyssel: Champ Vallon, 2001.

Hamy, Ernest. "Les dernier jours du jardin du roi et la fondation du Muséum d'Histoire naturelle." *Centenaire de la fondation du Muséum d'Histoire naturelle.* Paris, 1893.

Heitzmann, Annick. "Les jardins du Petit Trianon." In *Les Jardins de Versailles et de Trianon d'André Le Nôtre à Richard Mique.* Exhibition catalogue, Château de Versailles. Paris: RMN, 1992.

Hoog, Simone. *Plan des jardins de Versailles et de Trianon: Relevé topographique du décor sculpté.* Versailles: Editions d'art Lys, 1987.

Les Jardins de Versailles d'André Le Nôtre à Richard Mique. Exhibition catalogue, Château de Versailles. Paris: RMN, 1992.

Jardins en France, 1760–1820: Pays d'illusion, terre d'expérience. Paris: RMN, 1977.

Lablaude, Pierre-André. "Restauration et régénération de l'architecture végétale des jardins de Versailles." *Monumental* 4 (September 1993): 76–84.

Ledoux-Lebard, Denise. *Le Petit Trianon.* Paris: Editions de l'Amateur, 1989.

Morel, Jean-Marie. *Théorie des jardins.* Paris, 1776.

Morey, Mathieu, Prosper. *Richard Mique, architecte de Stanislas, roi de Pologne et de la reine Marie-Antoinette*. Nancy, 1868.

Mosser, Monique. "Les architectures paradoxales ou petit traité des fabriques." In Monique Mosser and G. Teyssot, *Histoire des jardins de la Renaissance à nos jours*. Paris: Flammarion, 1992. 259–76.

Nolhac, Pierre de. *Histoire du Château de Versailles: Versailles au XVIIIe siècle*. Paris, 1926.

———. *La résurrection de Versailles: Souvenirs d'un conservateur, 1887–1920*. Paris: Plon, 1937.

Scott, Barbara. "Madame's Pavillon de musique." *Apollo* 45 (May 1972): 123.

Taylor-Leduc, Susan B. "Louis XVI's Public Gardens: The Replantation of Versailles in the Eighteenth Century." *Journal of Garden History* 14, no. 2 (1994): 67–91.

Versailles vu par les peintres de Demachy à Lévy-Dhurmer. Exhibition catalogue. Versailles: Musée Lambinet, 1992.

Walpole, Horace. *Essai sur l'art des jardins modernes*. Trans. le duc de Nivernois. London, 1785. Reprint, Paris: Gérard Monfort, 2000.

Wiebenson, Dora. *The Picturesque Garden in France*. Princeton, N.J.: Princeton University Press, 1985.

INDEX

ACKNOWLEDGMENTS

As WAS THE case for the French edition of *The Gardens of Versailles*, thanks for this edition are due to Hubert Astier, the former president of the Etablissement Public de Versailles, and to his successor, Christine Albanel; to Pierre Arizzoli-Clémentel, director-general of the Château de Versailles; and to Béatrix Saule, chief conservator at the Château de Versailles. I would also like to thank Pierre-André Lablaude, chief architect of the Monuments historiques, for his help and for the plans he allowed me to reproduce; Thierry Mariage, architect of the Bâtiments de France, whose book on Le Nôtre remains one of the best on the subject; Sylvie Messinger, director of publications of the Etablissement Public de Versailles, and her colleagues Florence Renouf and Rachel Coudray. I am also indebted to the staff at the Service des Fontaines de Versailles, Marly et Saint-Cloud. I would also like to express my gratitude to Aurélia Rostaing, and to Magnus Olaussen and Linda Henrikkson of the Nationalmuseum of Stockholm.

Special thanks are due to Jean-Baptiste Leroux for allowing me to use eight of the 115 photographs that illustrated the first French edition of this book. It was a particular pleasure to work with him because, like the true artist he is, he perceived all the optical effects the gardens were meant to produce, and he captured them in color photographs whose sheer beauty was a constant inspiration while I was working on the book.